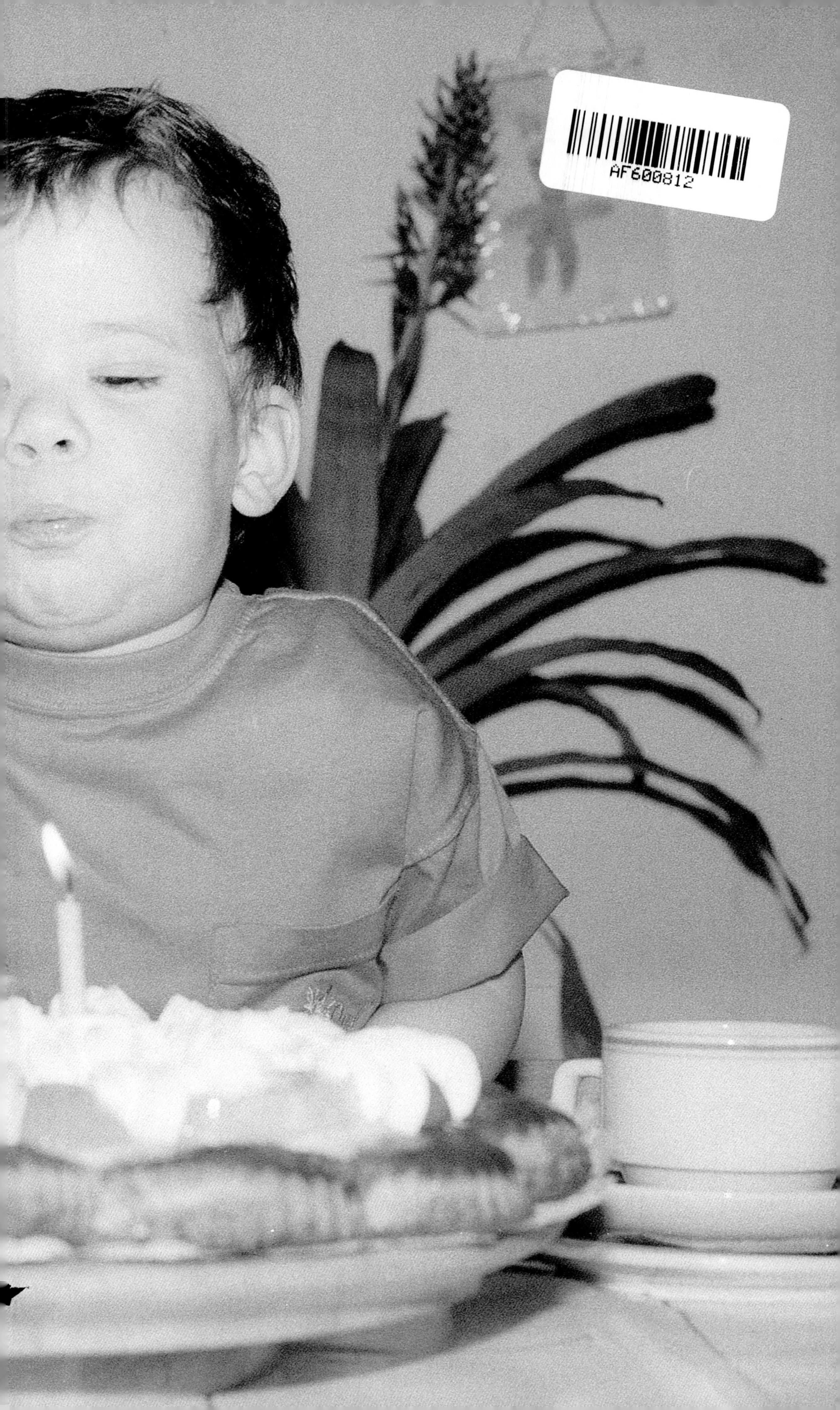

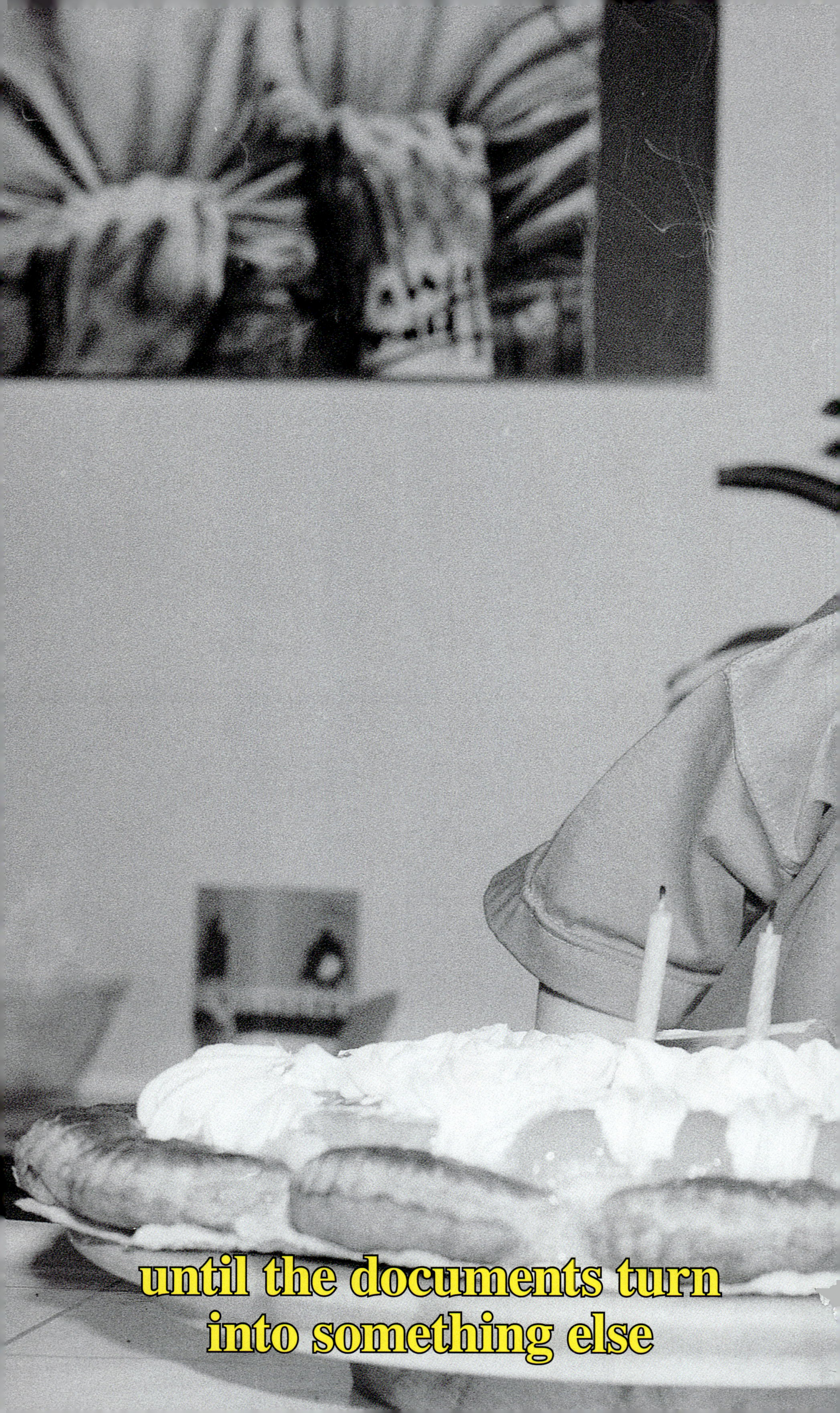
until the documents turn
into something else

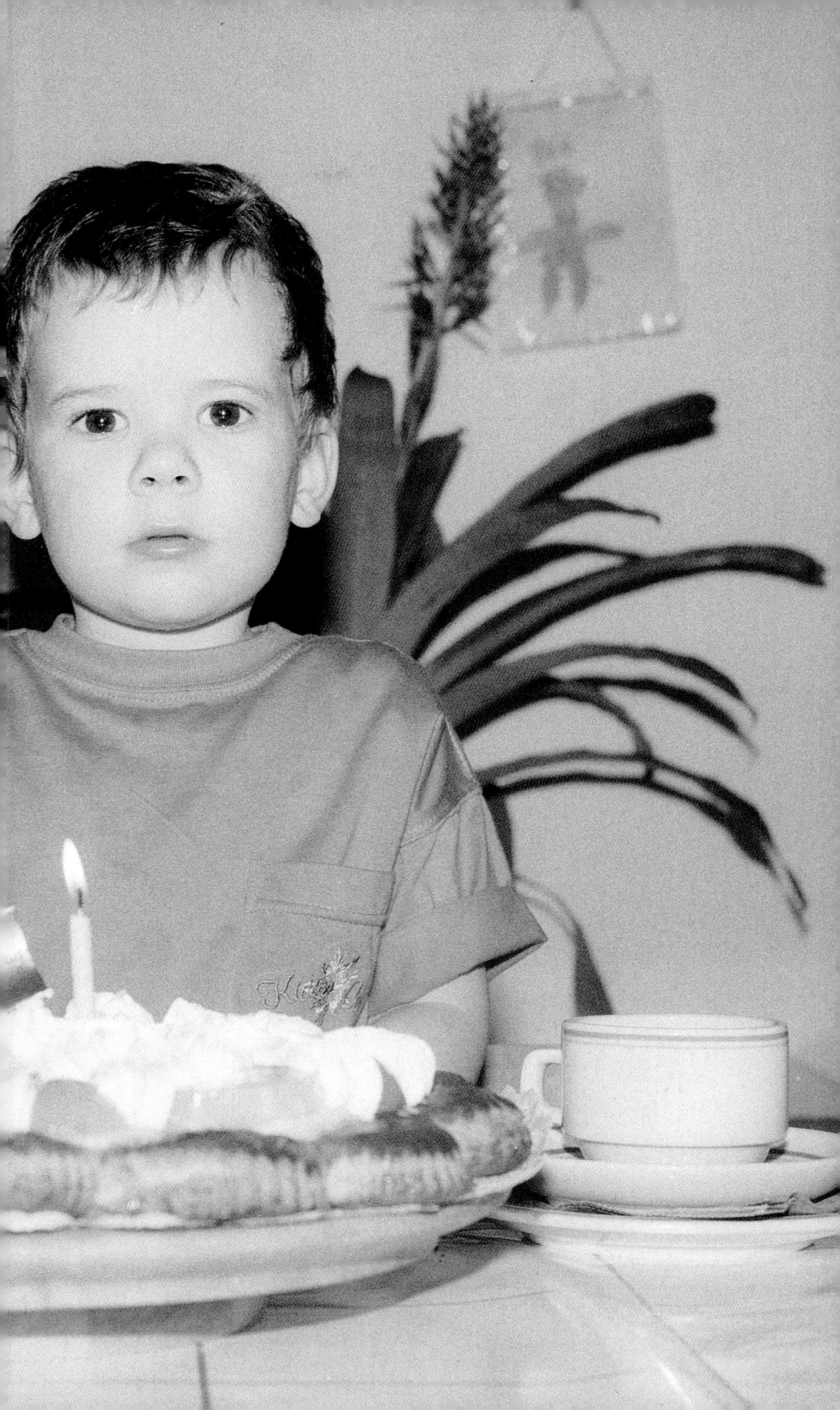

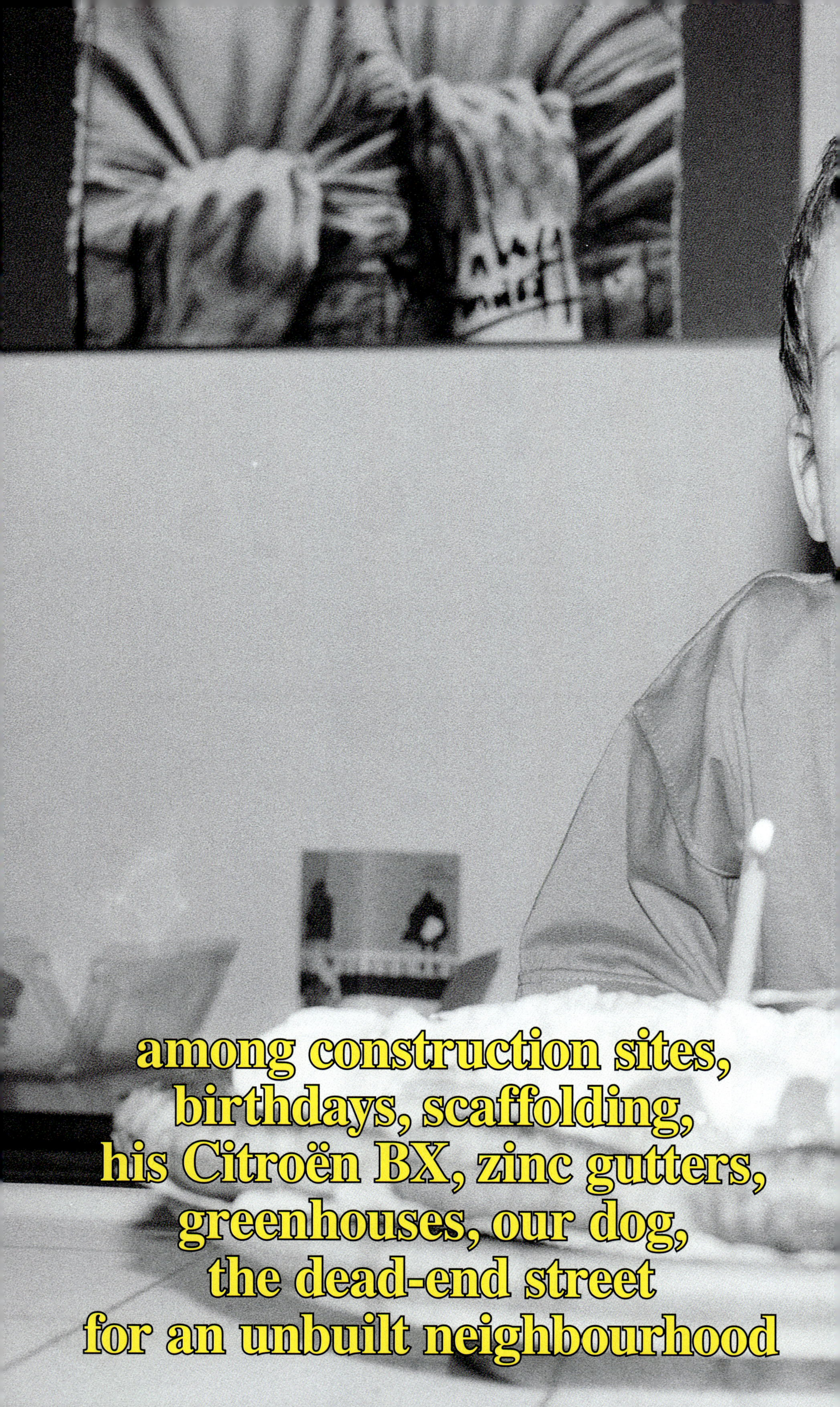

among construction sites,
birthdays, scaffolding,
his Citroën BX, zinc gutters,
greenhouses, our dog,
the dead-end street
for an unbuilt neighbourhood

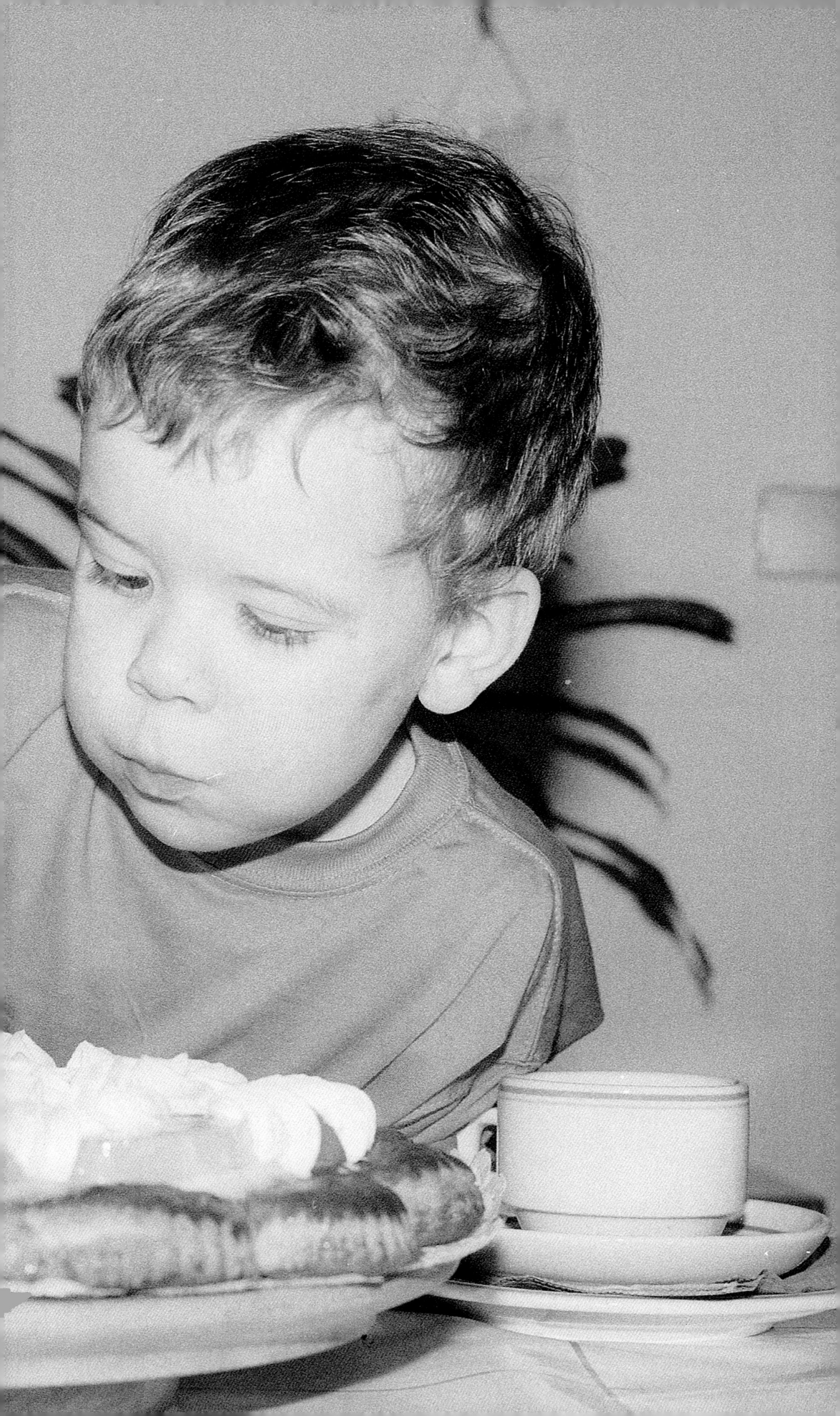

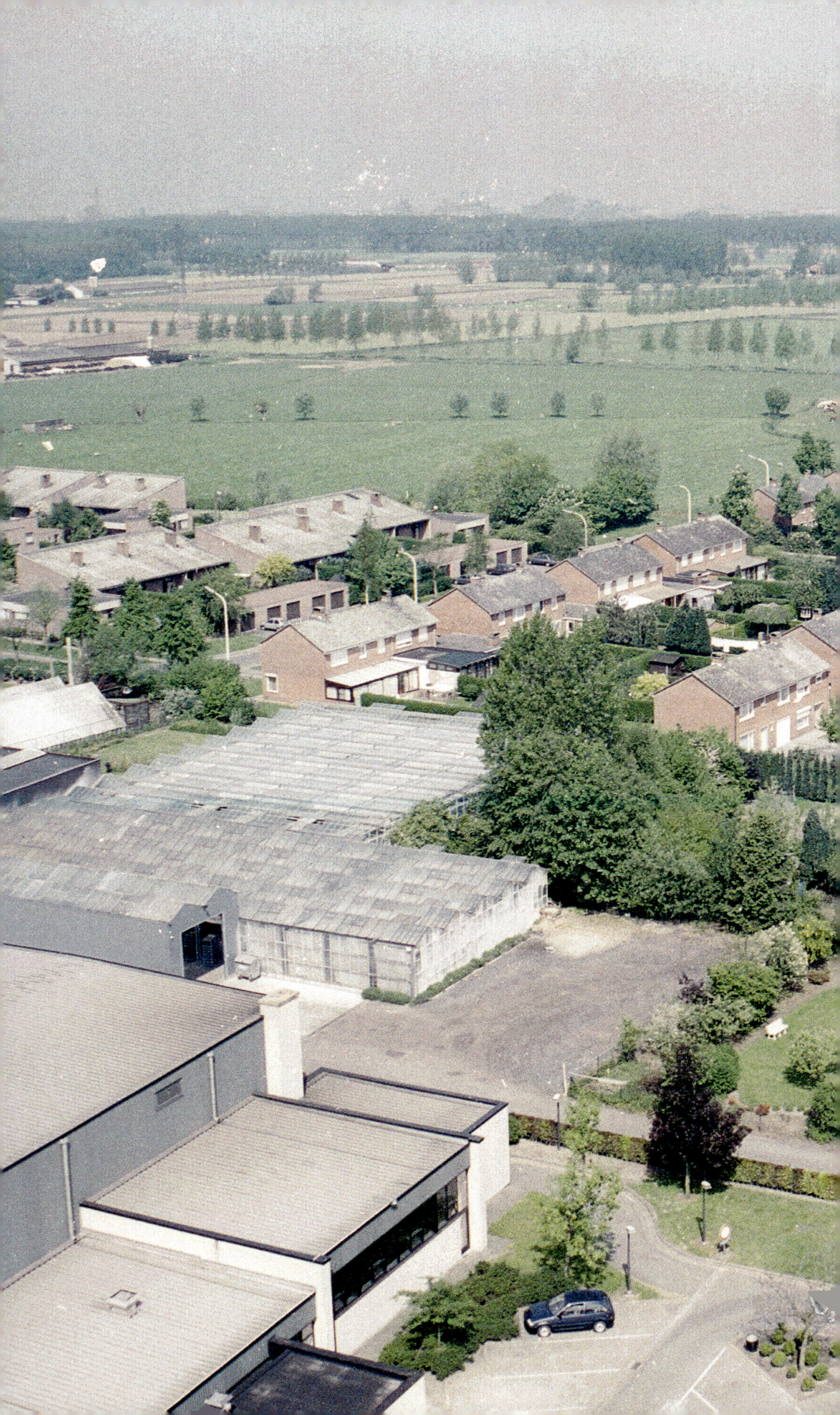

THE SITUATION

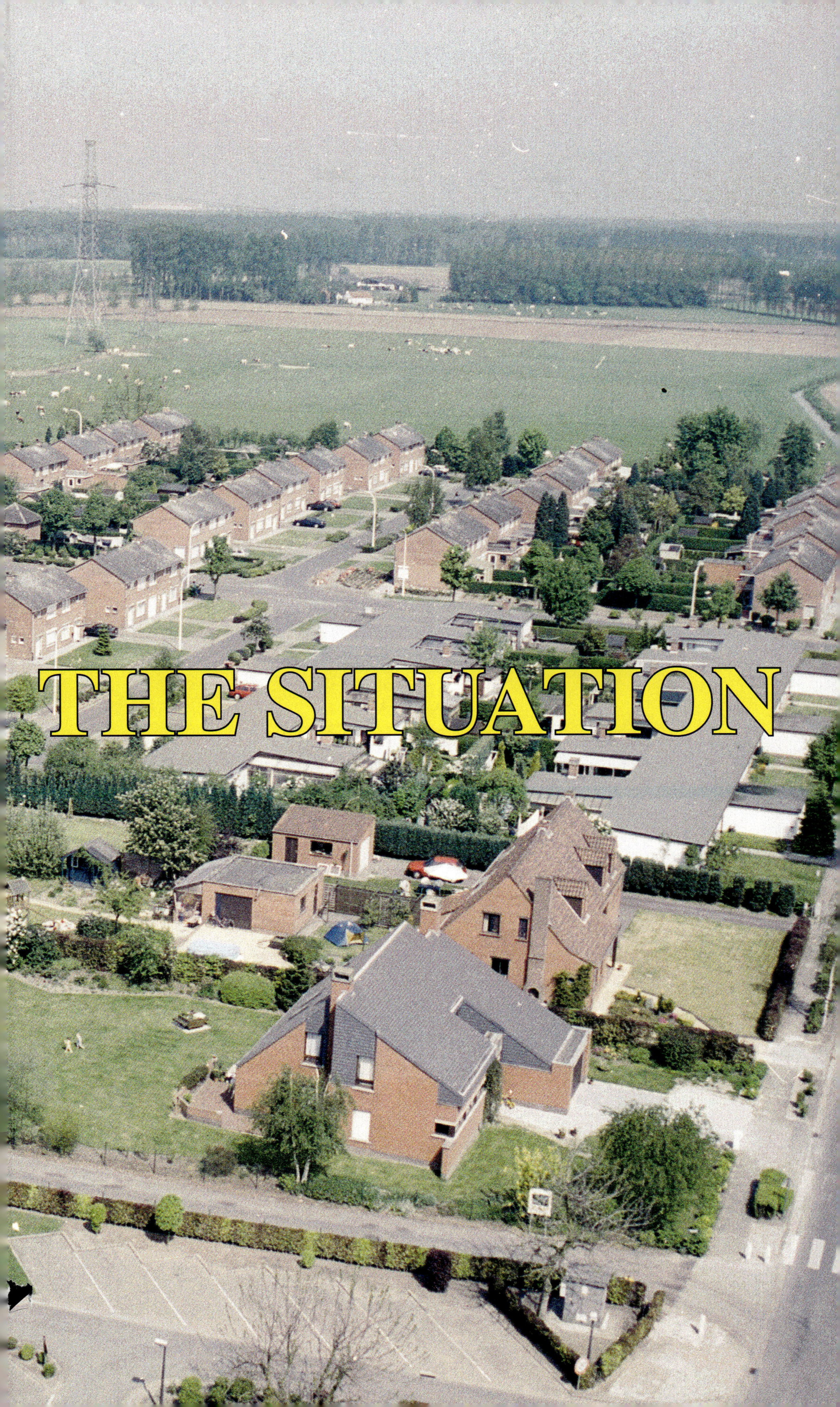

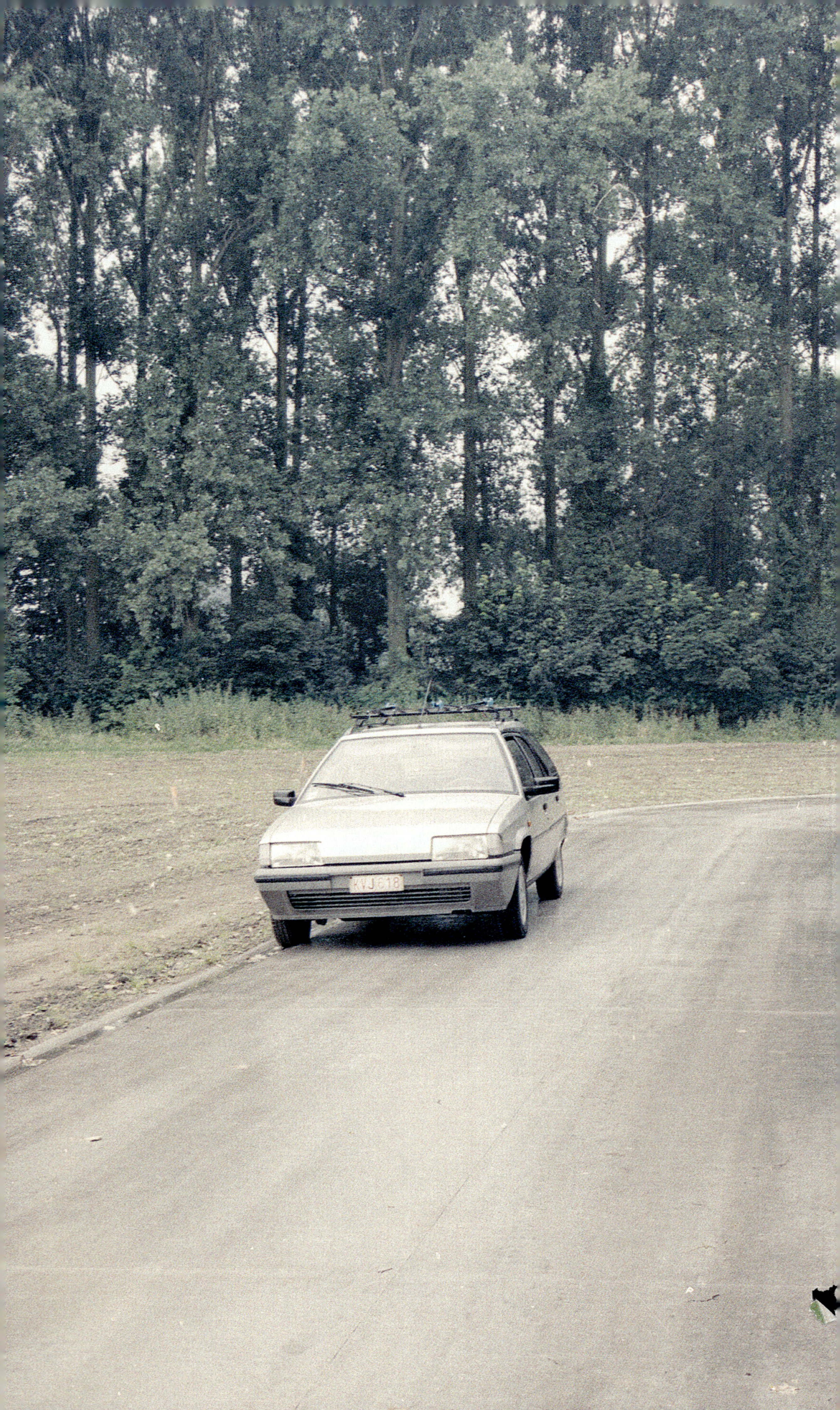

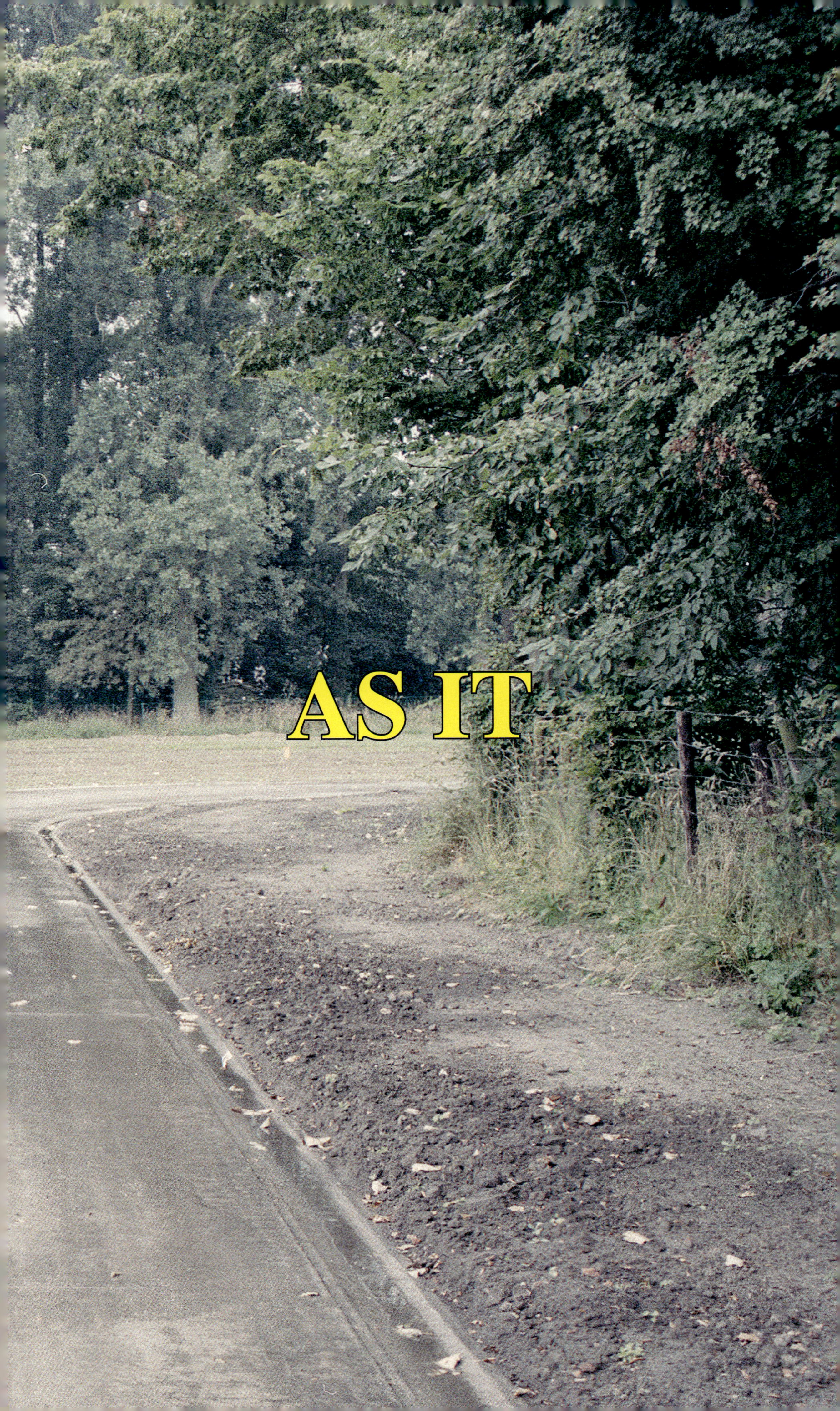
AS IT

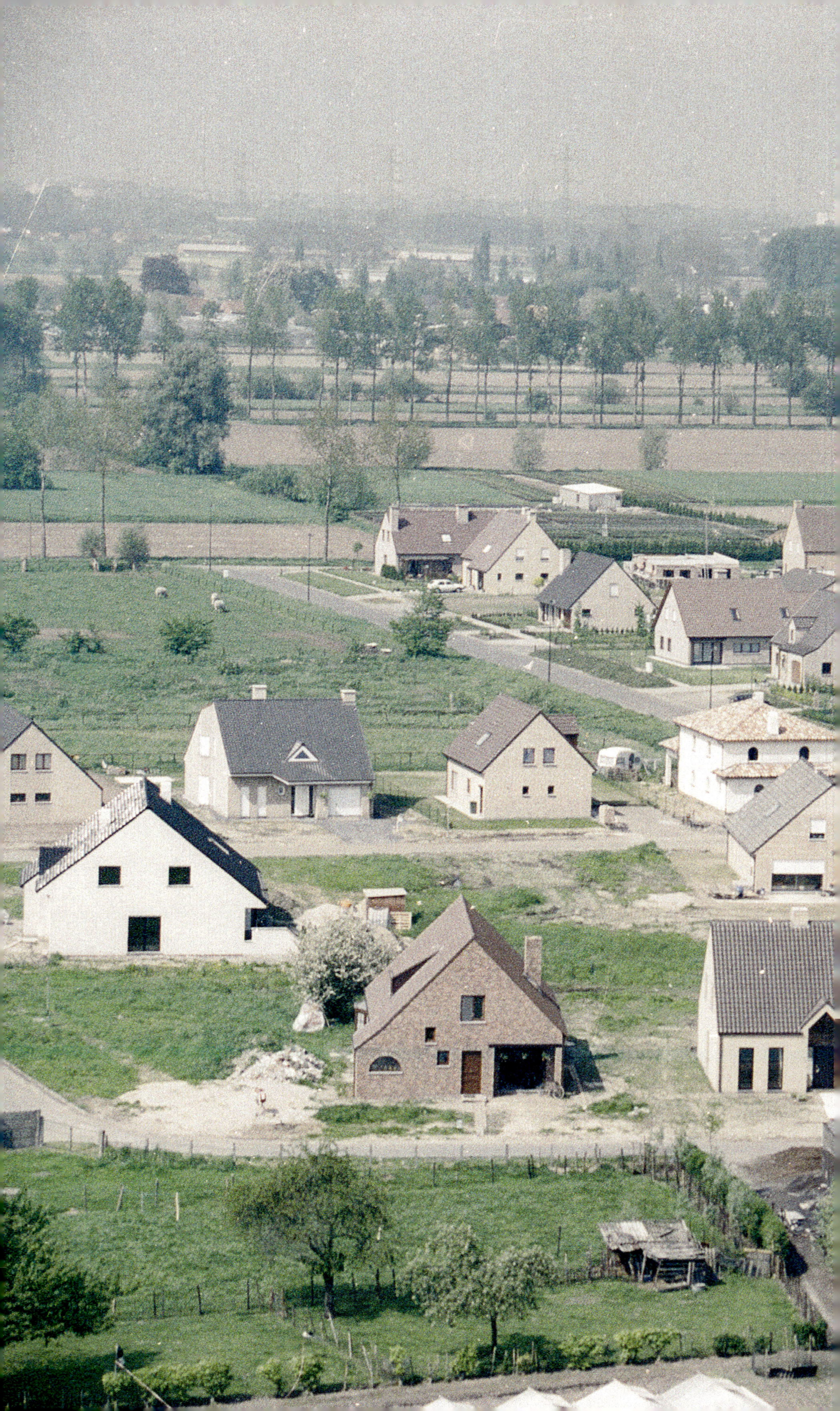

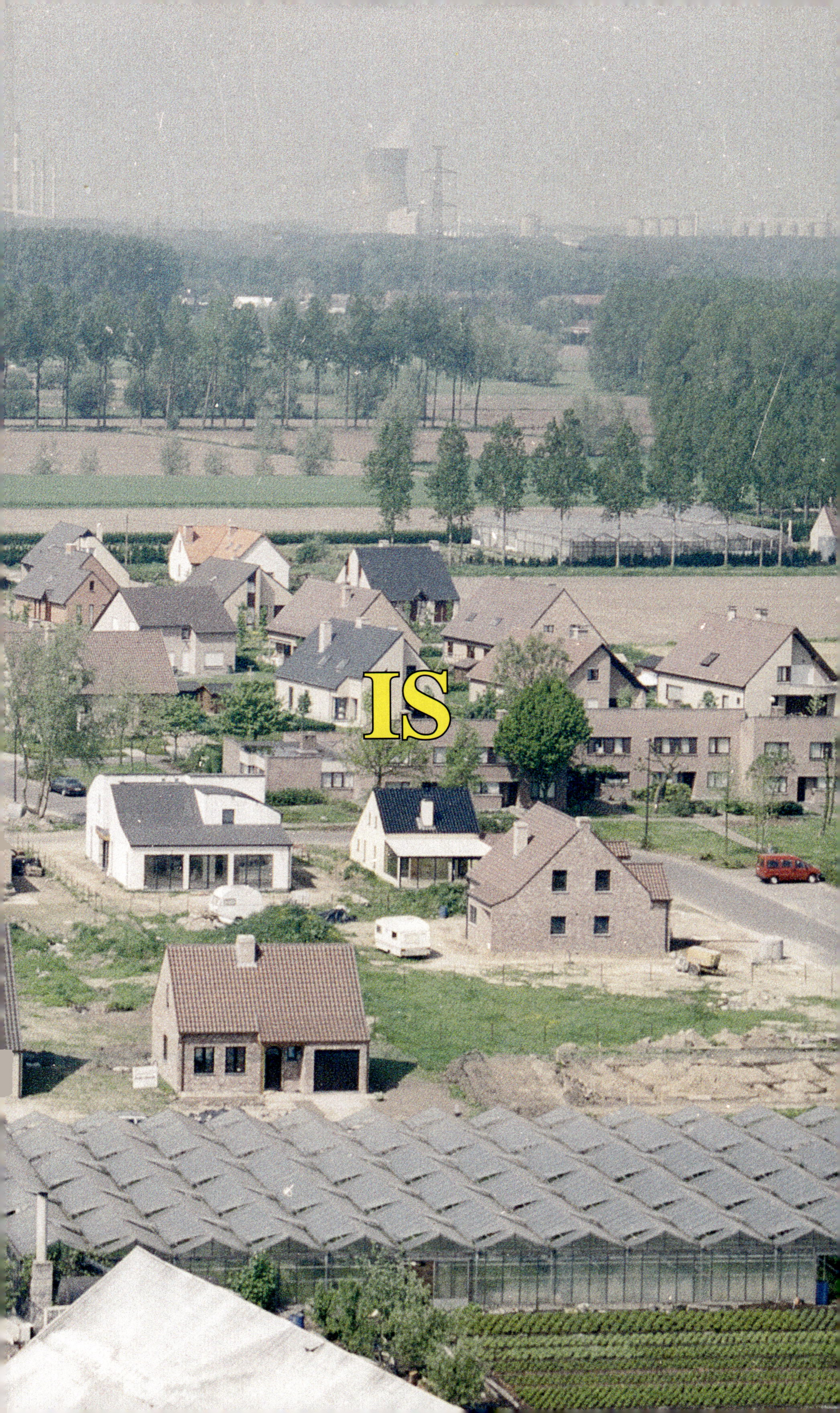
IS

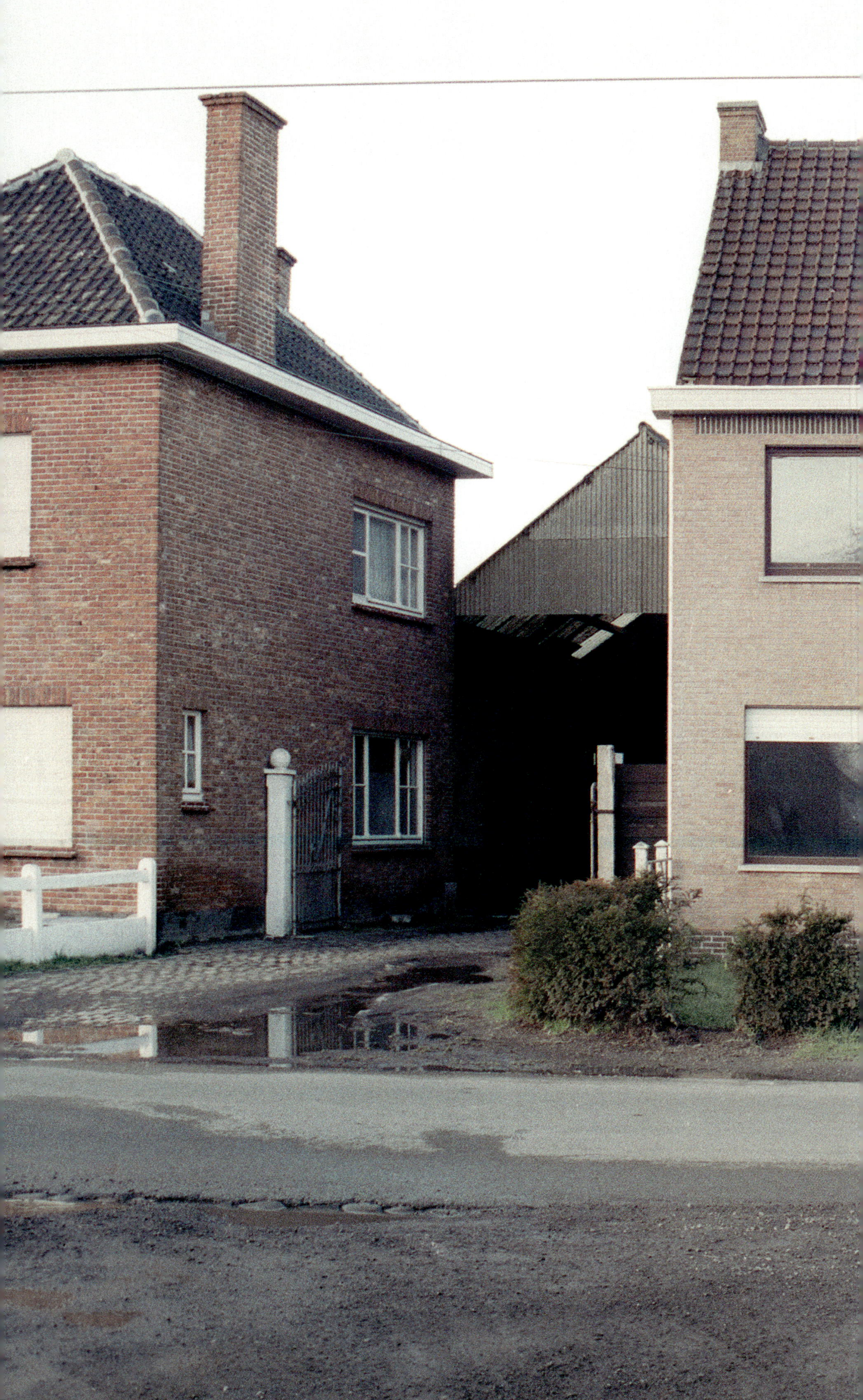

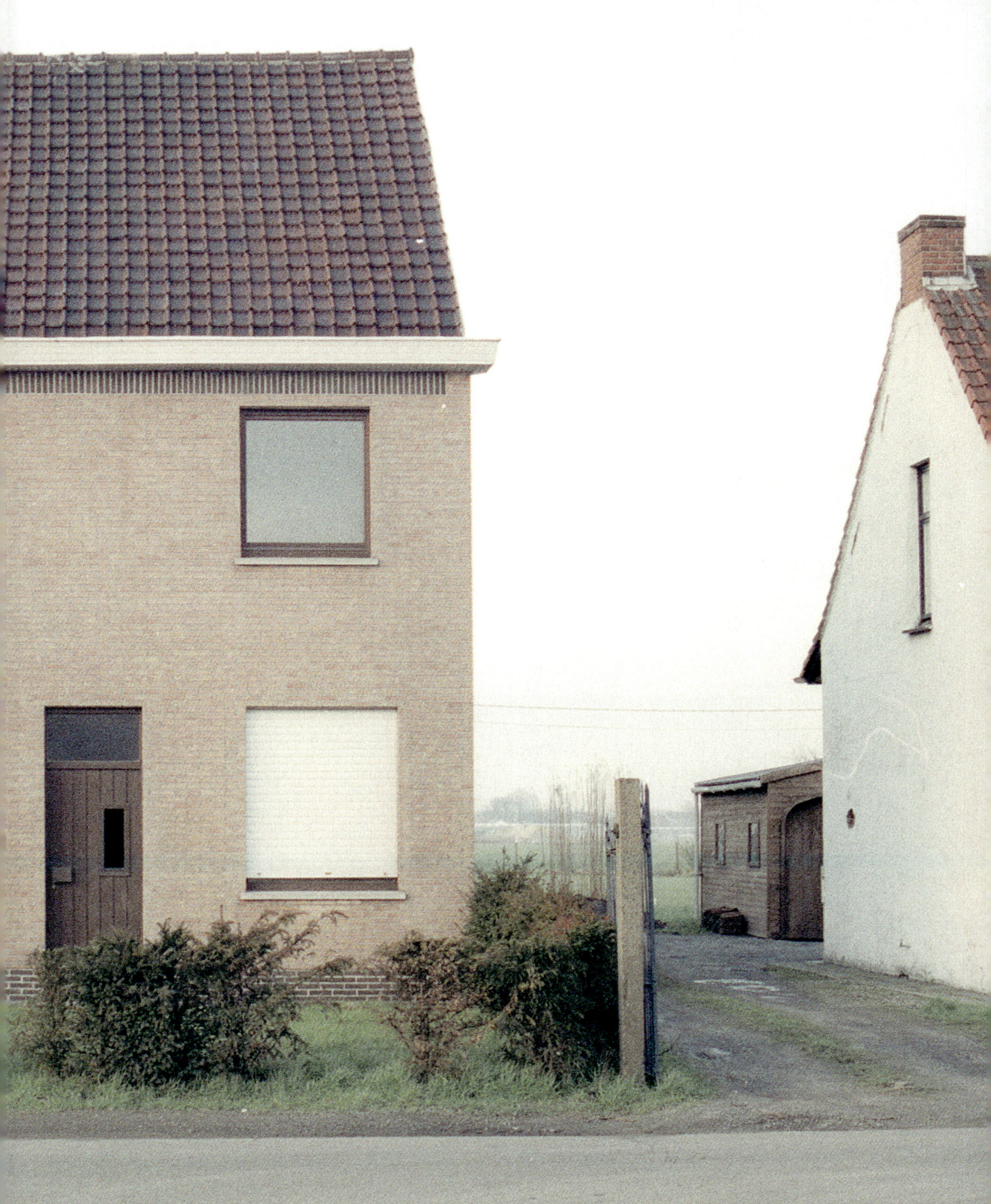

**for the houses he builds
for florists,
newlyweds and farmers**

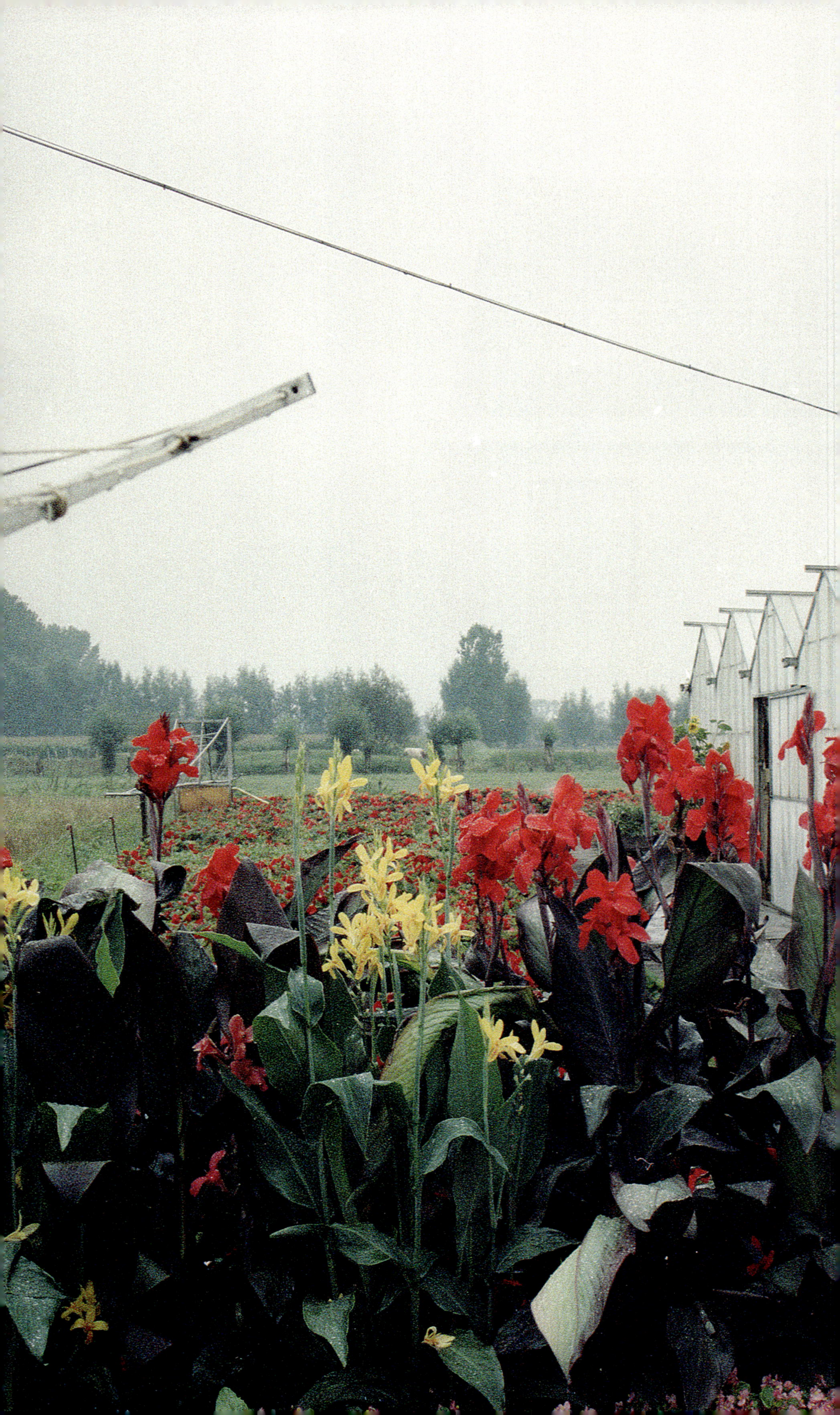

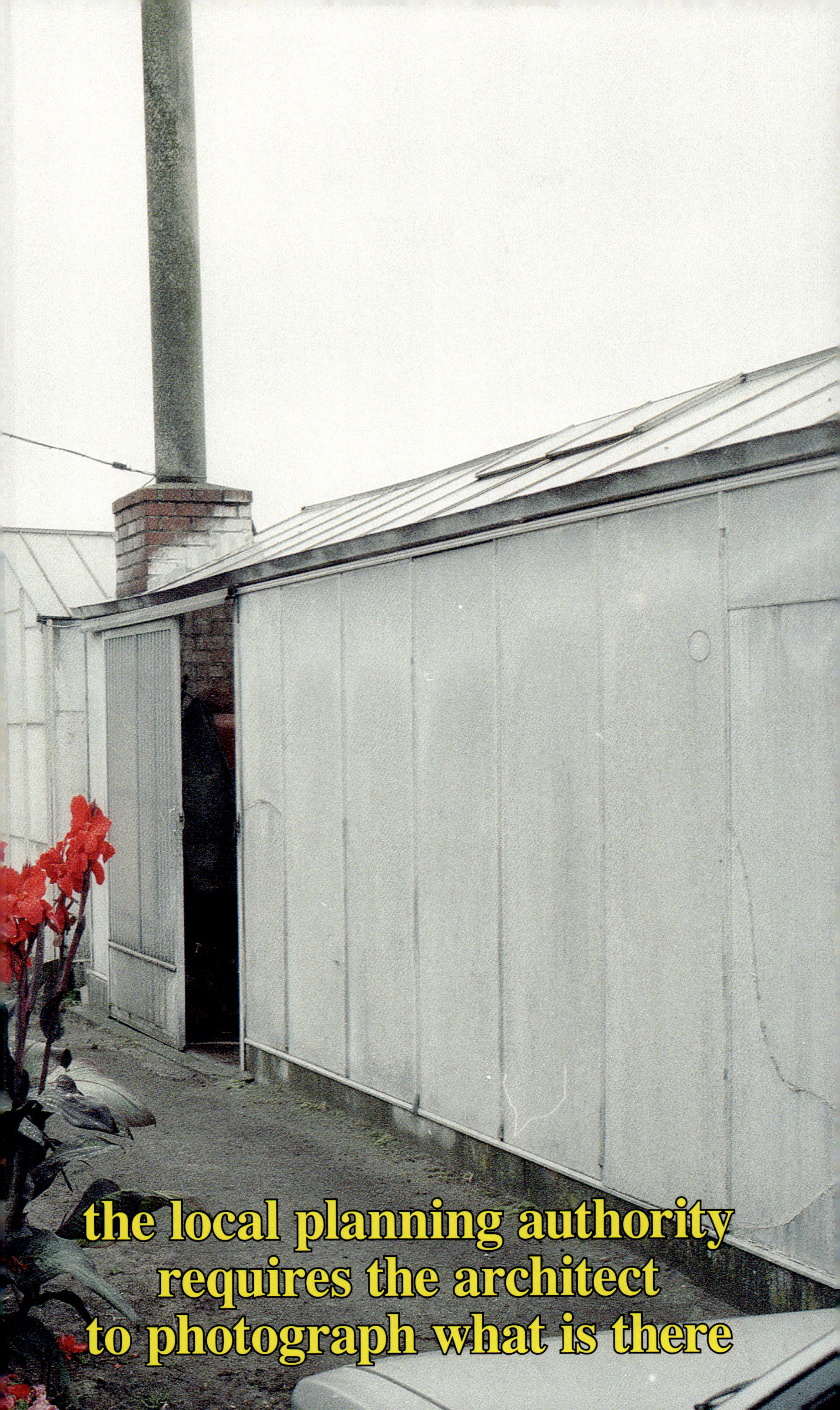
the local planning authority
requires the architect
to photograph what is there

now

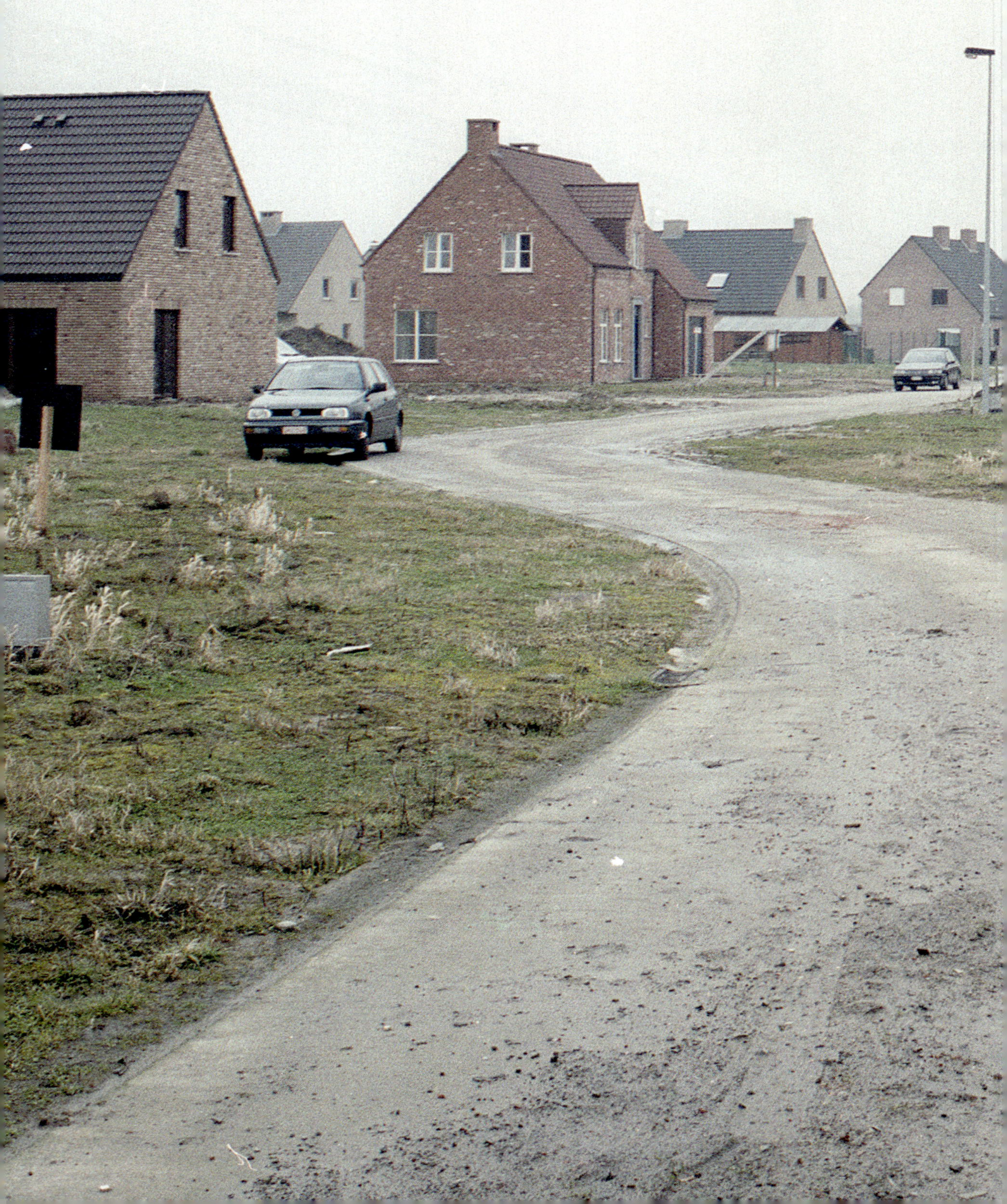

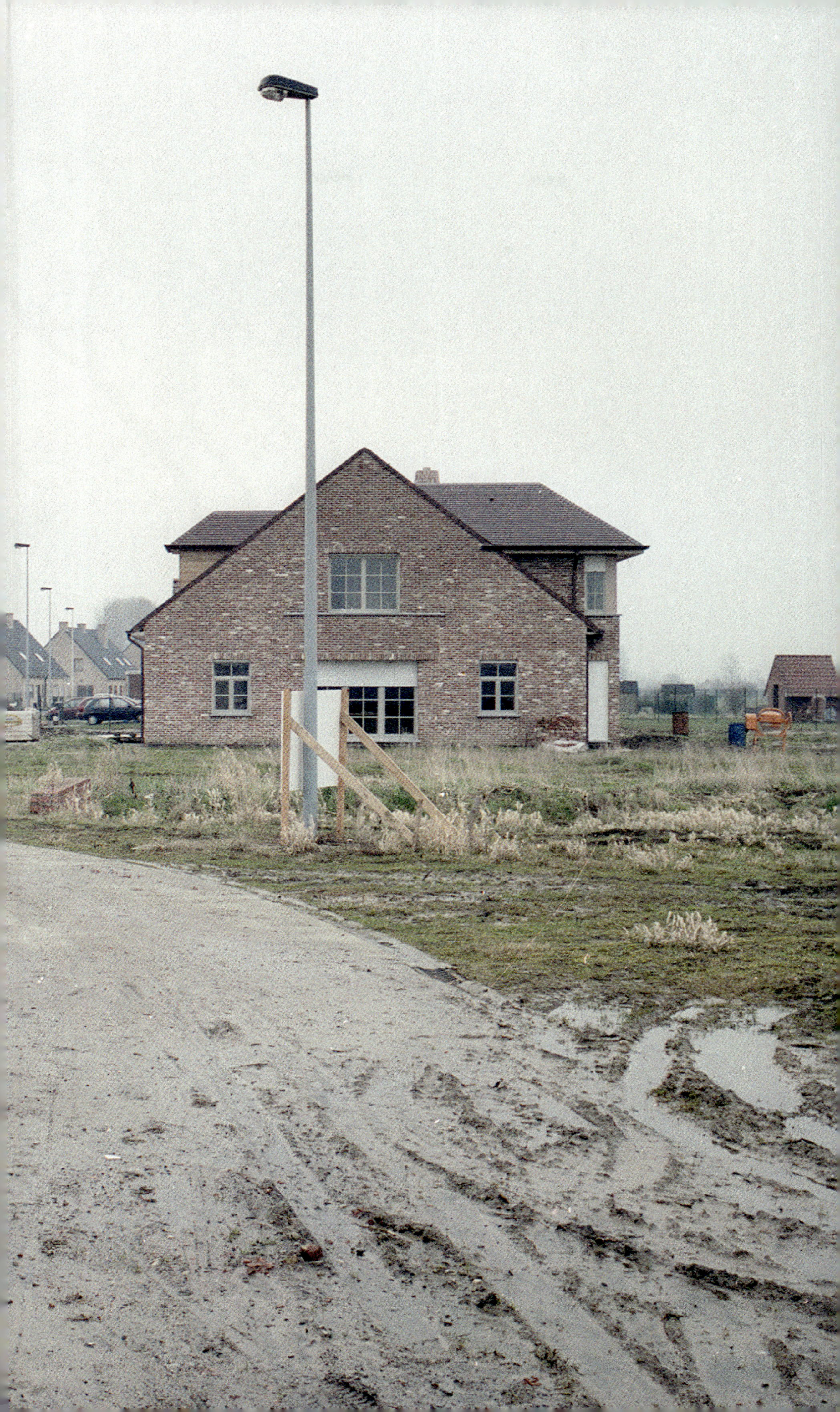

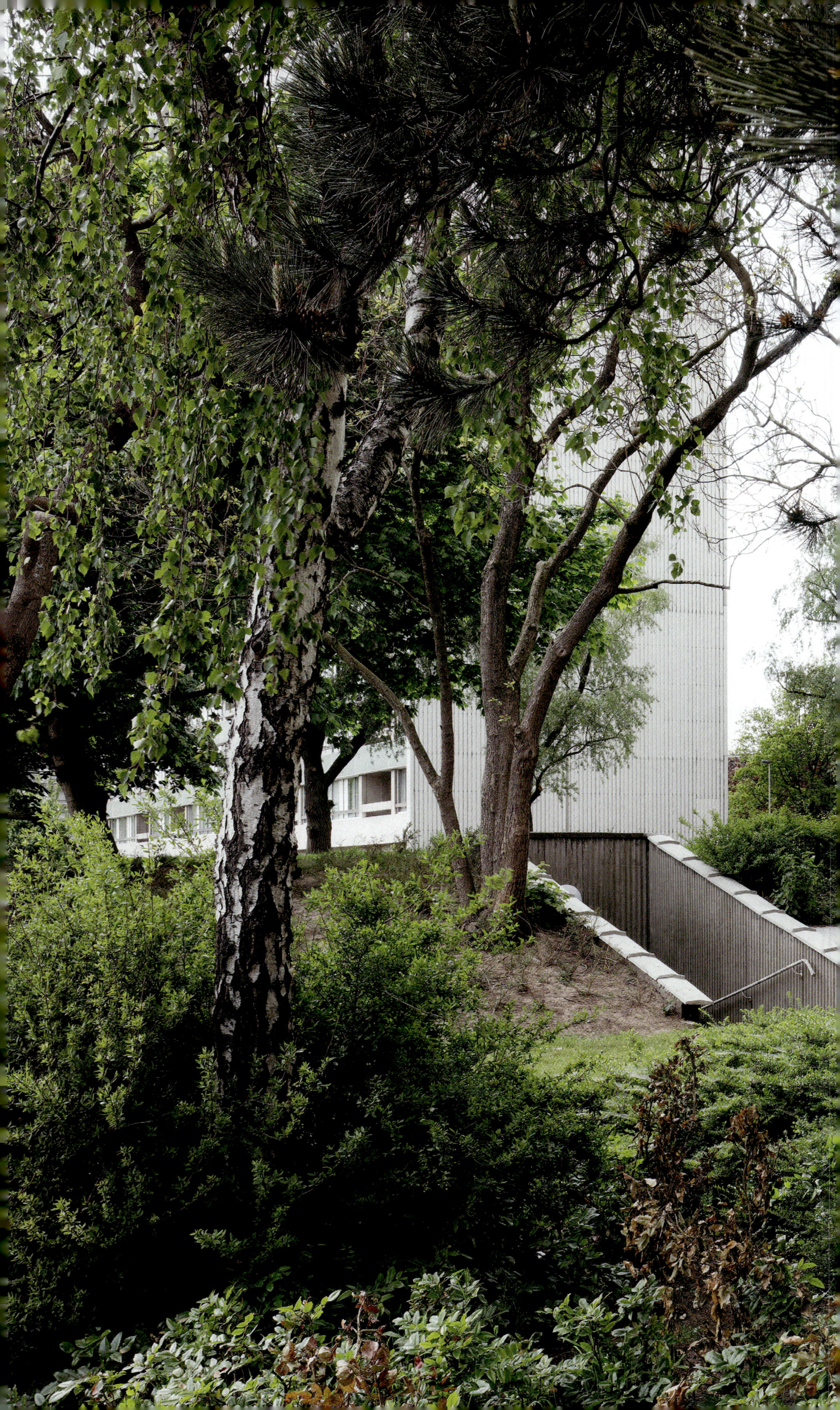

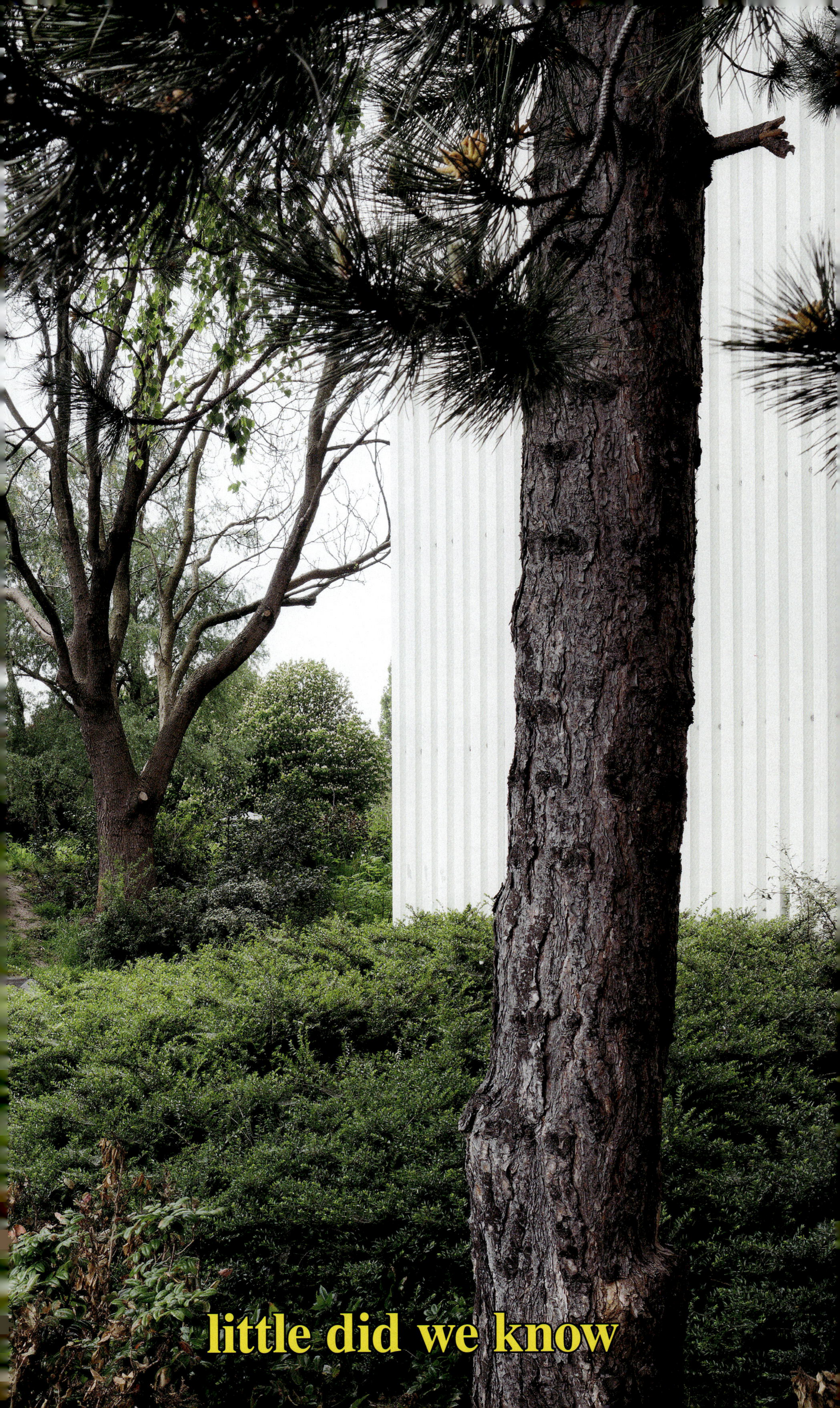
little did we know

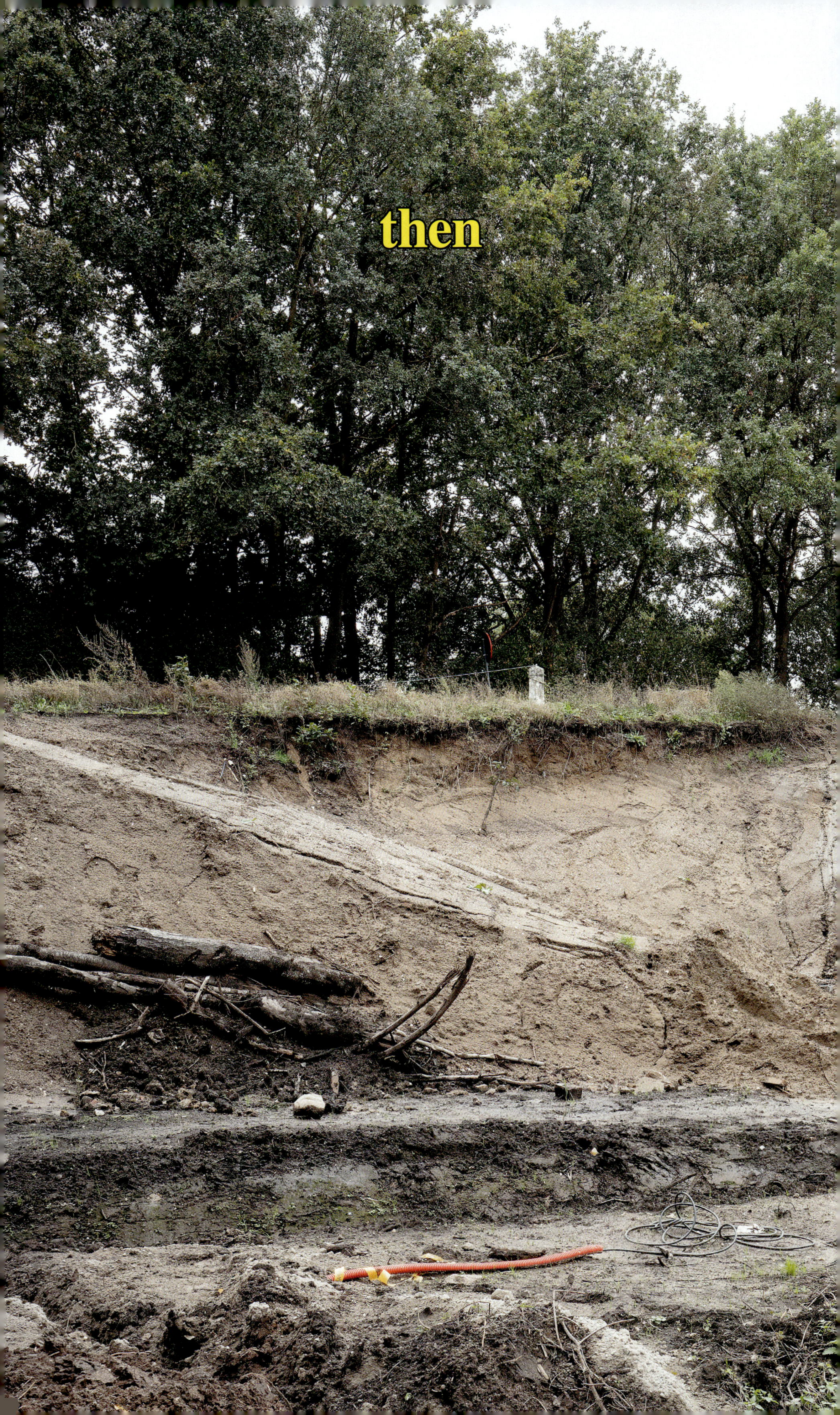

then

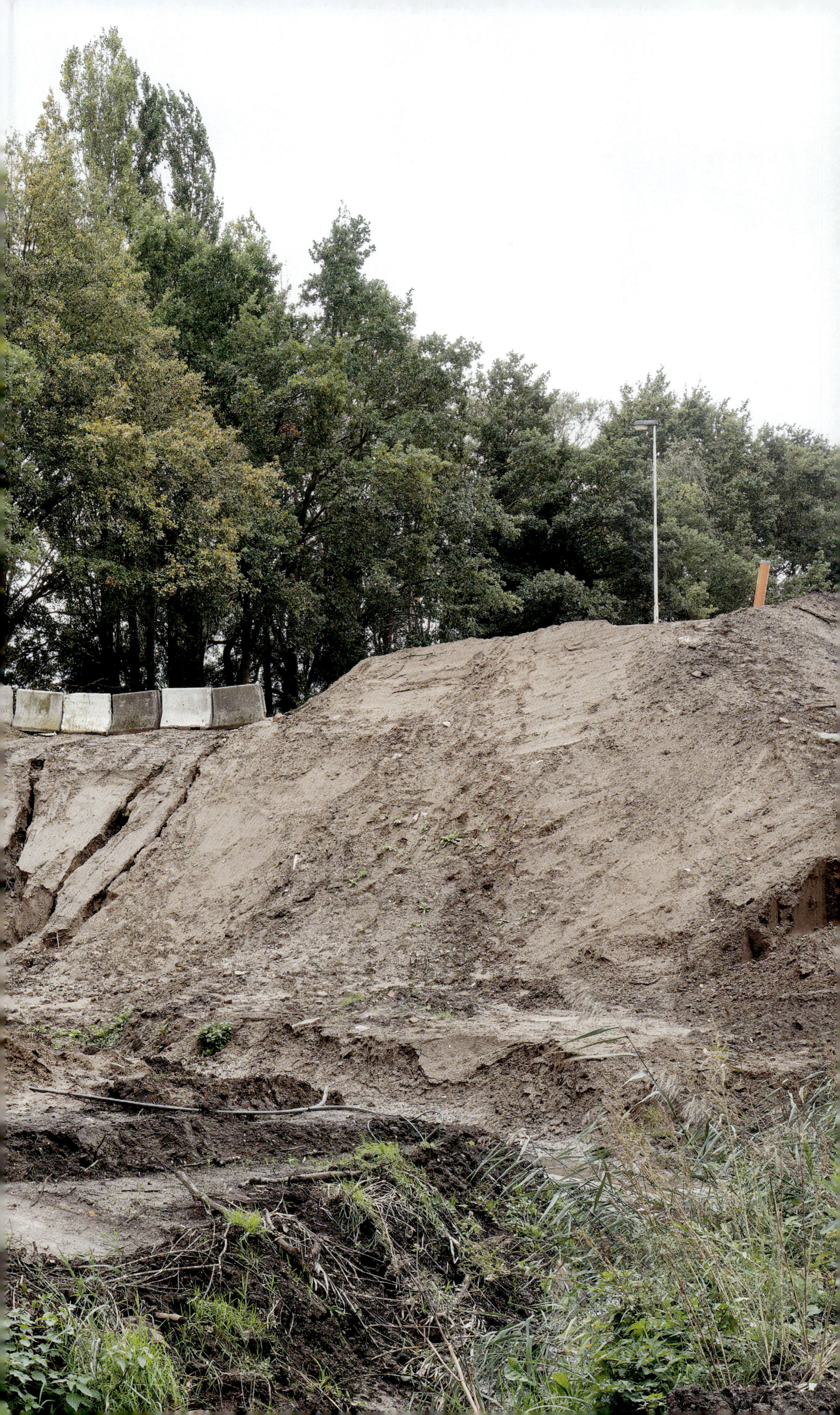

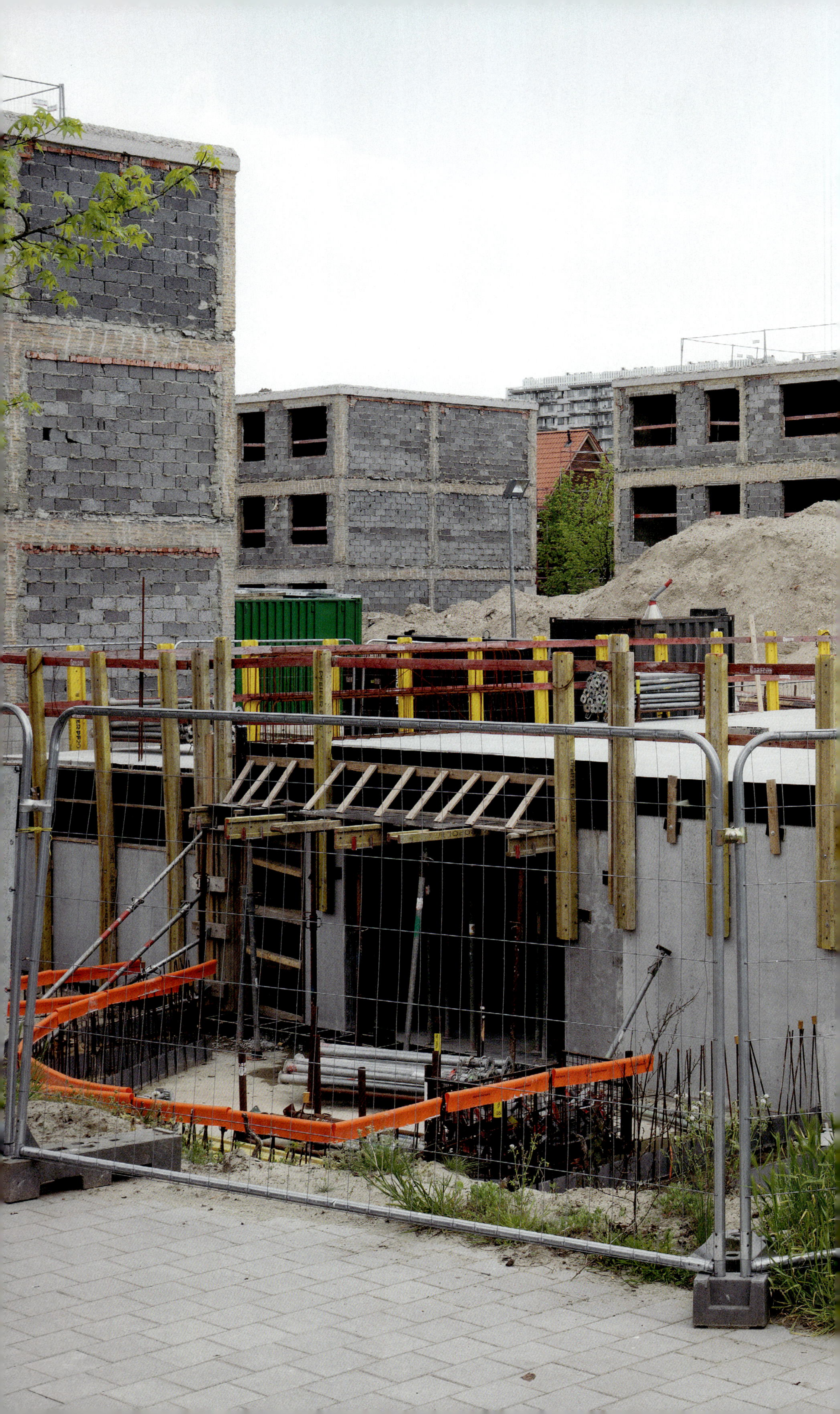

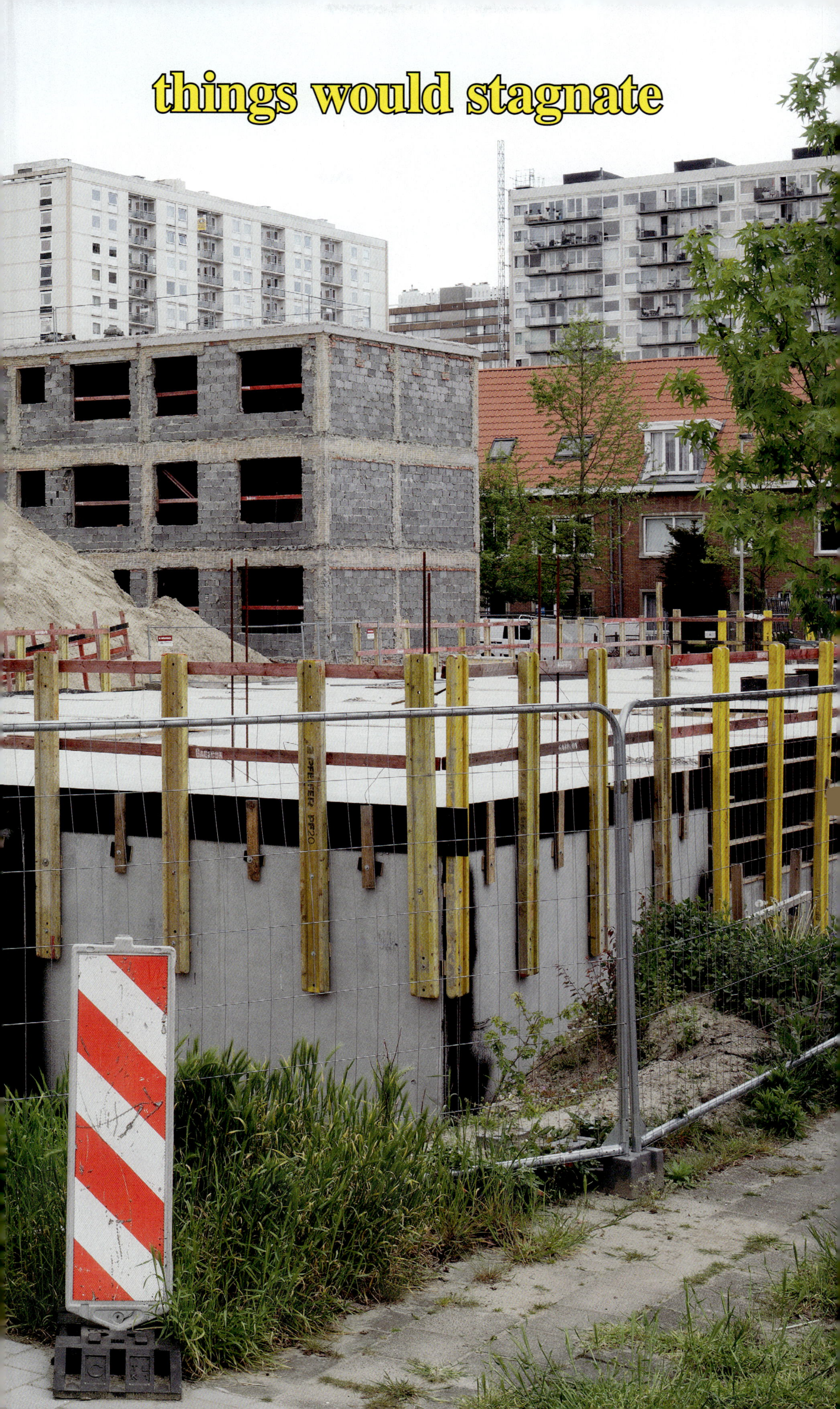
things would stagnate

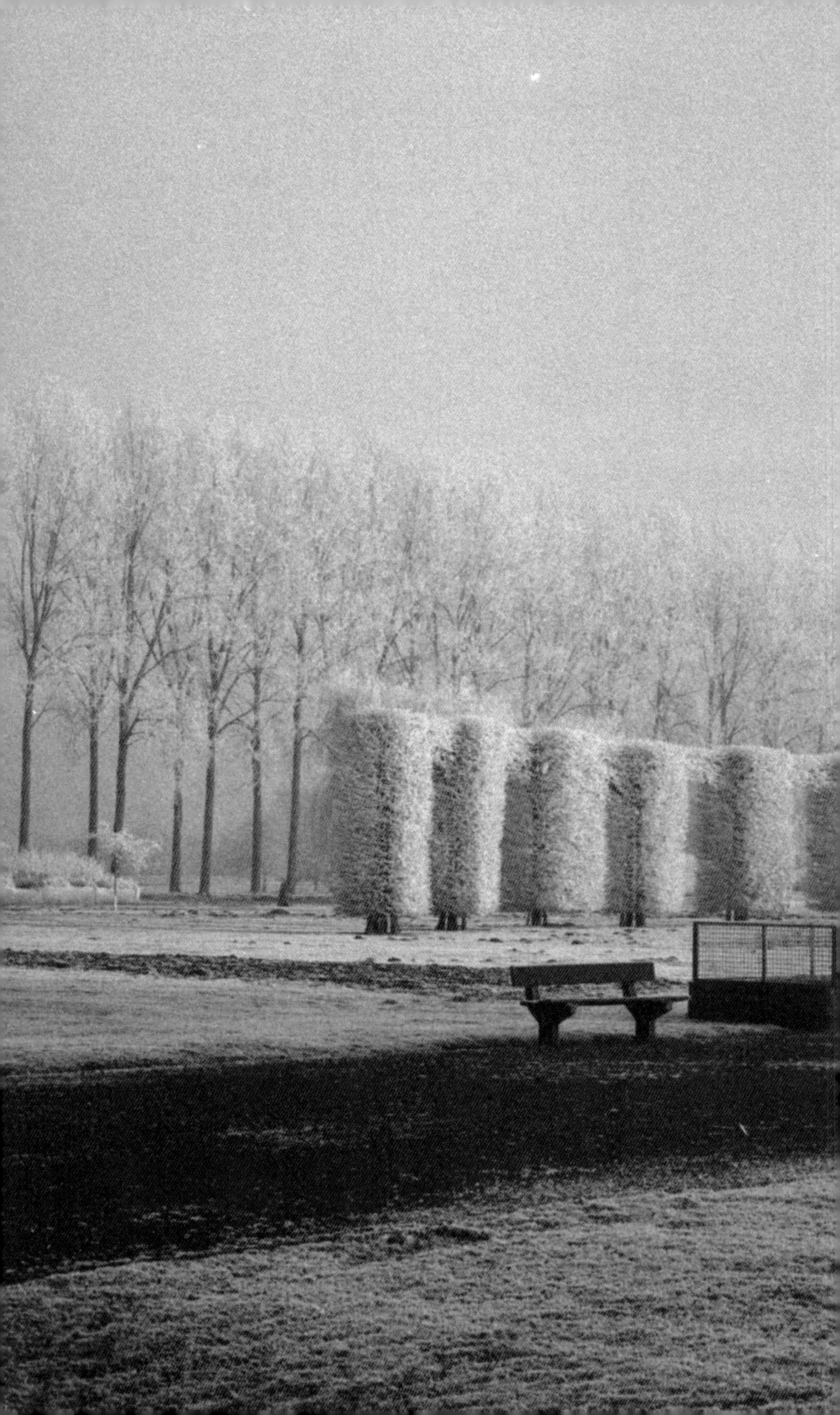

on Sunday

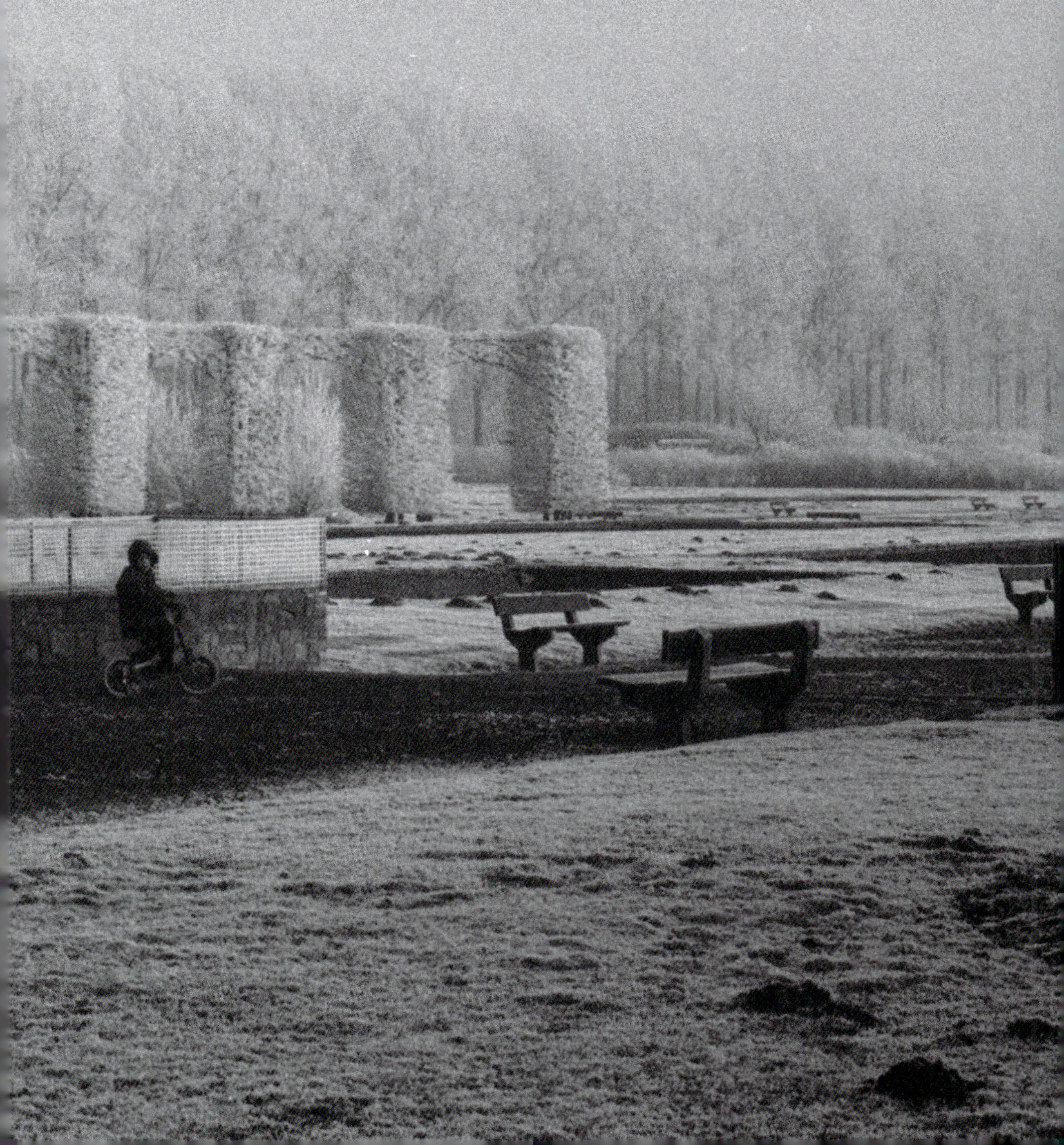

your pyjamas
are backwards

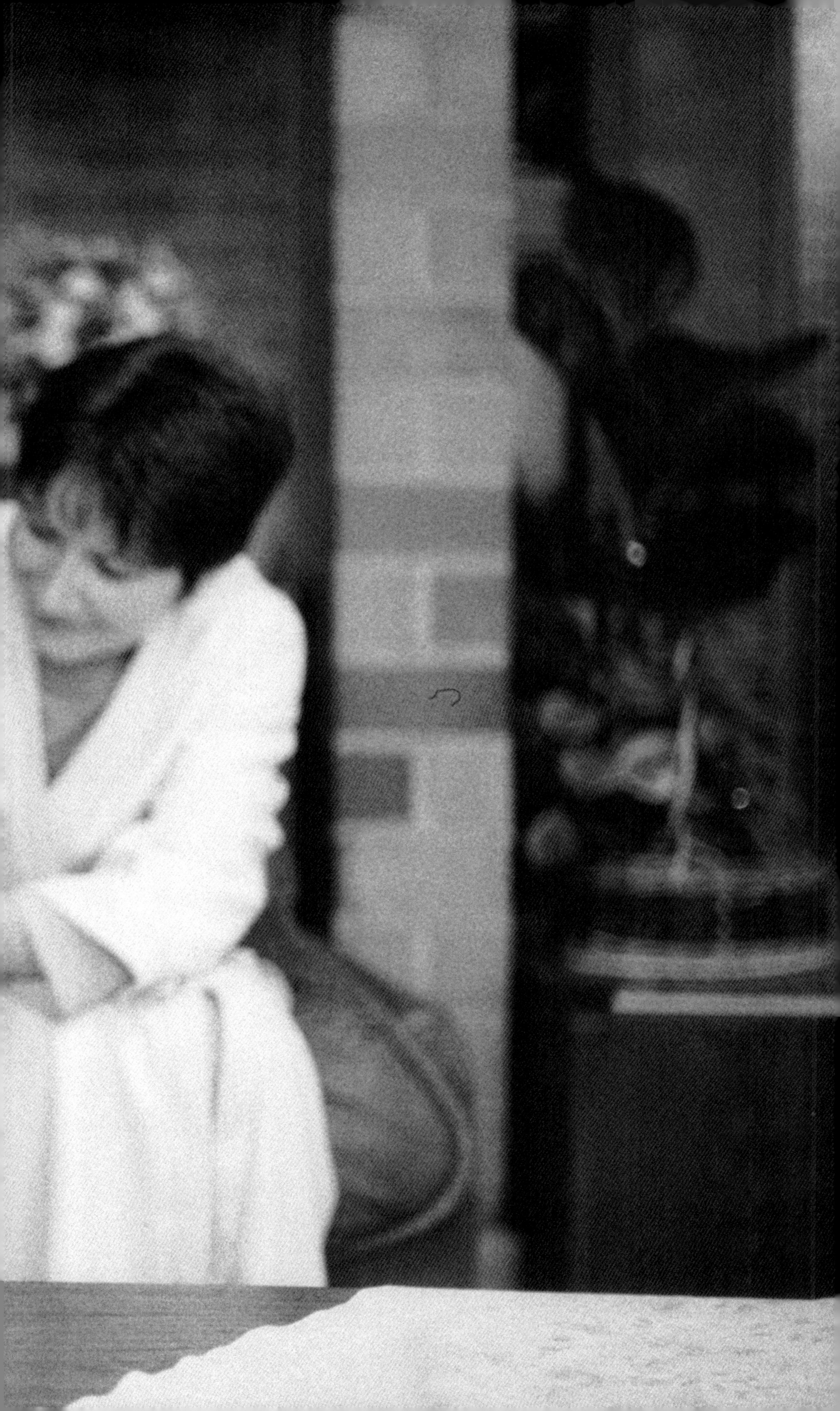

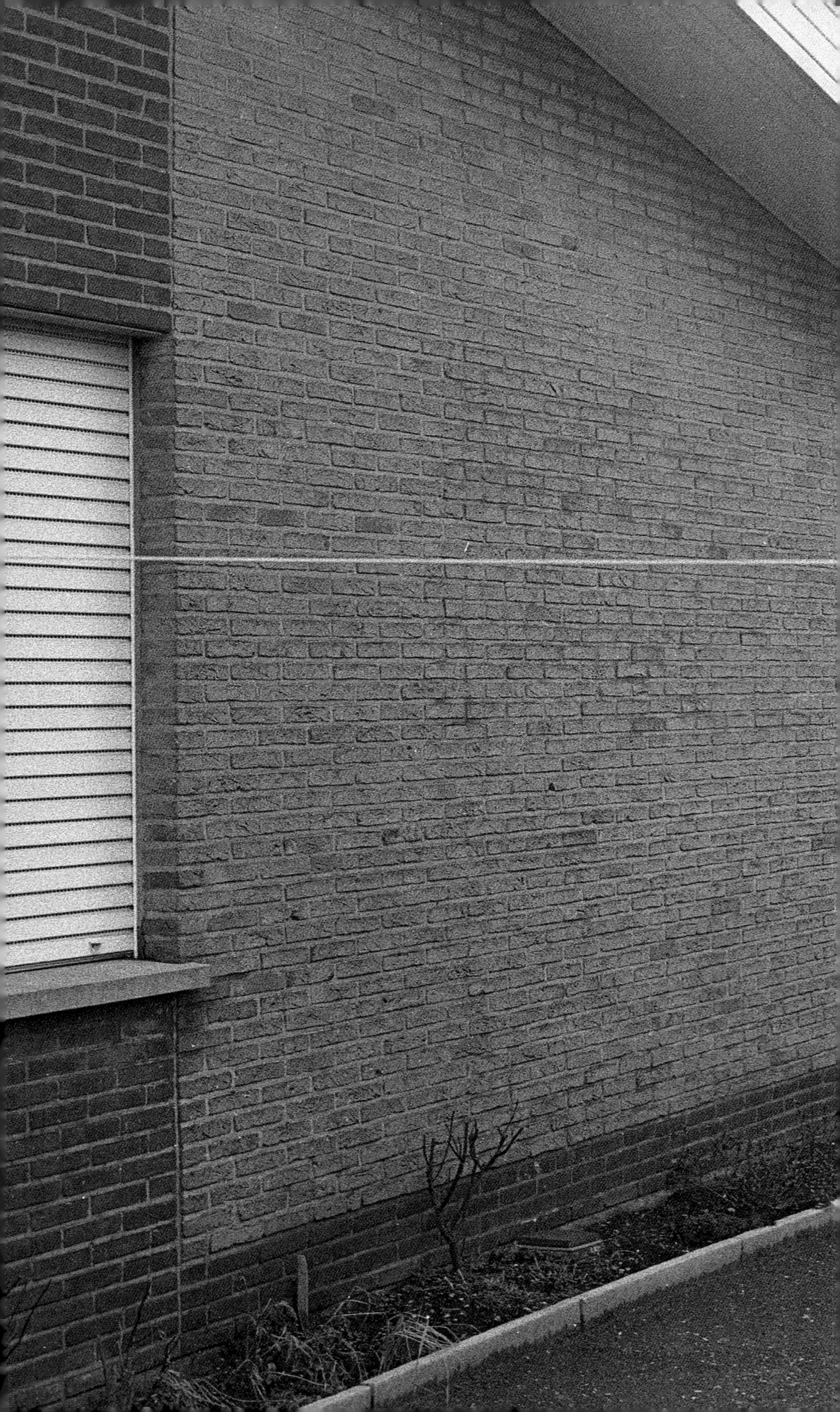

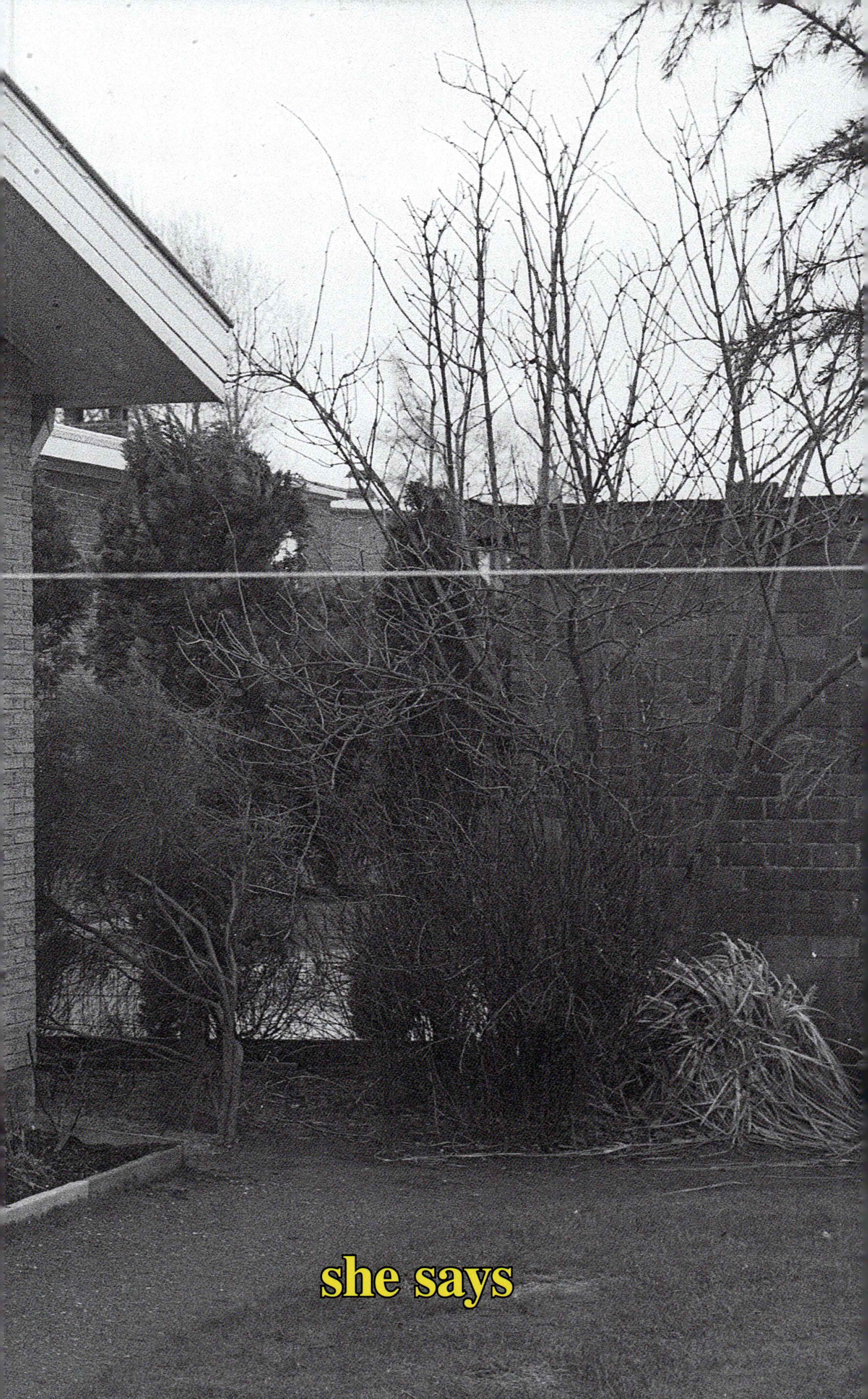

she says

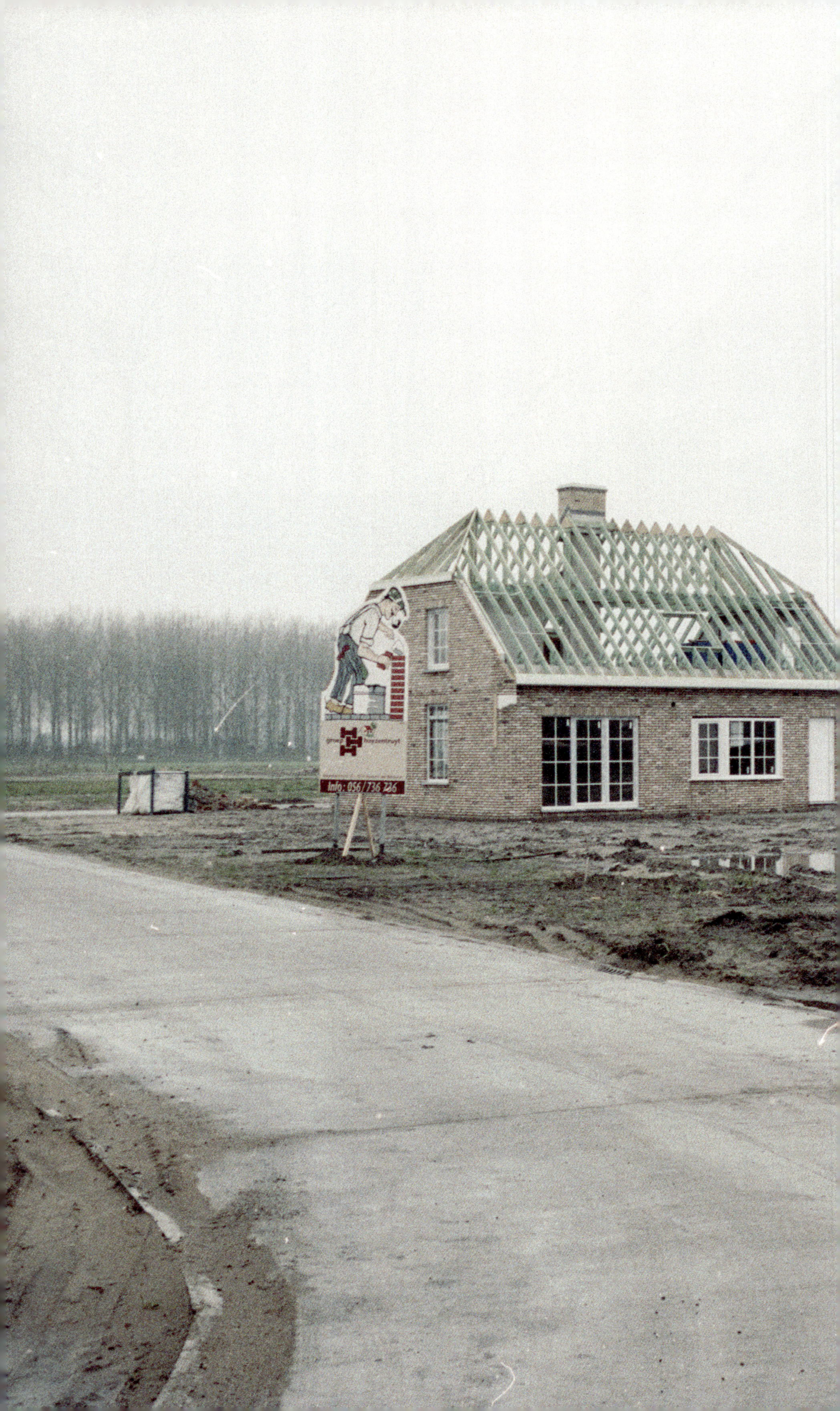

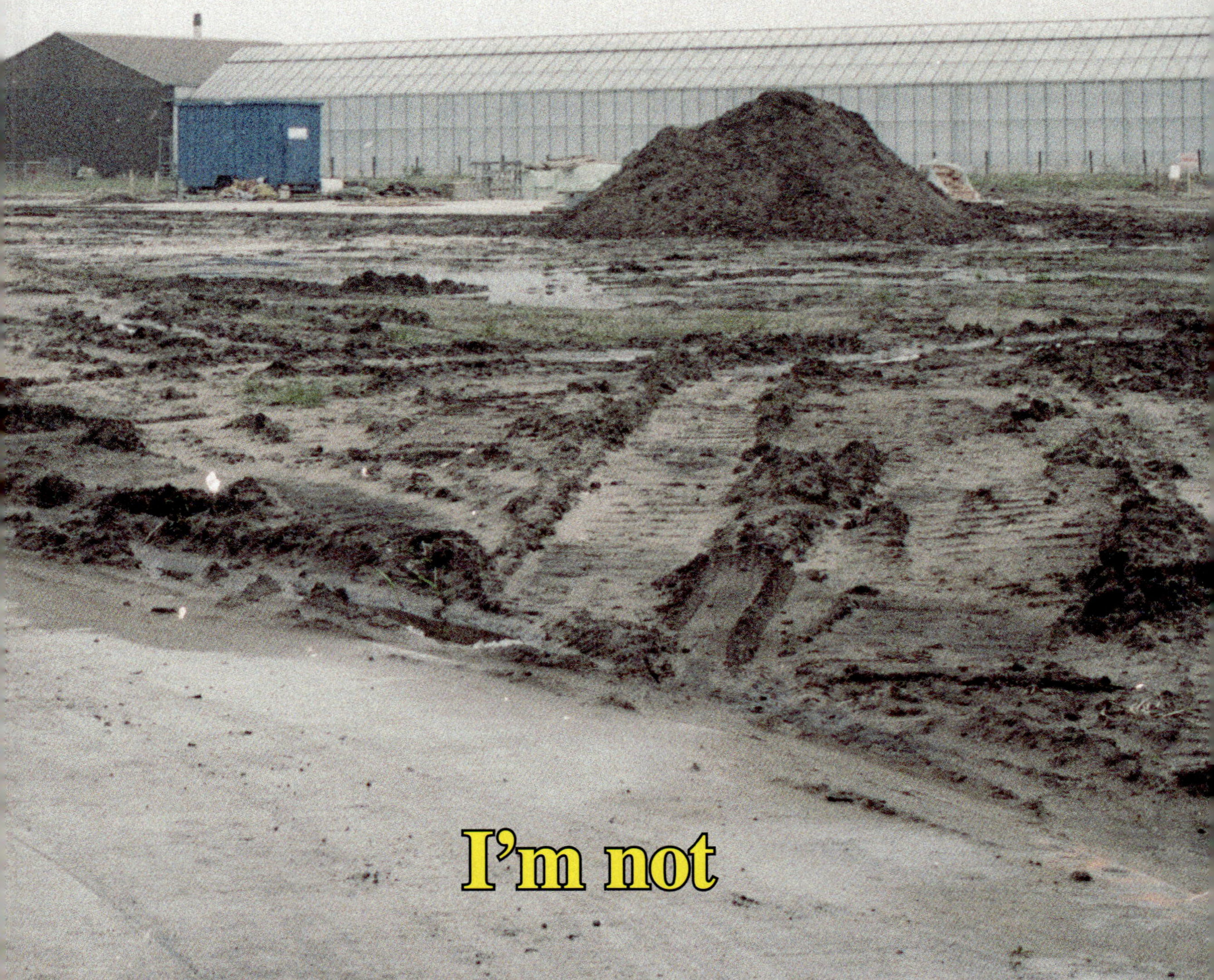

I’m not

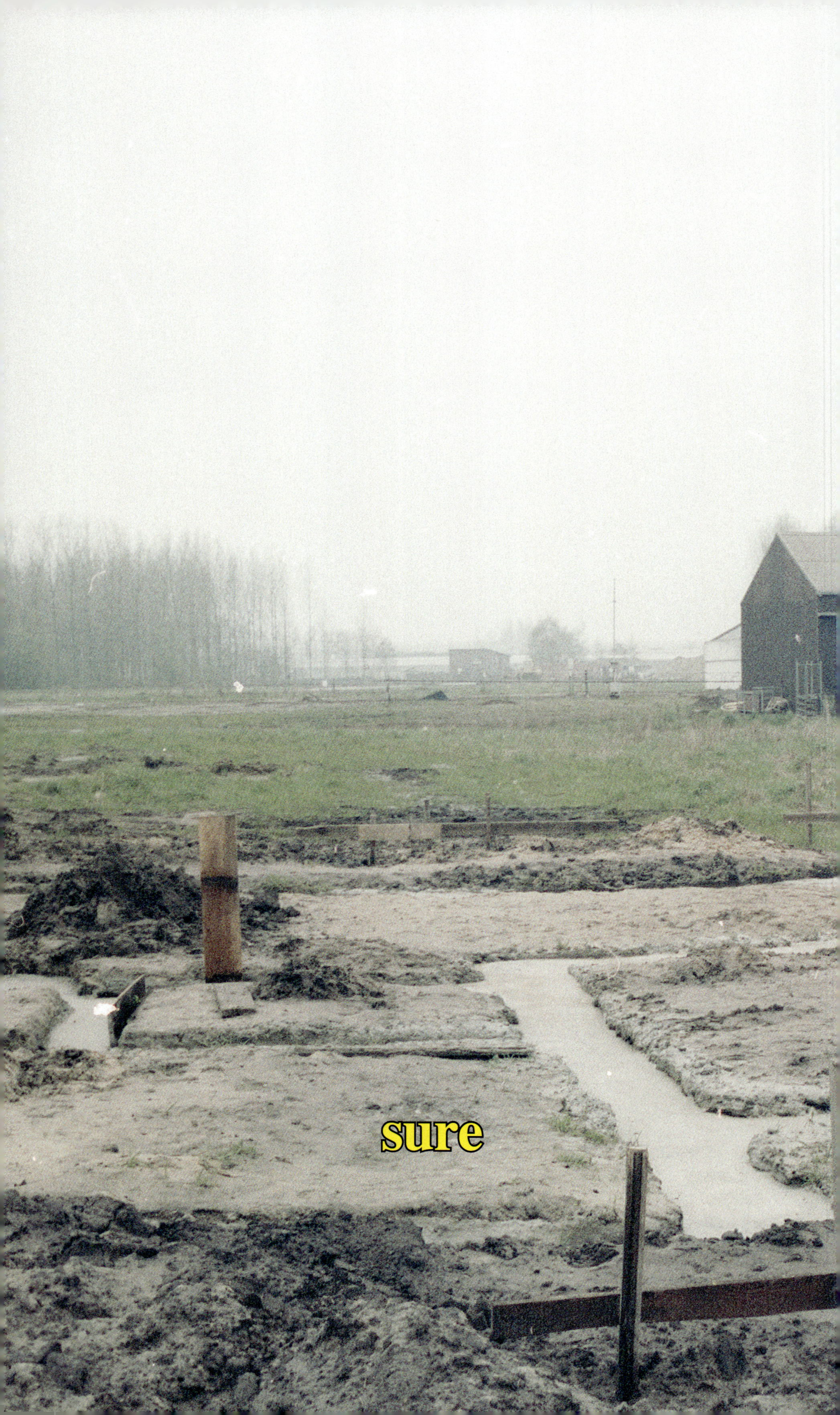
sure

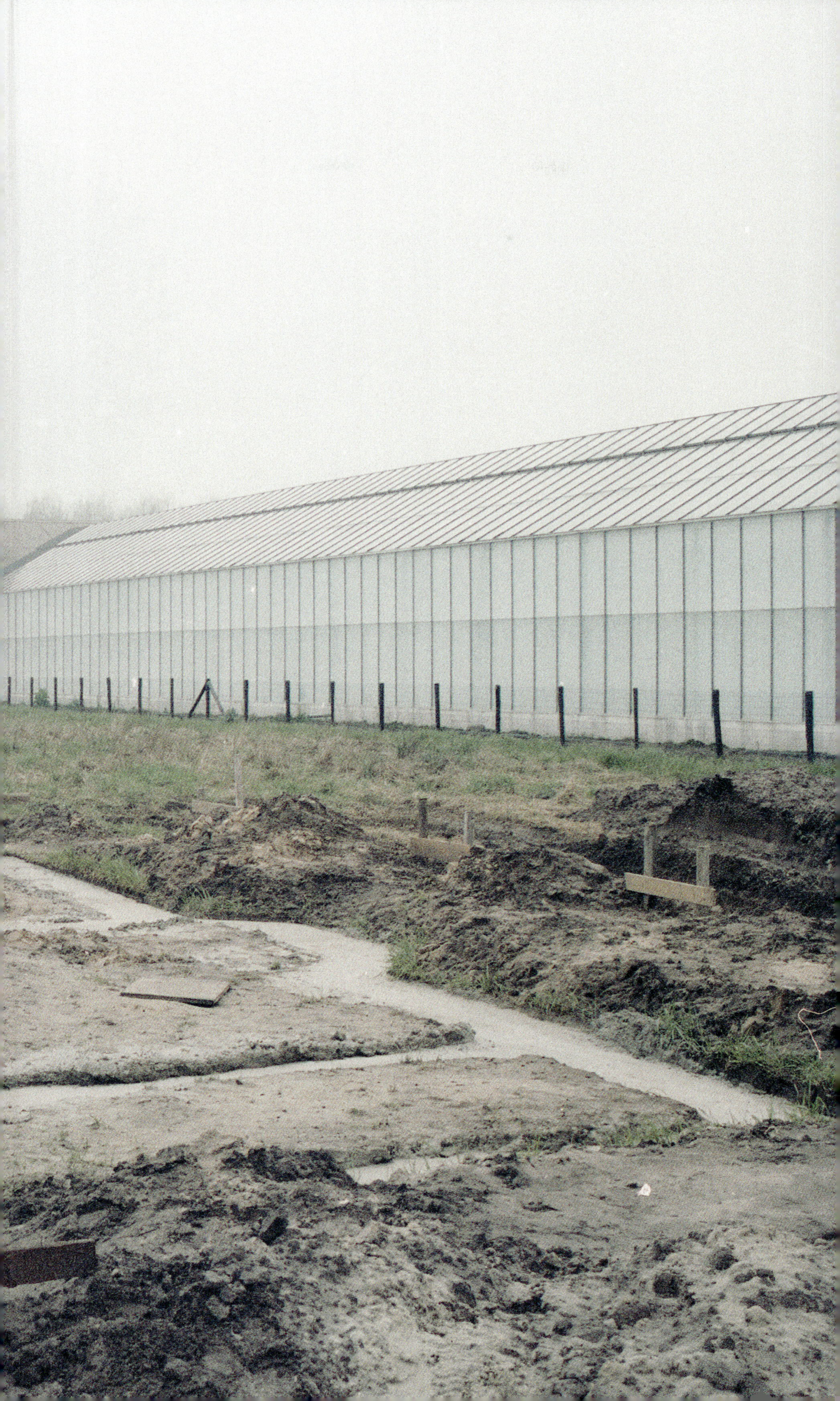

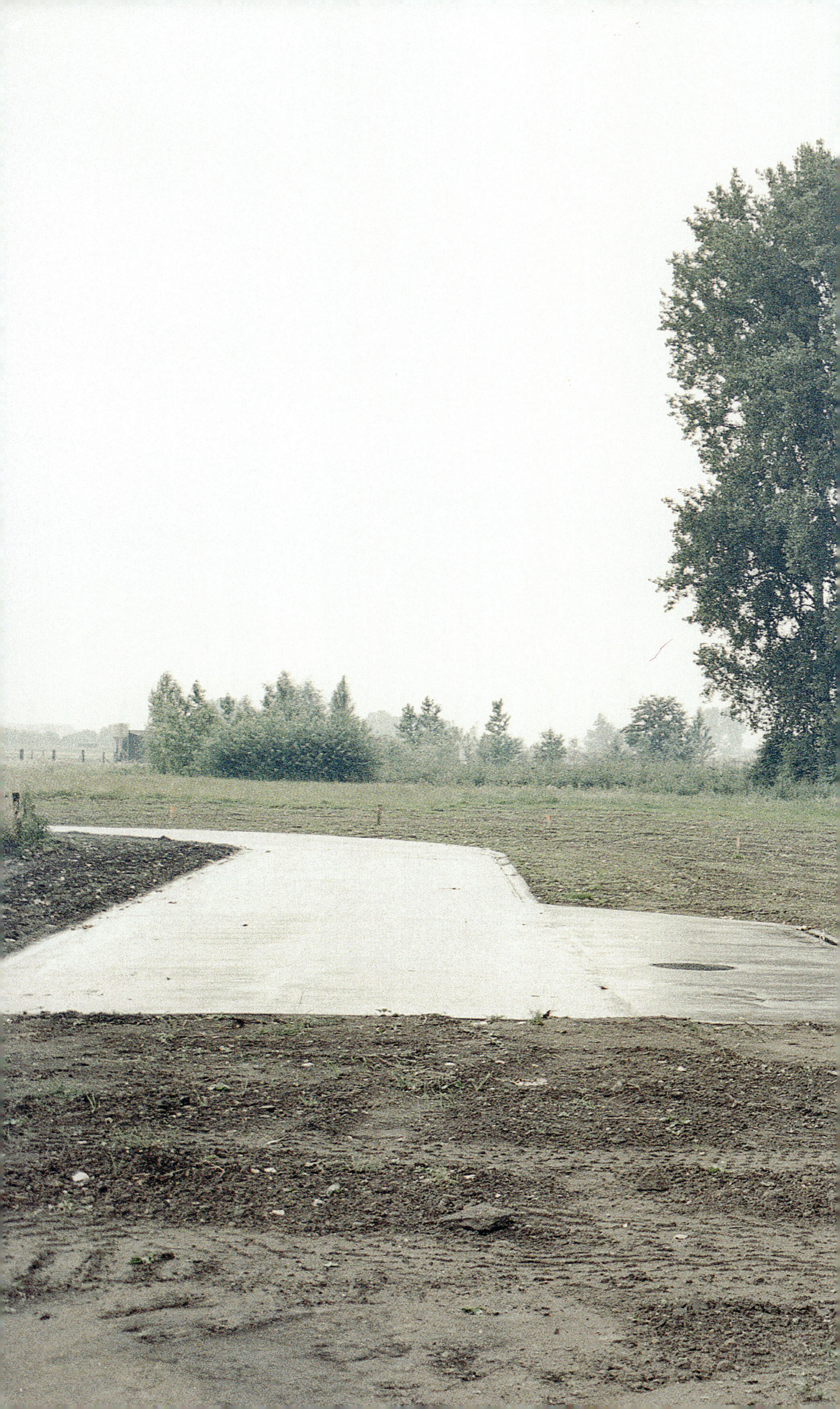

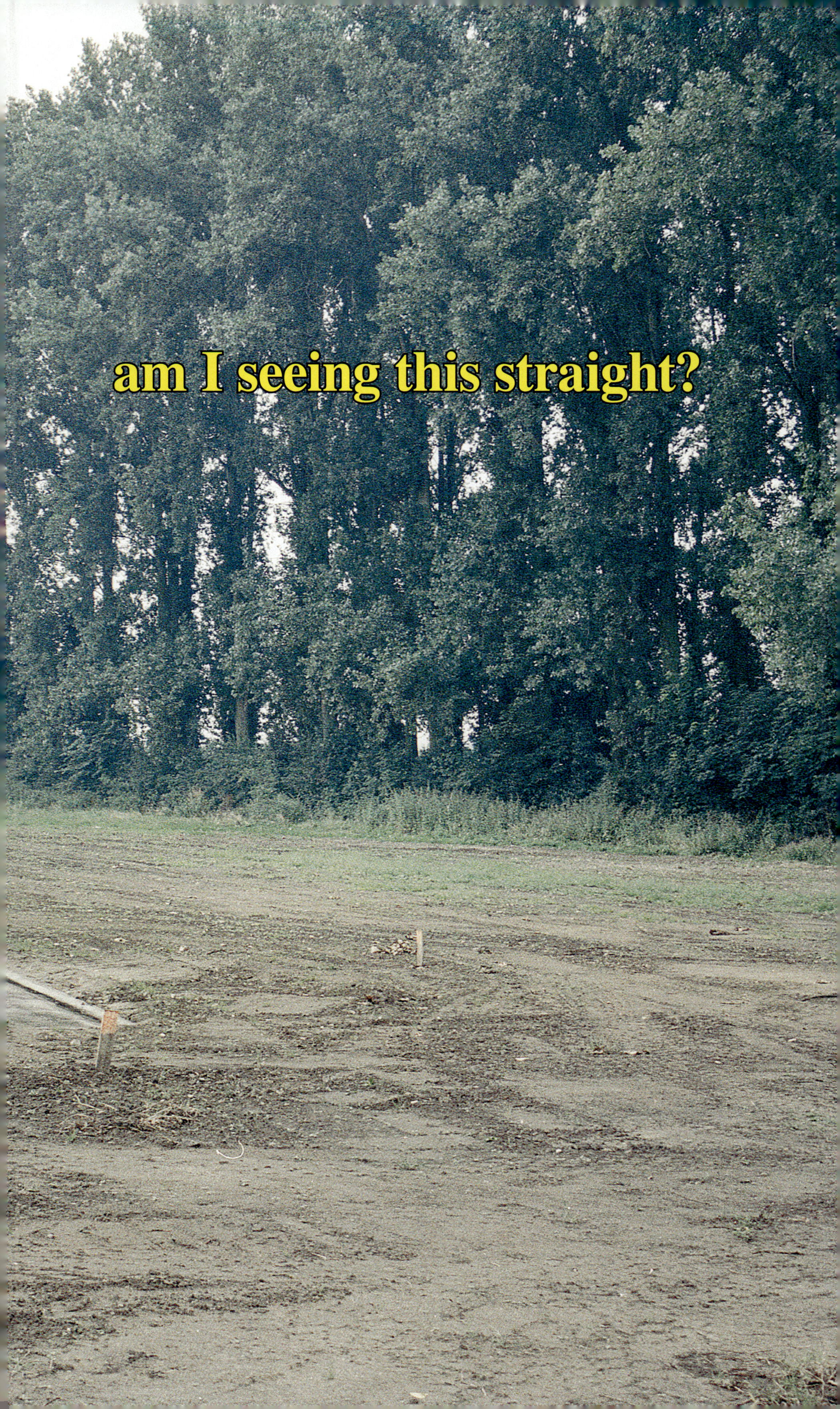
am I seeing this straight?

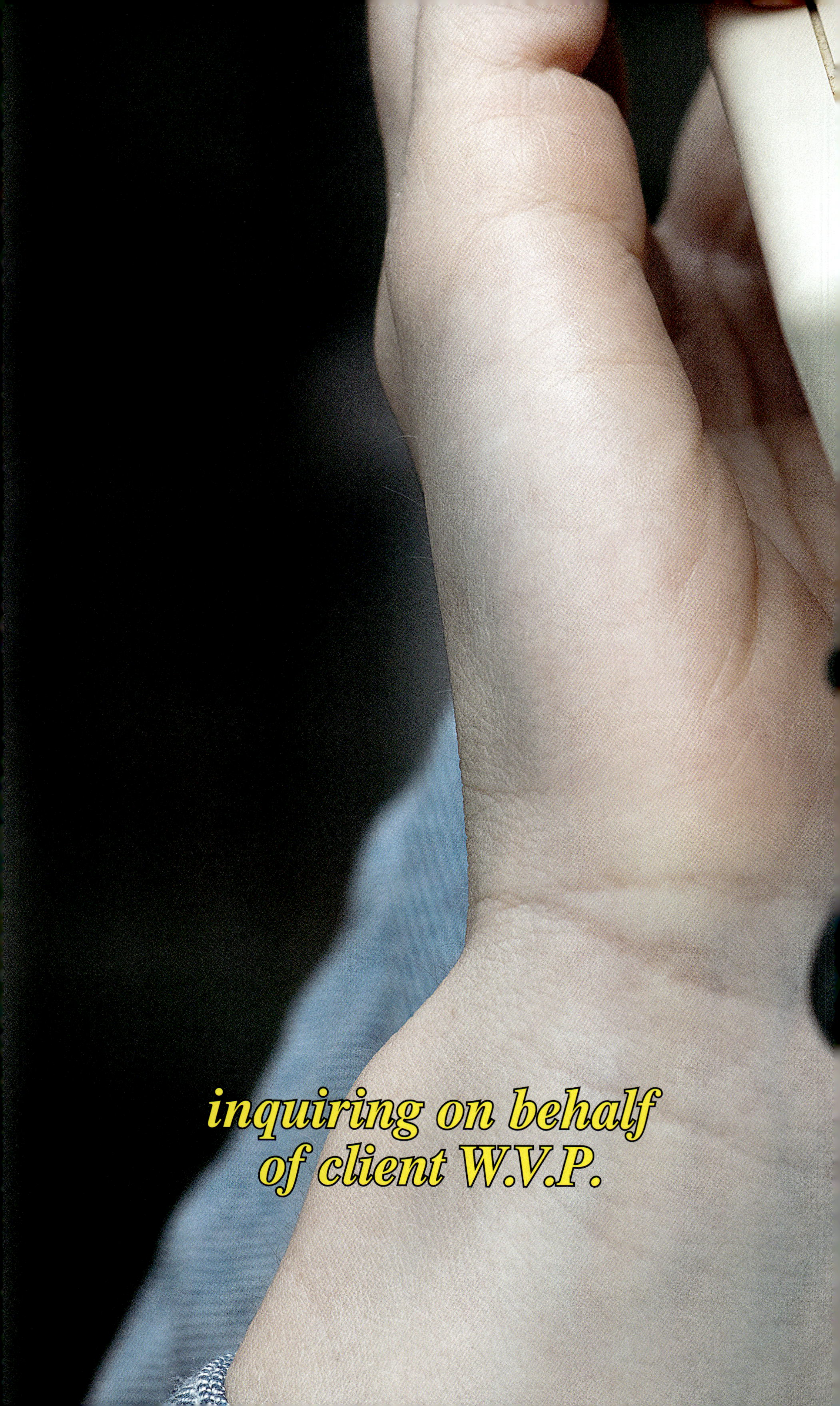
inquiring on behalf
of client W.V.P.

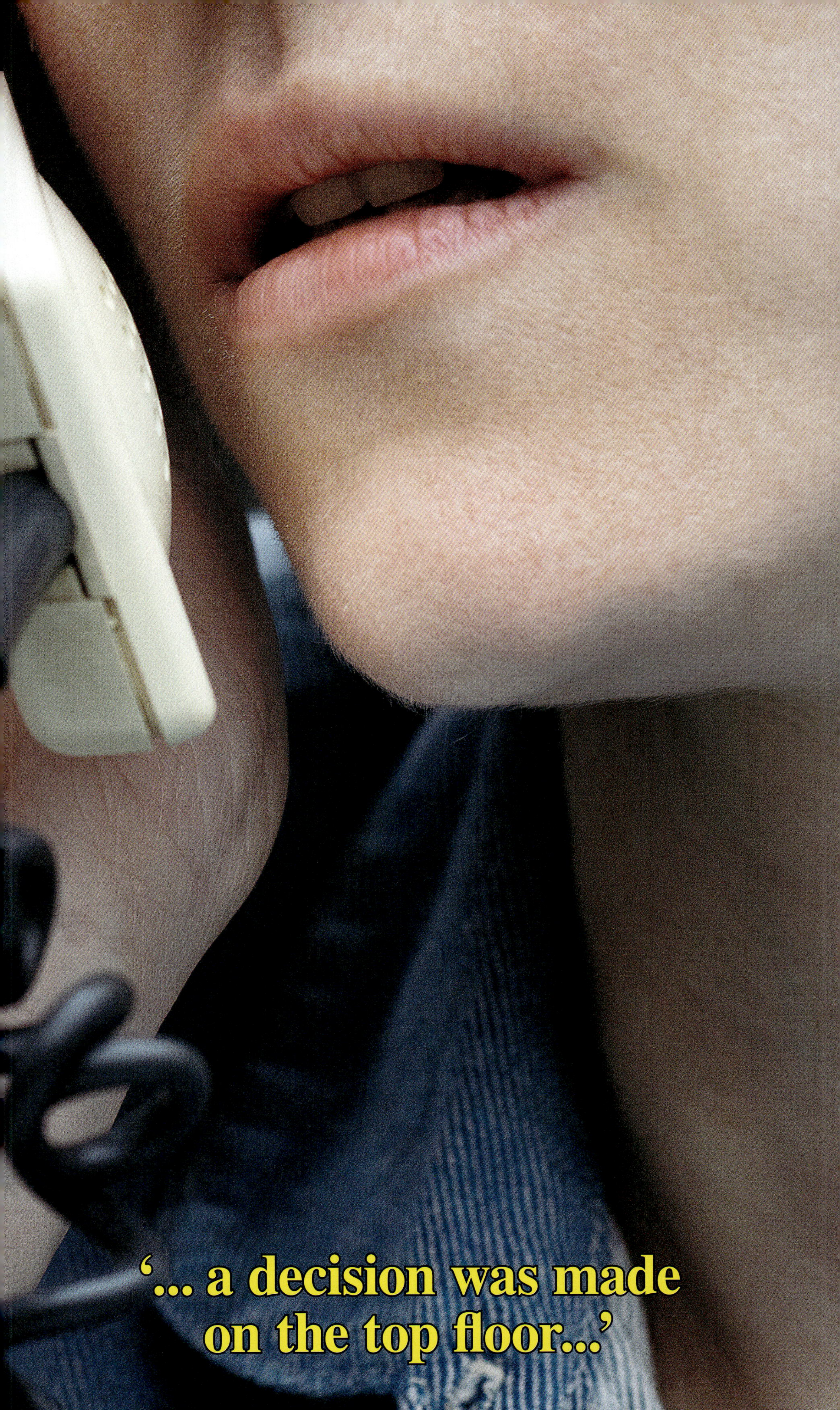
'... a decision was made
on the top floor...'

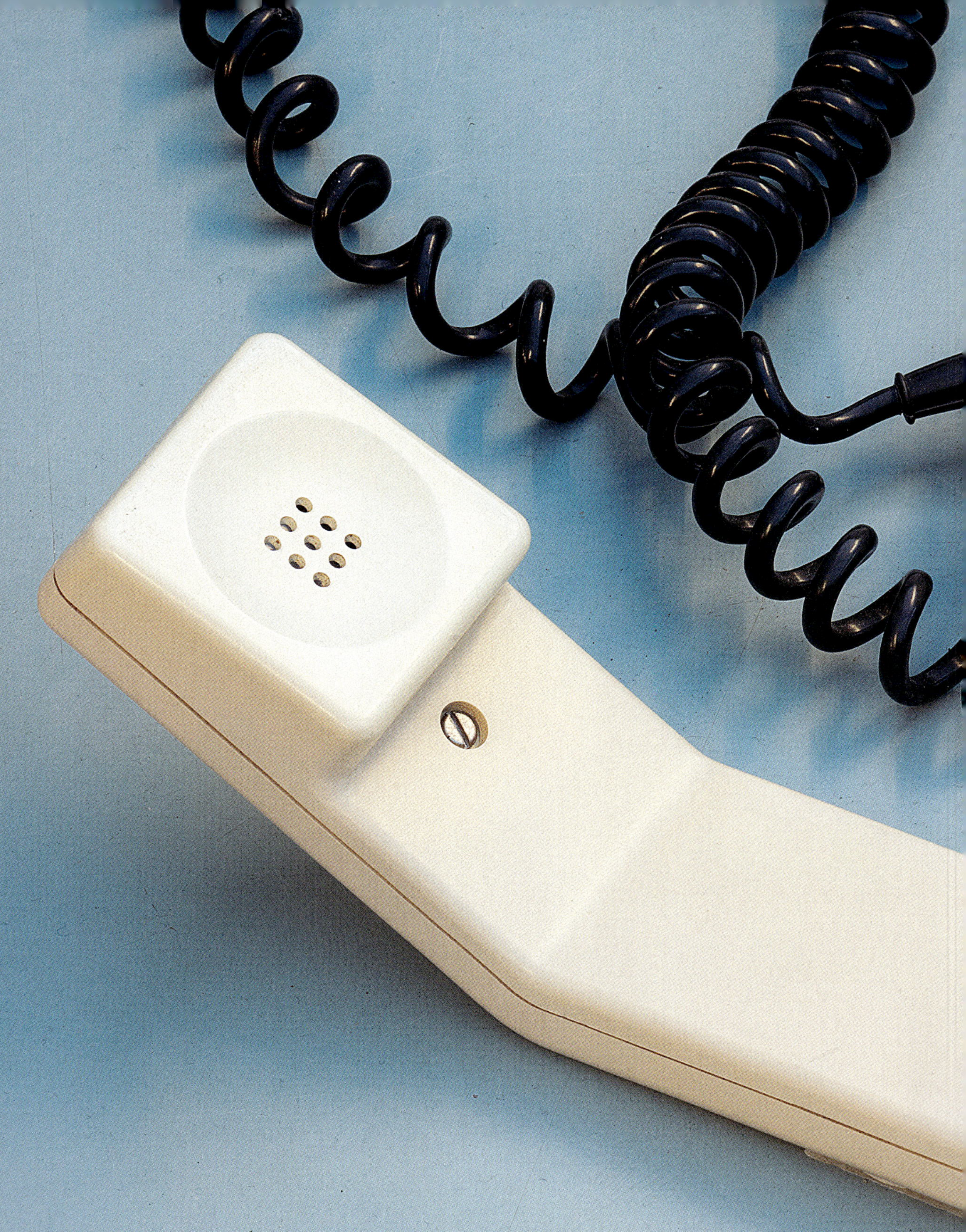

with regards to the refusal of the building application

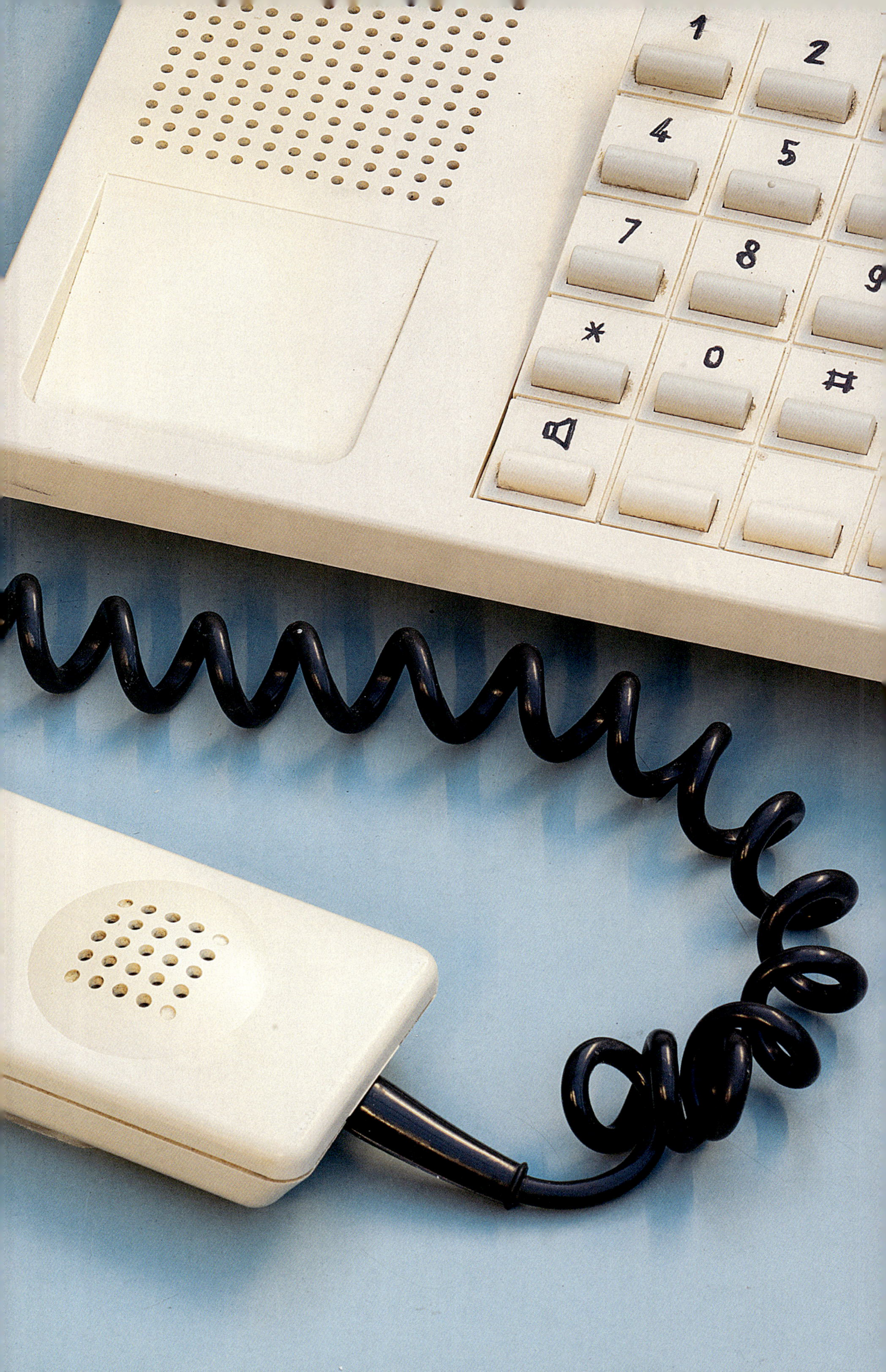

'... we no longer accept change...'

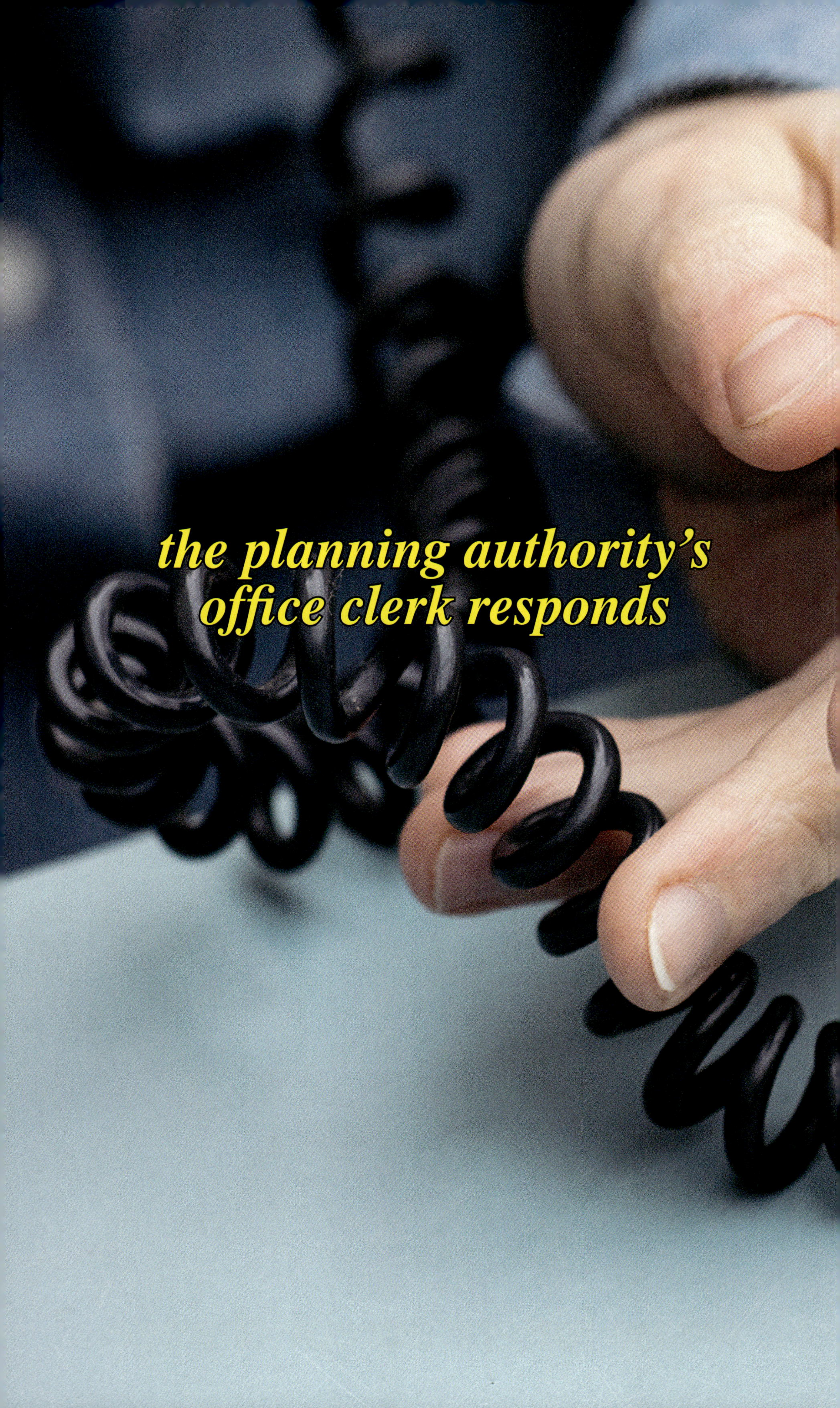
the planning authority's
office clerk responds

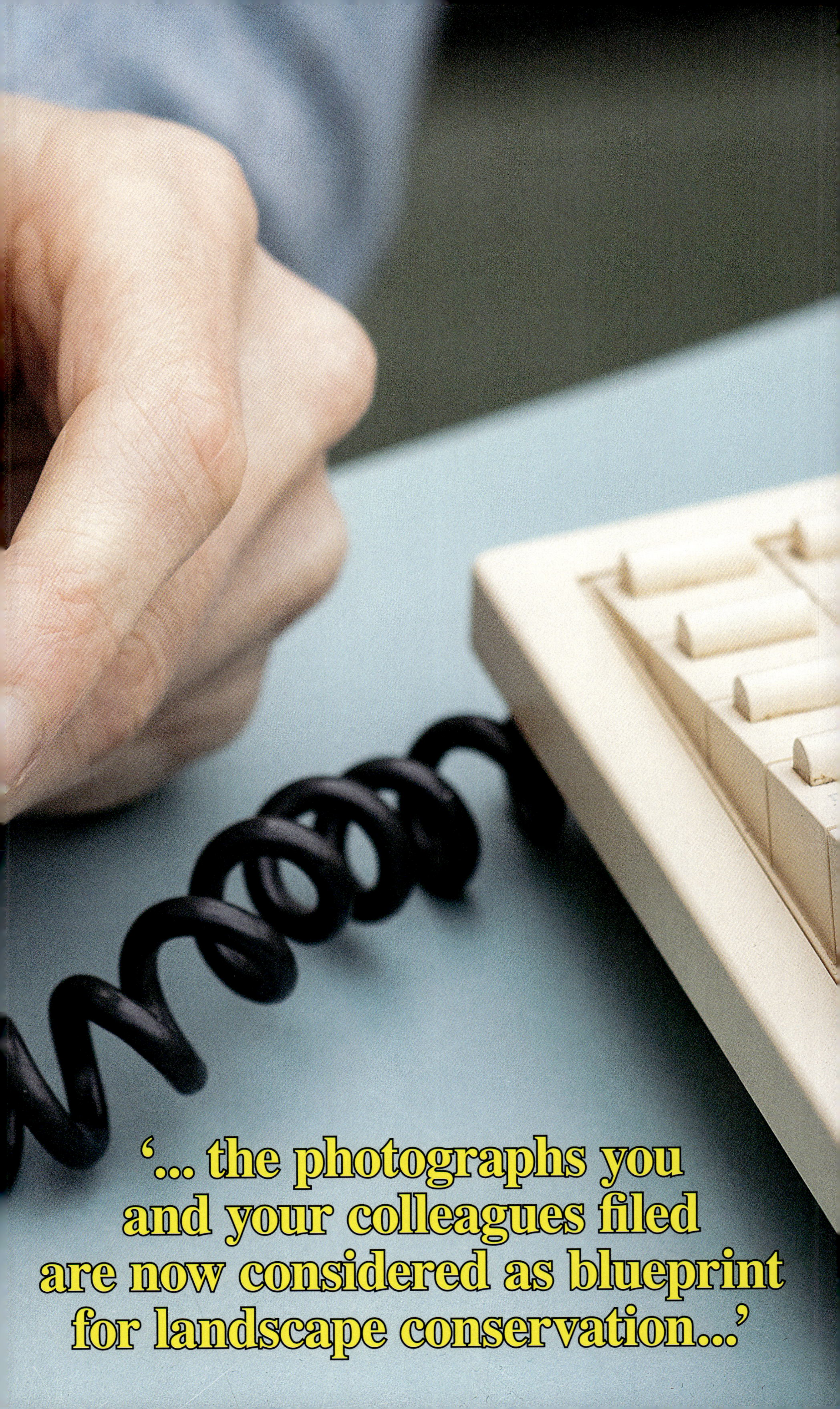
'... the photographs you
and your colleagues filed
are now considered as blueprint
for landscape conservation...'

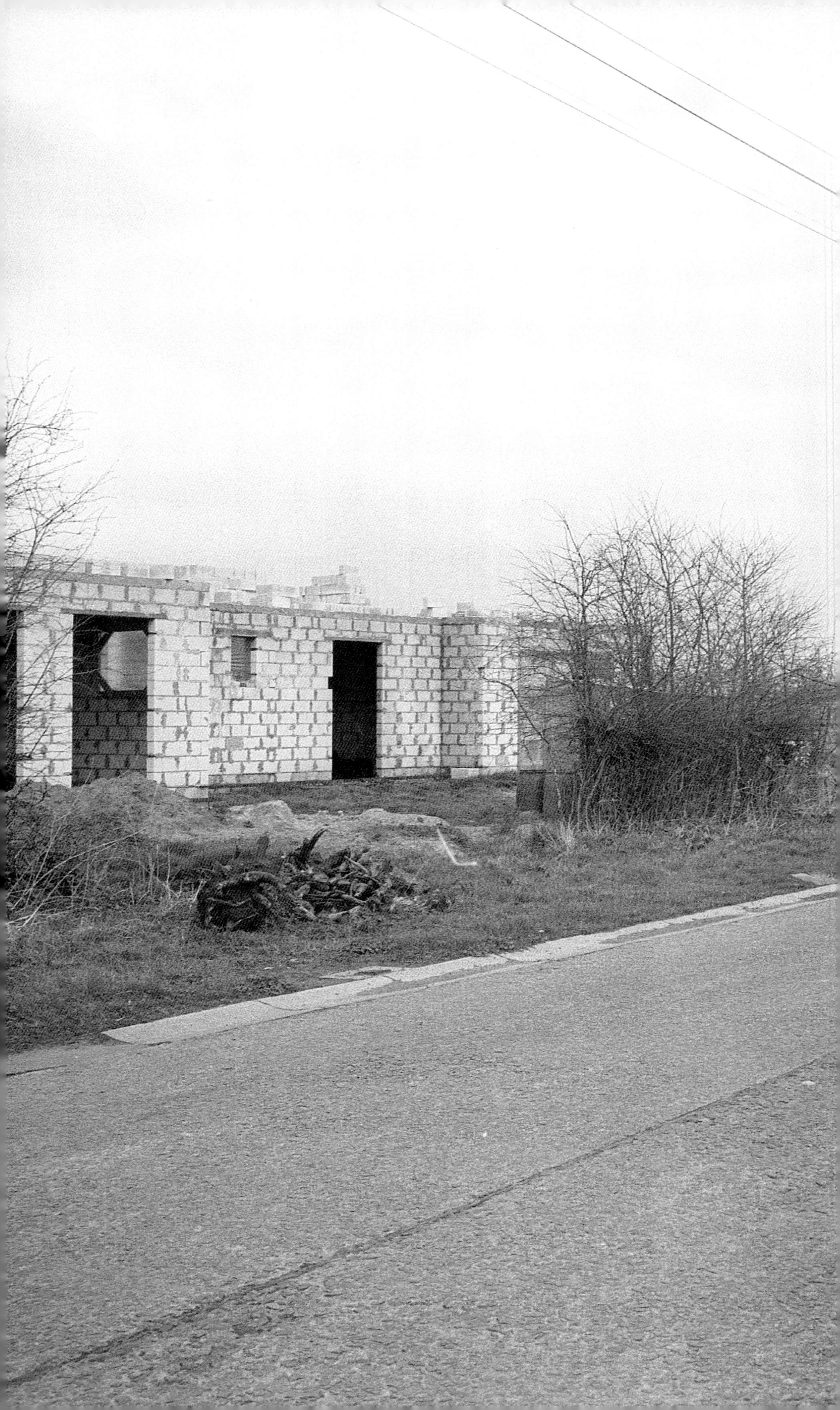

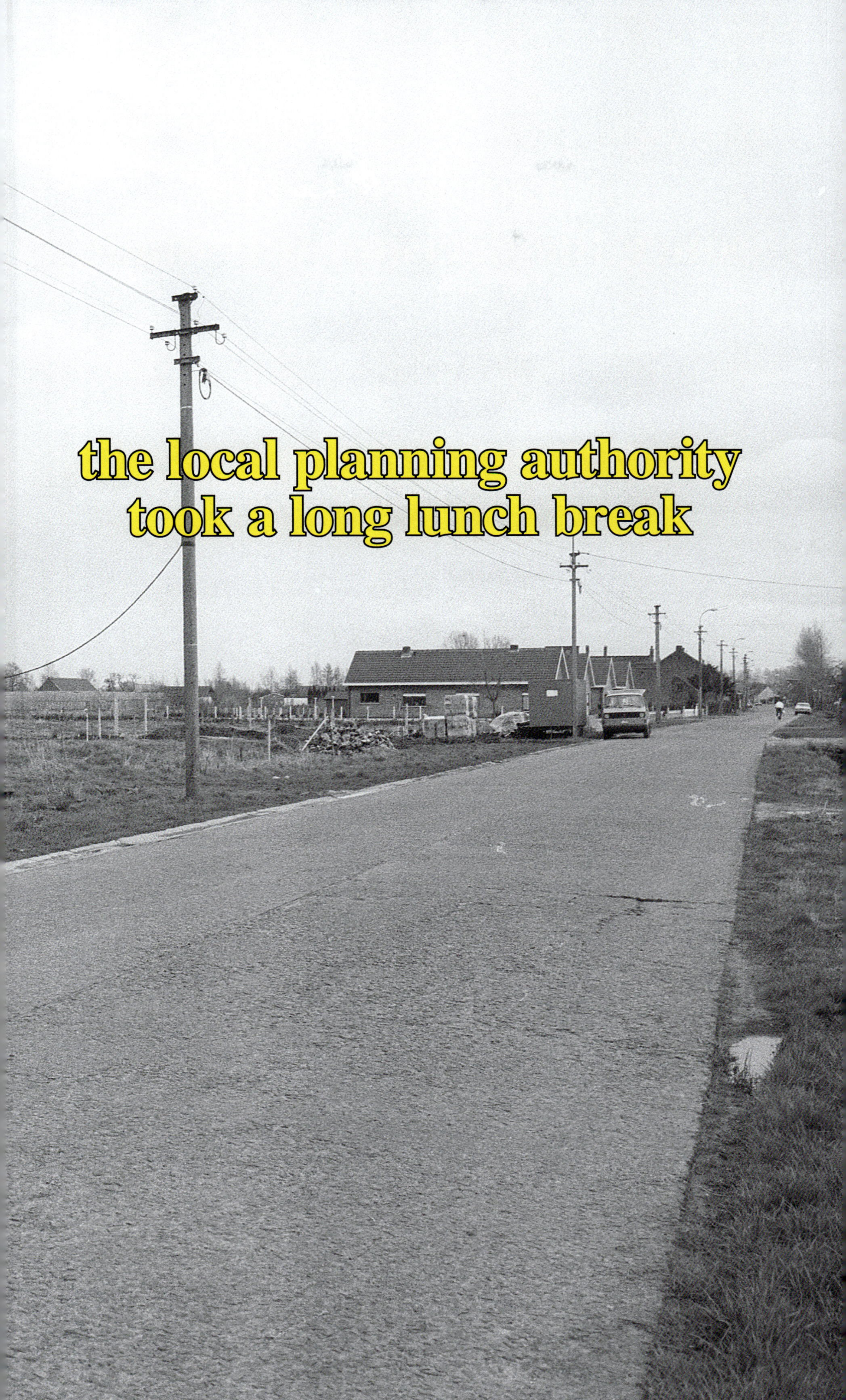
the local planning authority
took a long lunch break

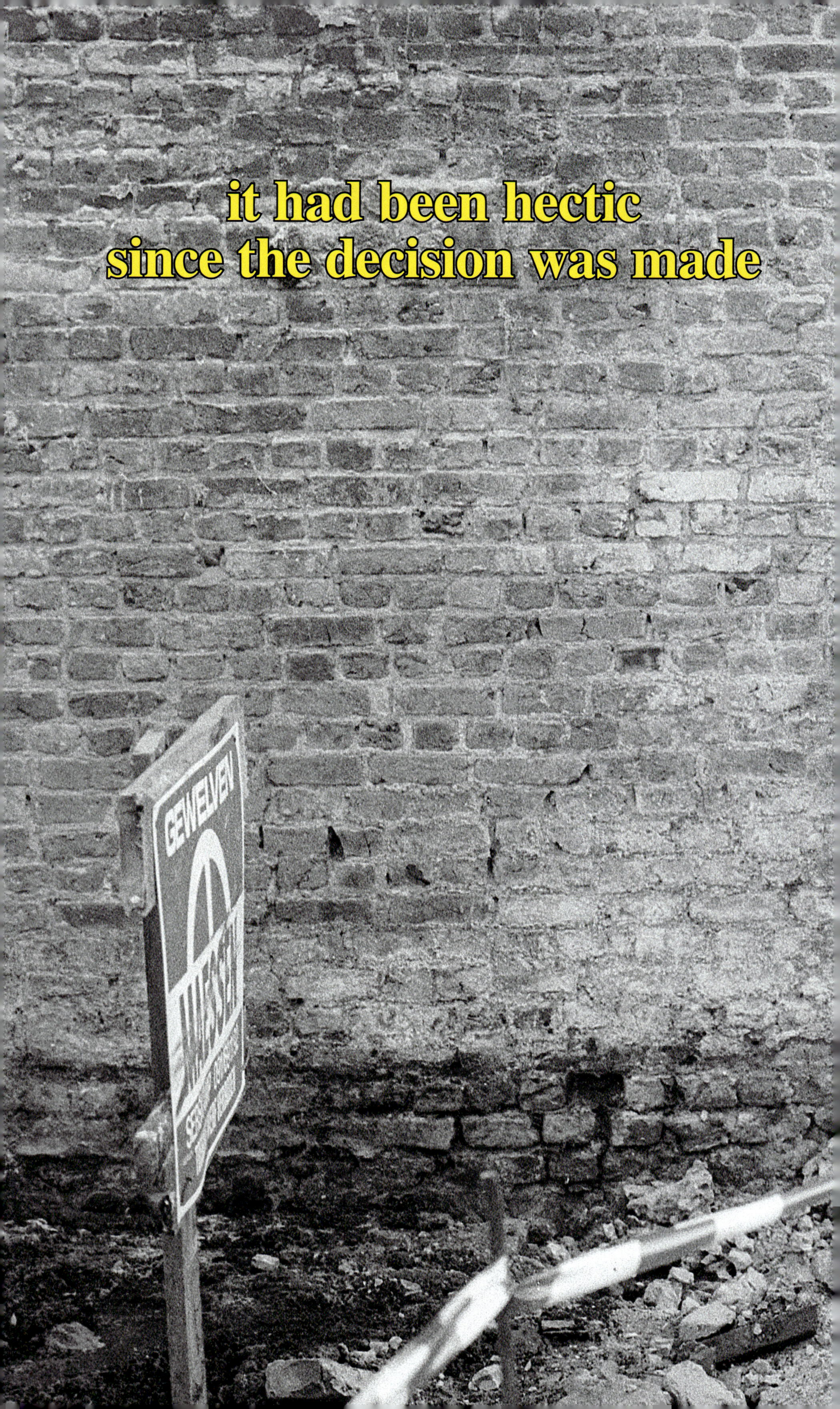

it had been hectic
since the decision was made

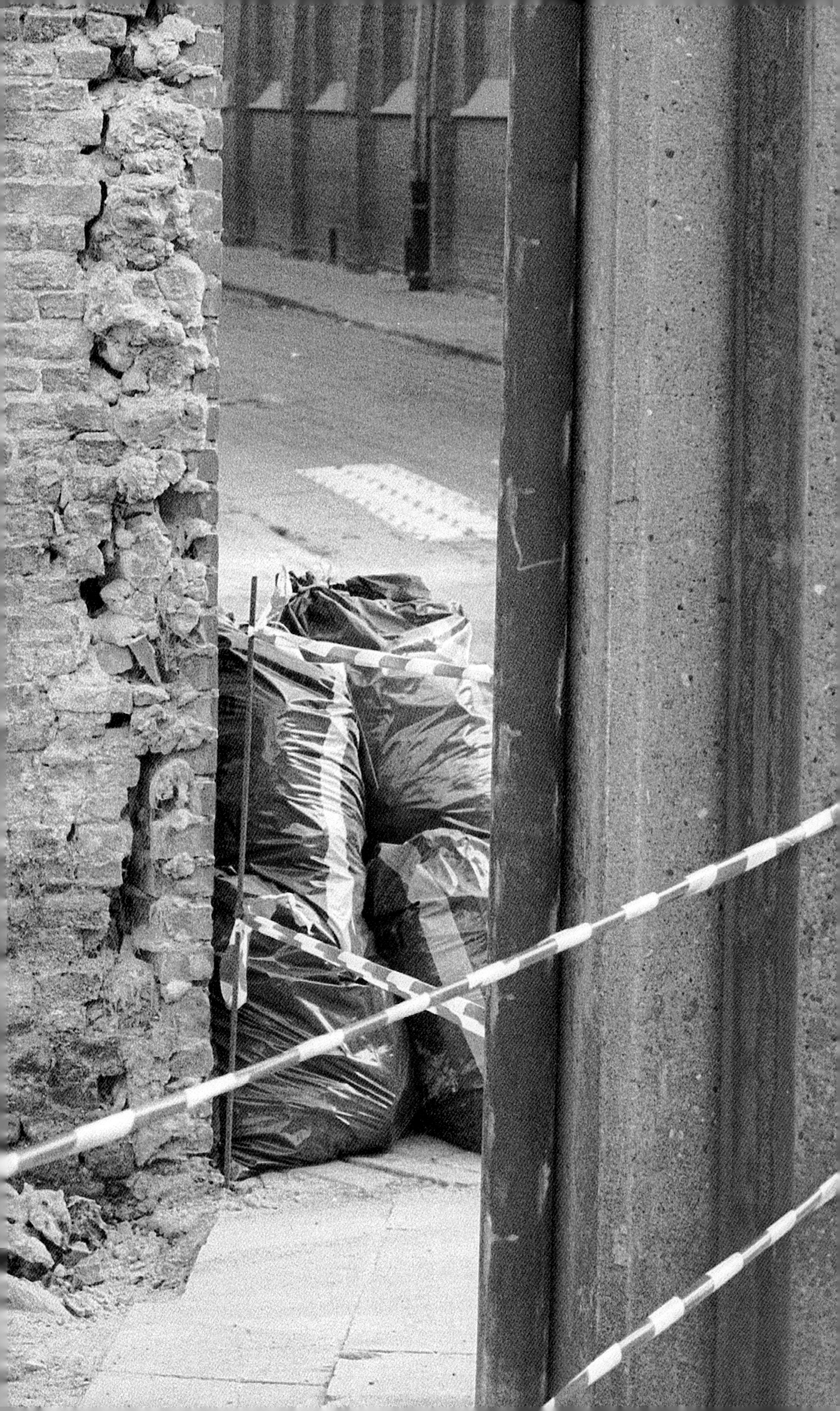

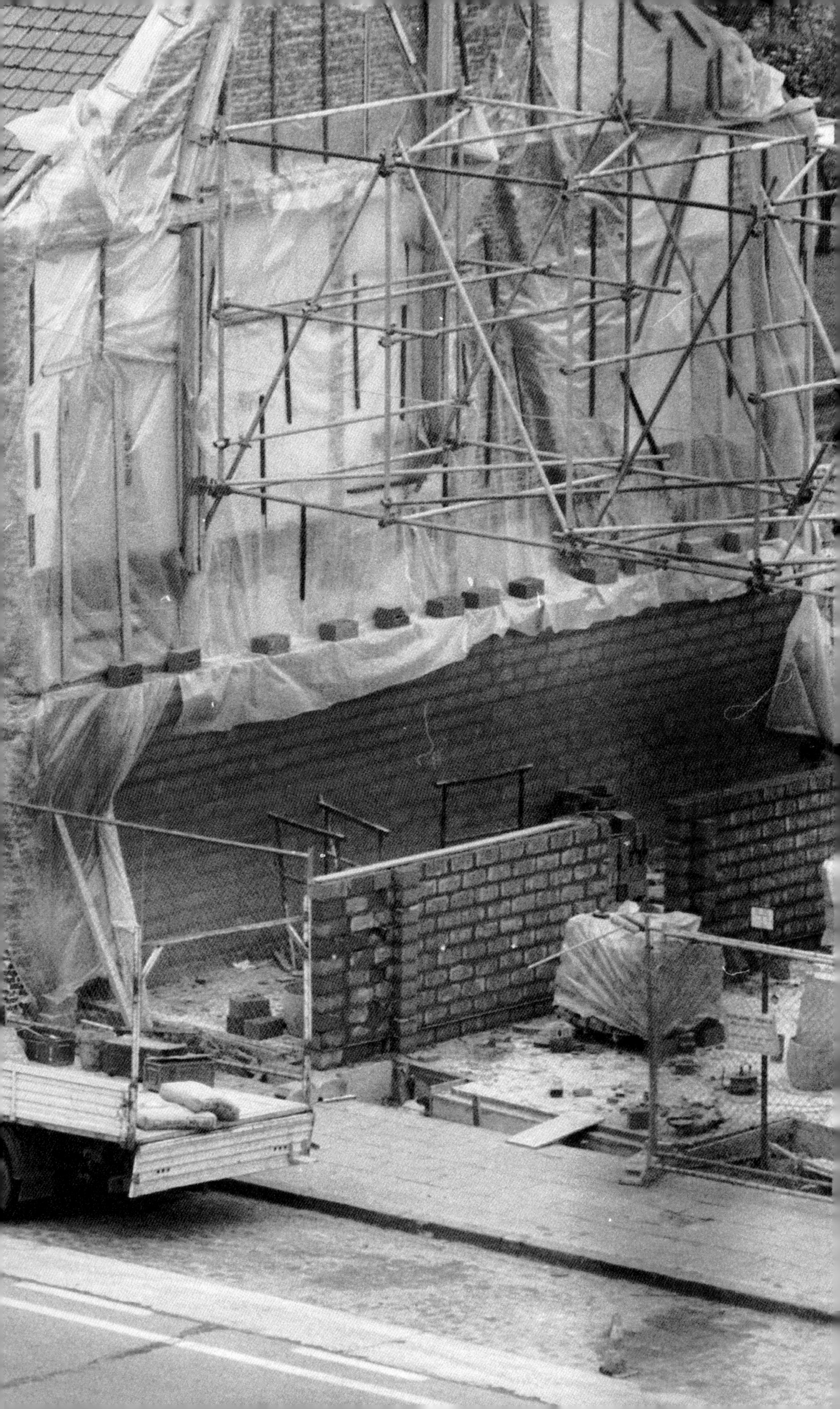

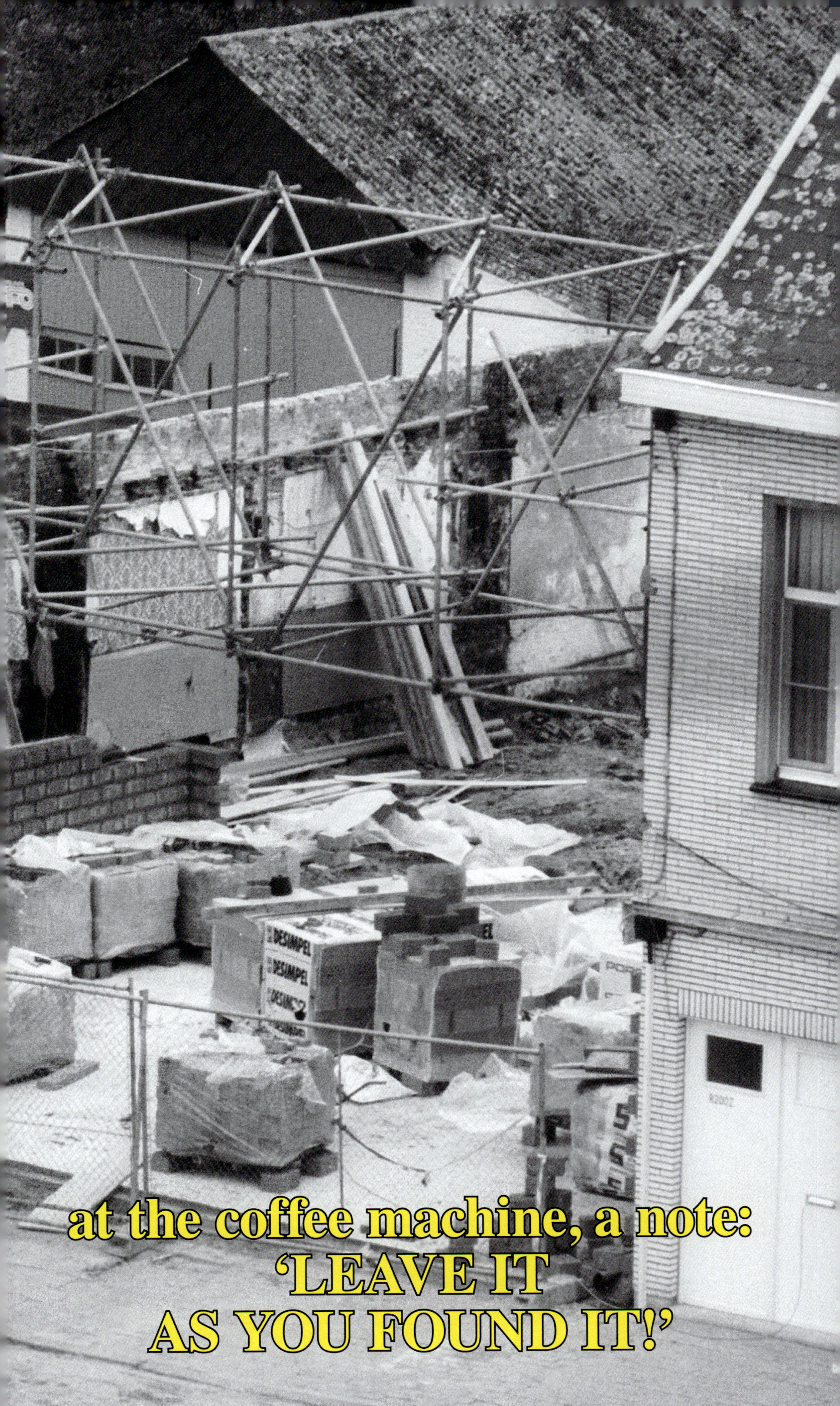

at the coffee machine, a note:
'LEAVE IT
AS YOU FOUND IT!'

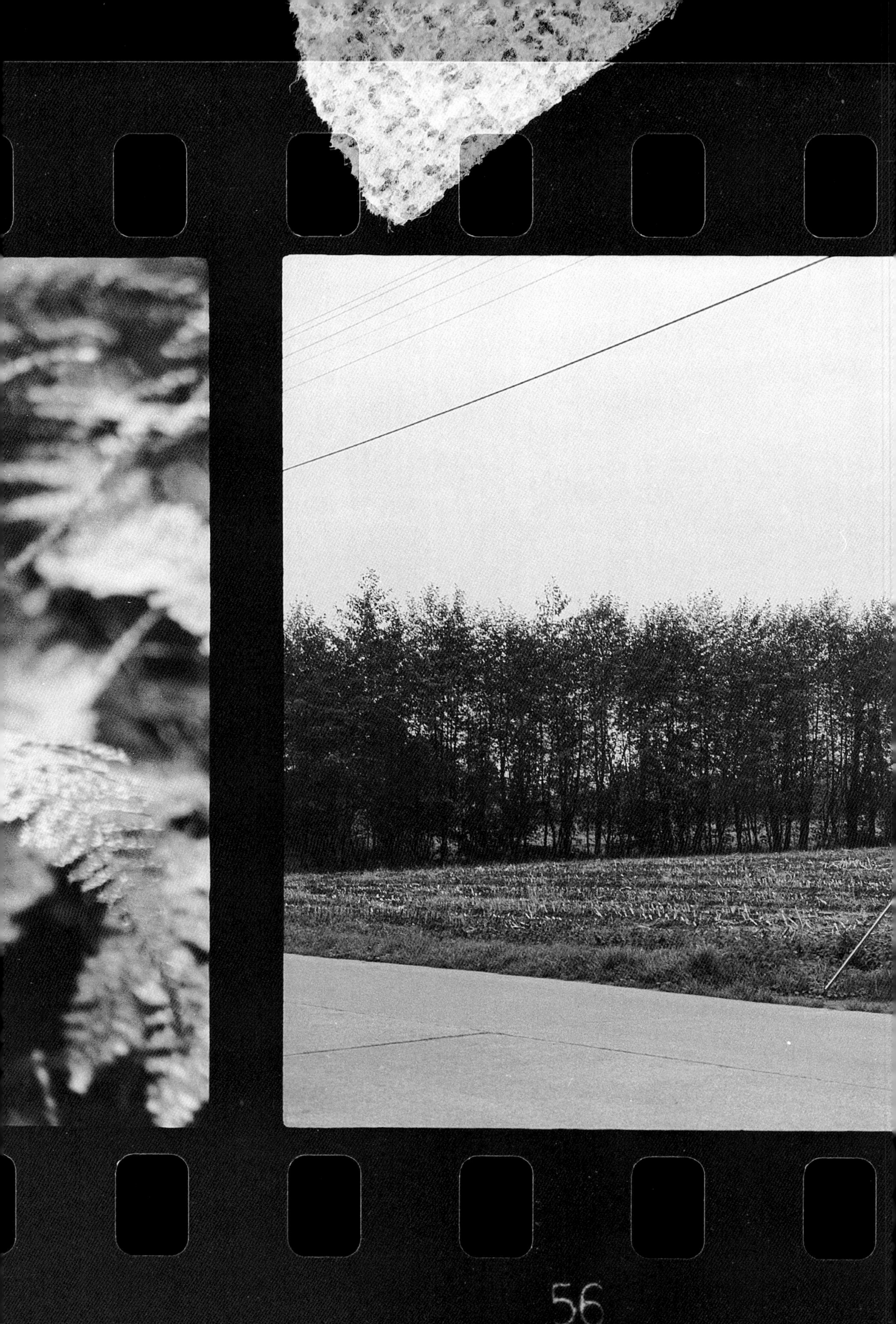

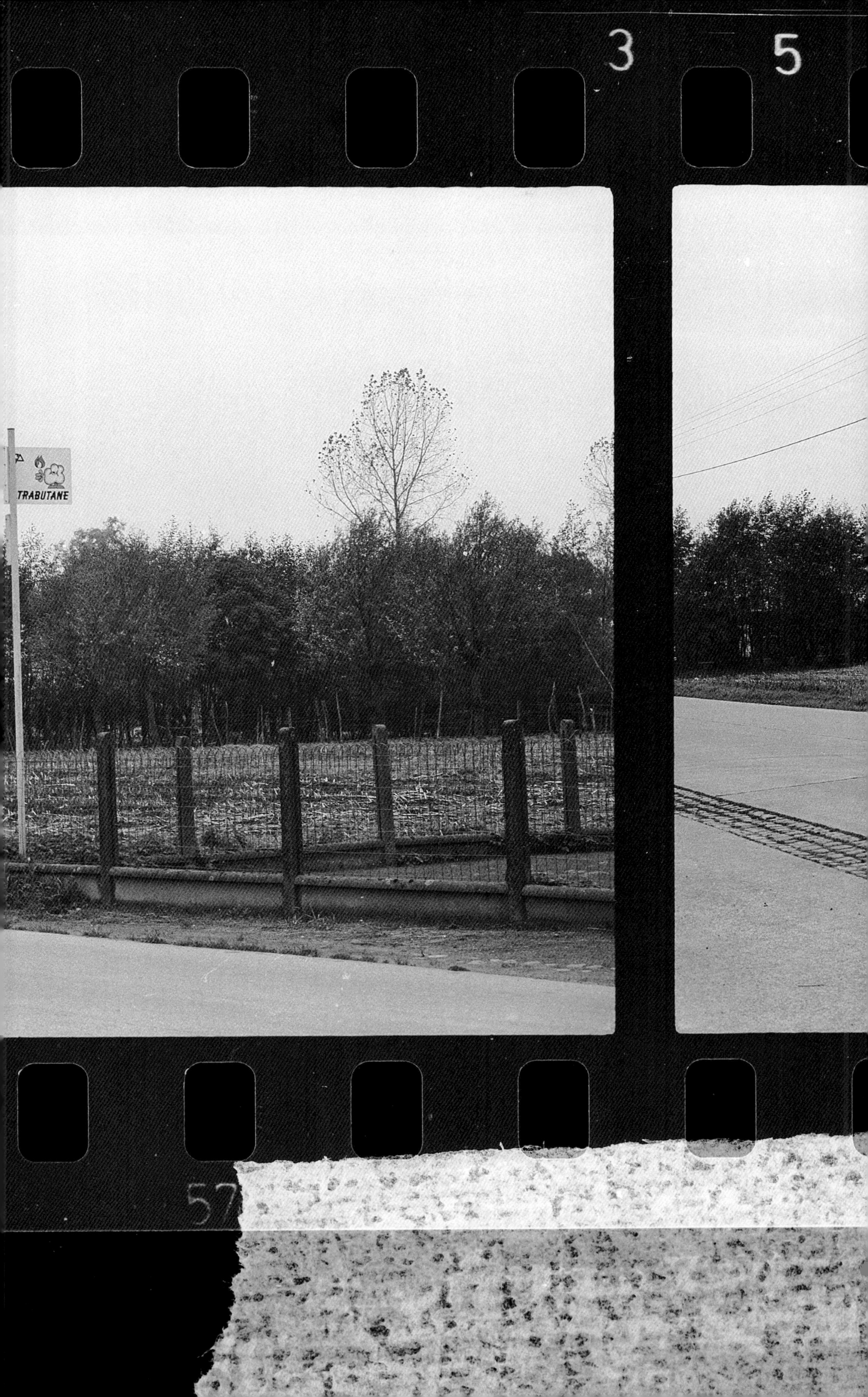
3 5
TRABUTANE
57

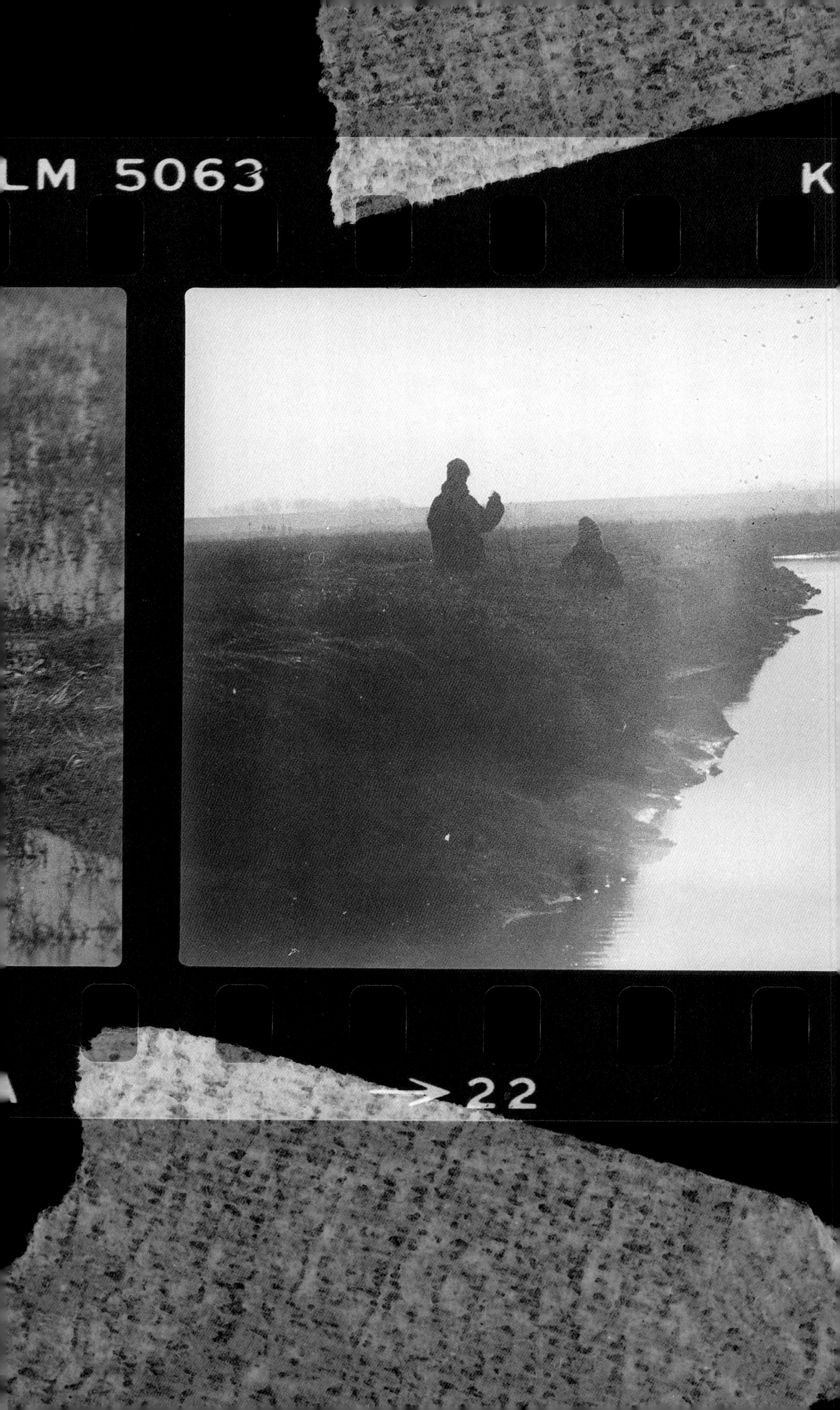

LM 5063 K

→22

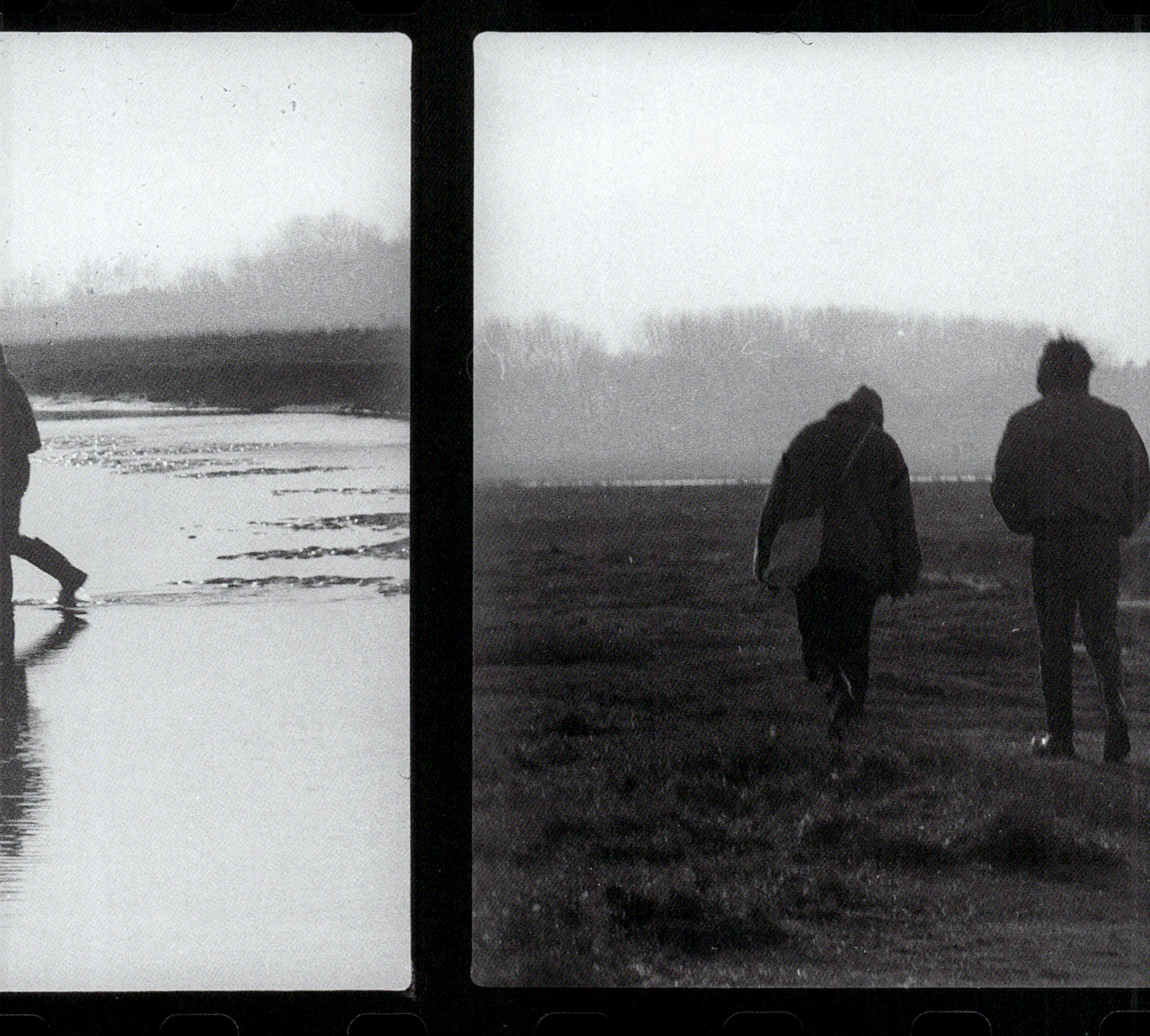

people trying to understand

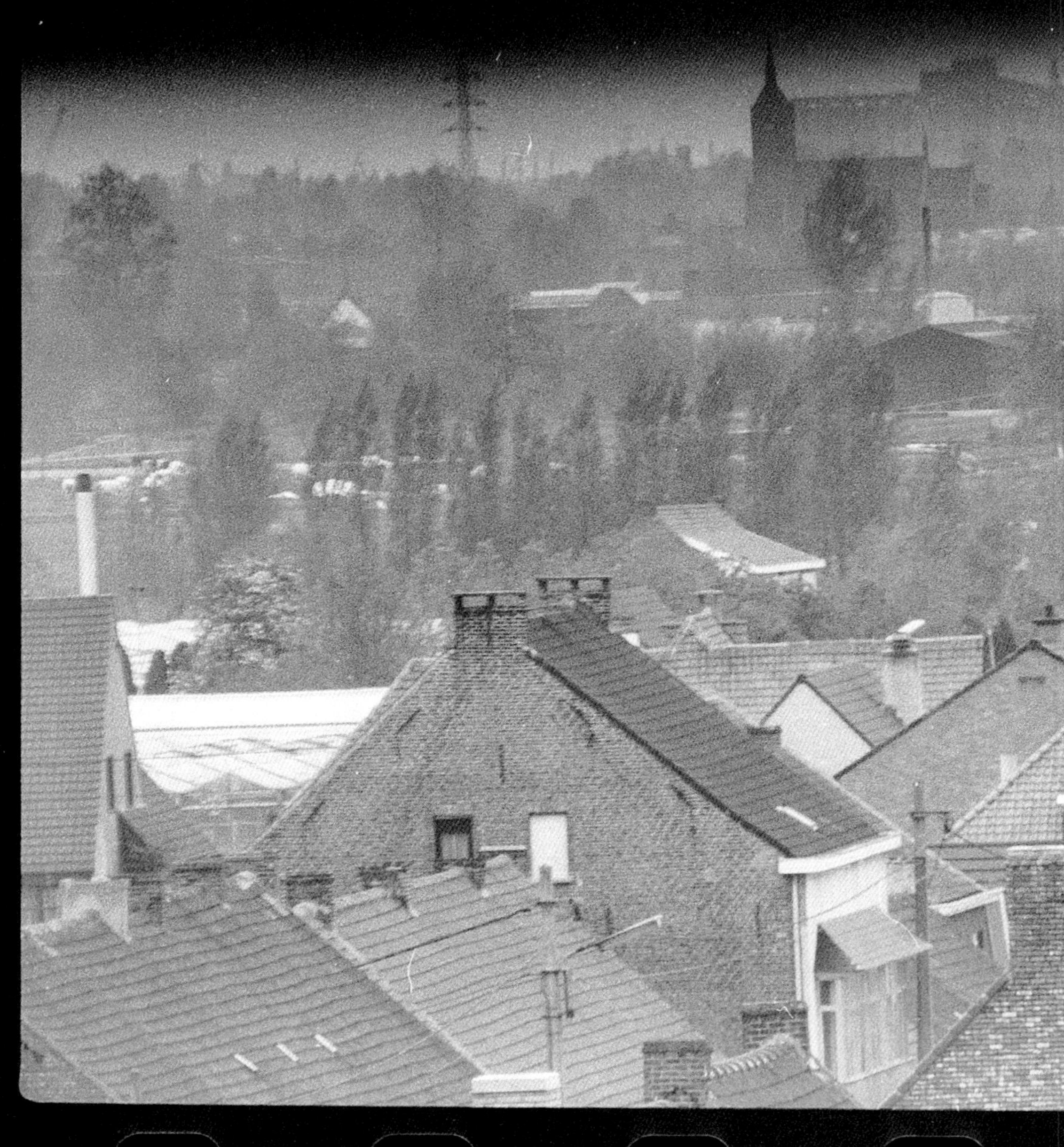
DAK 5053 TMY
18A

the landscape
they had shaped

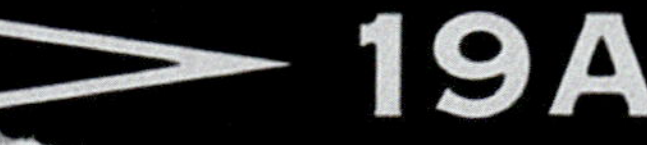

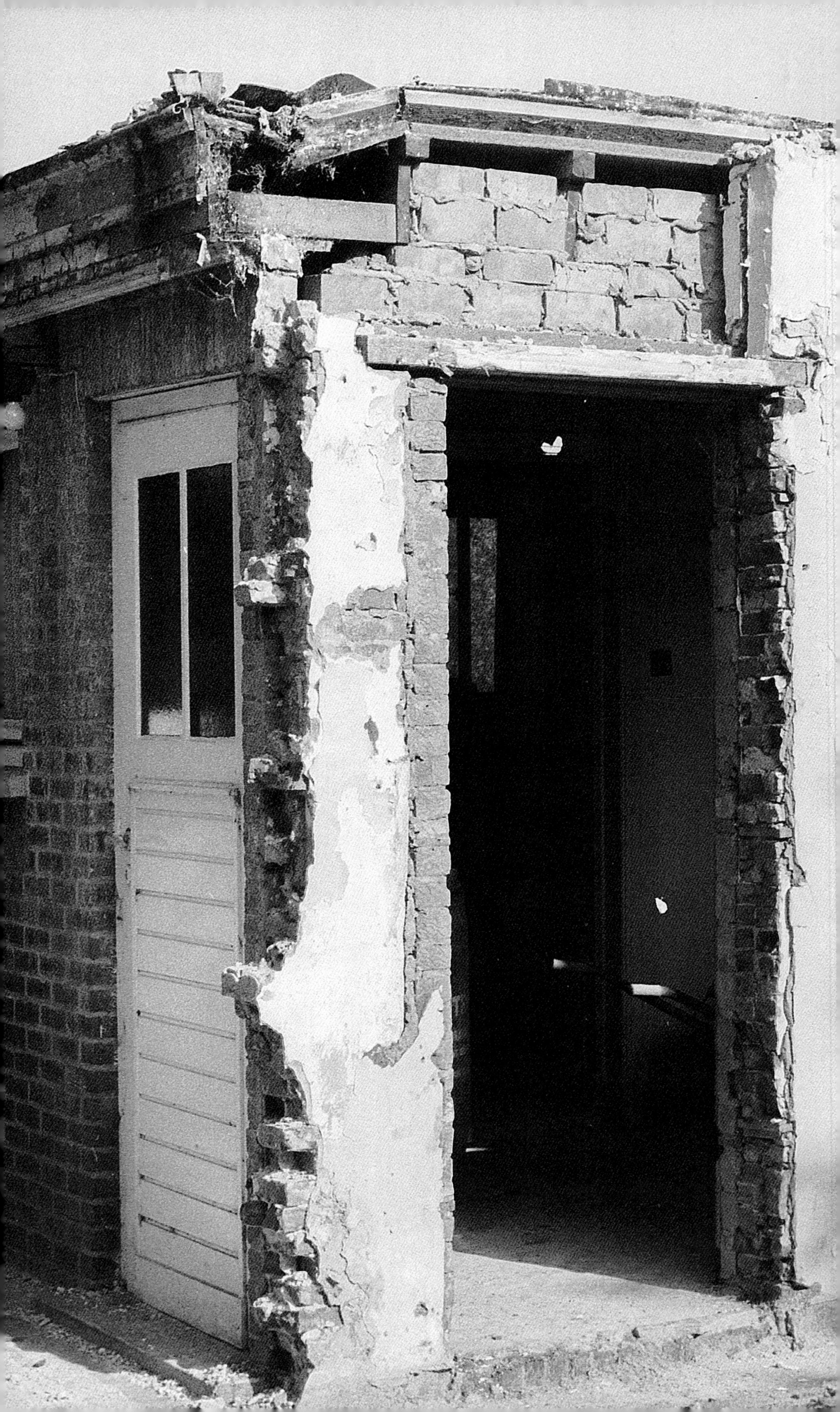

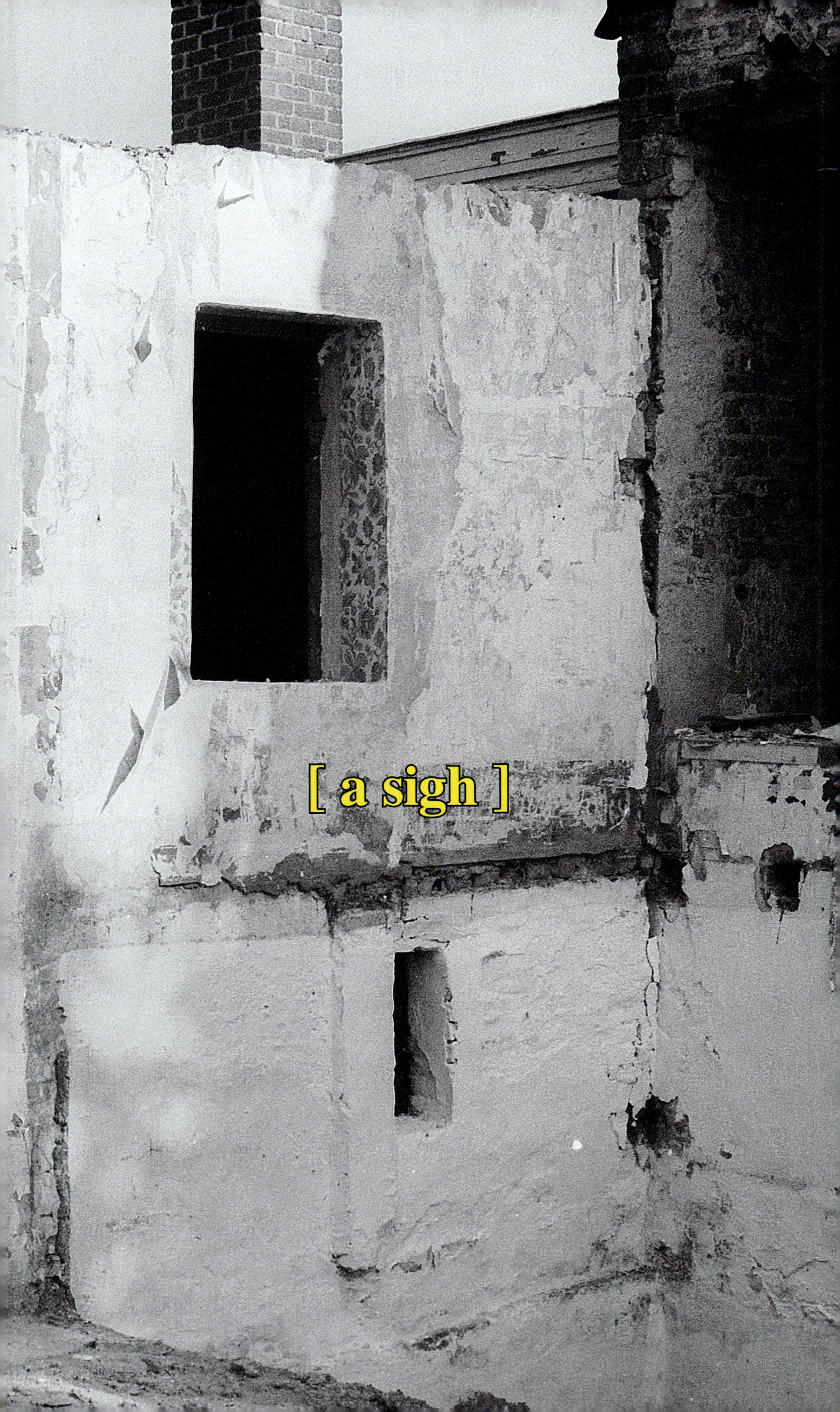
[a sigh]

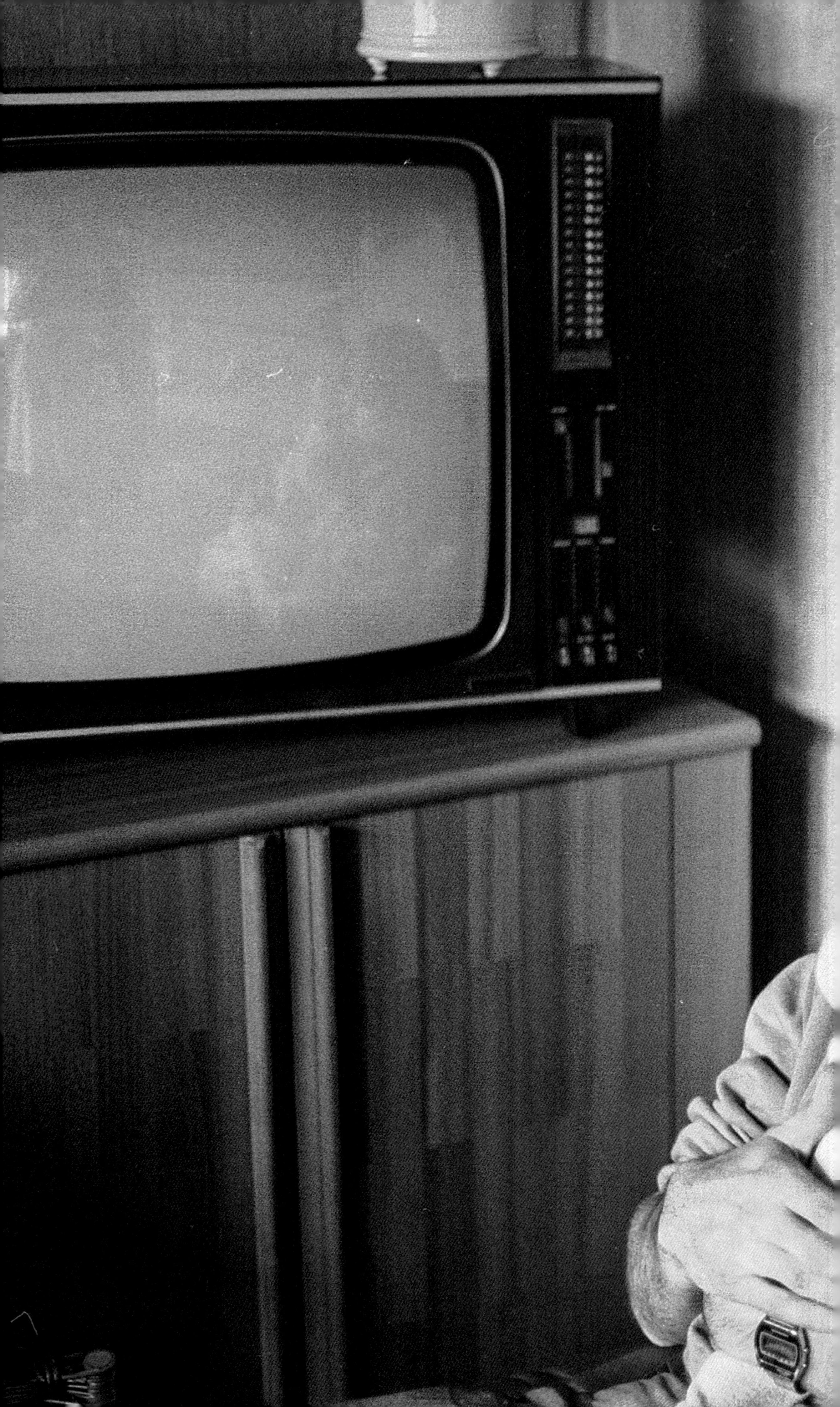

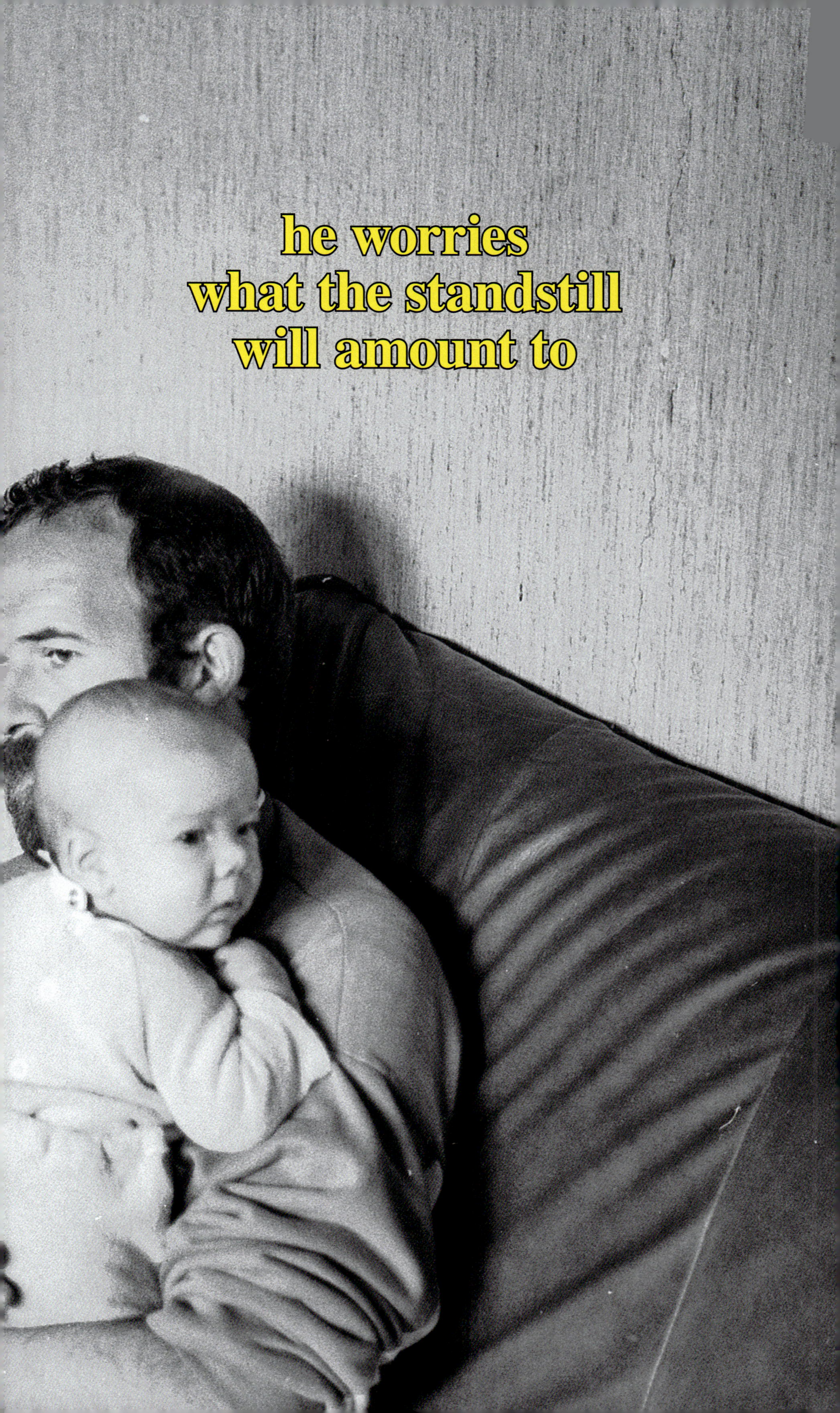
he worries
what the standstill
will amount to

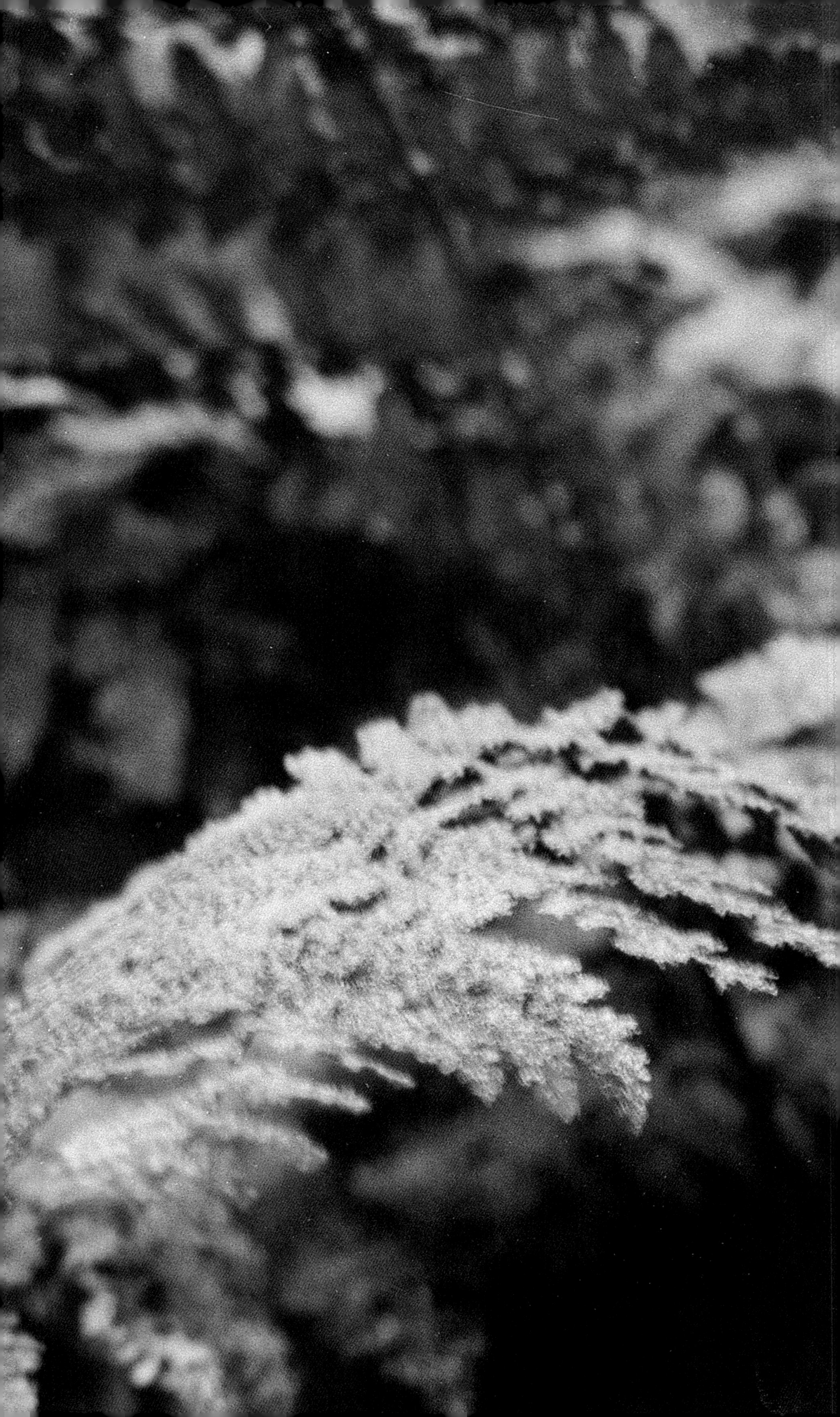

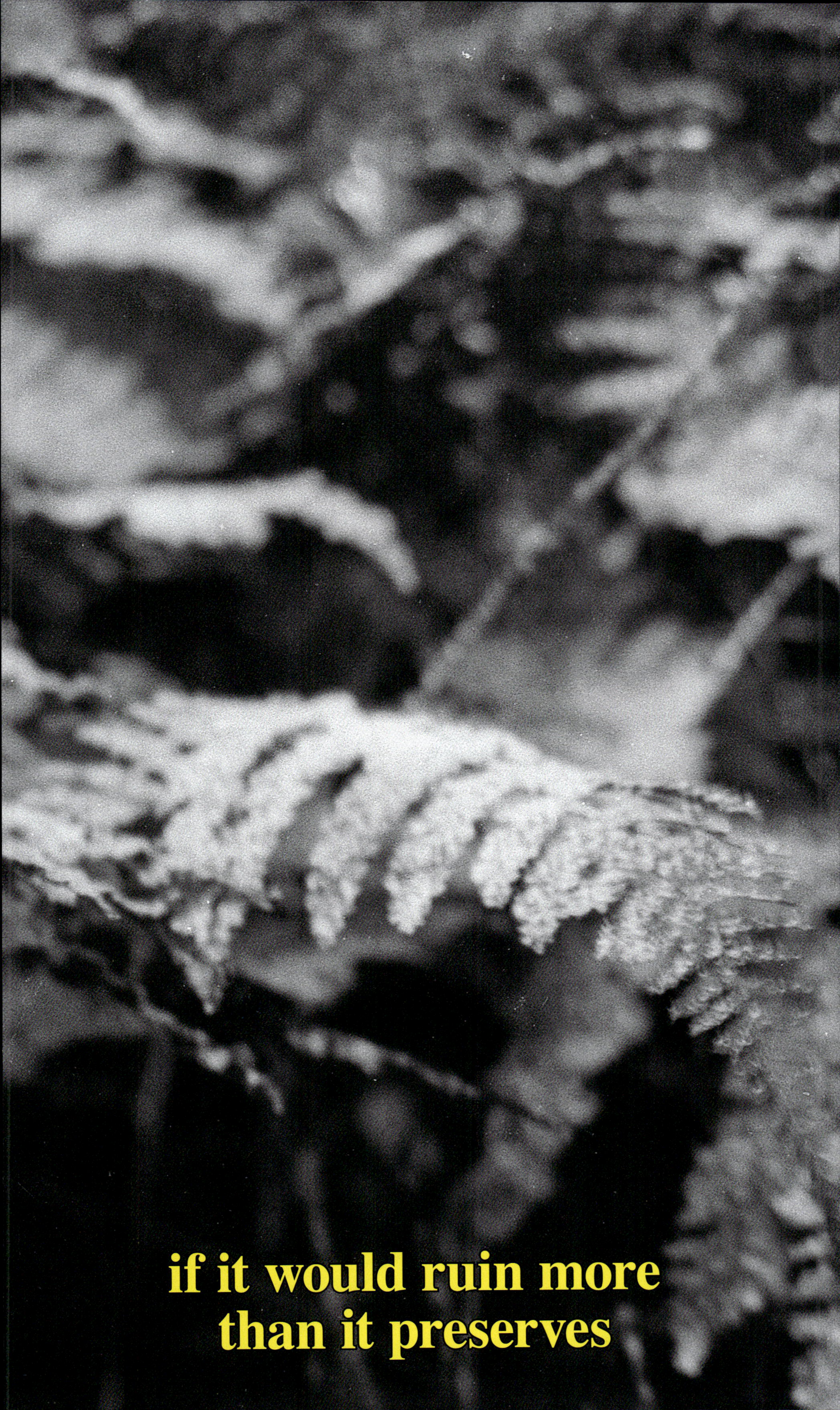
if it would ruin more
than it preserves

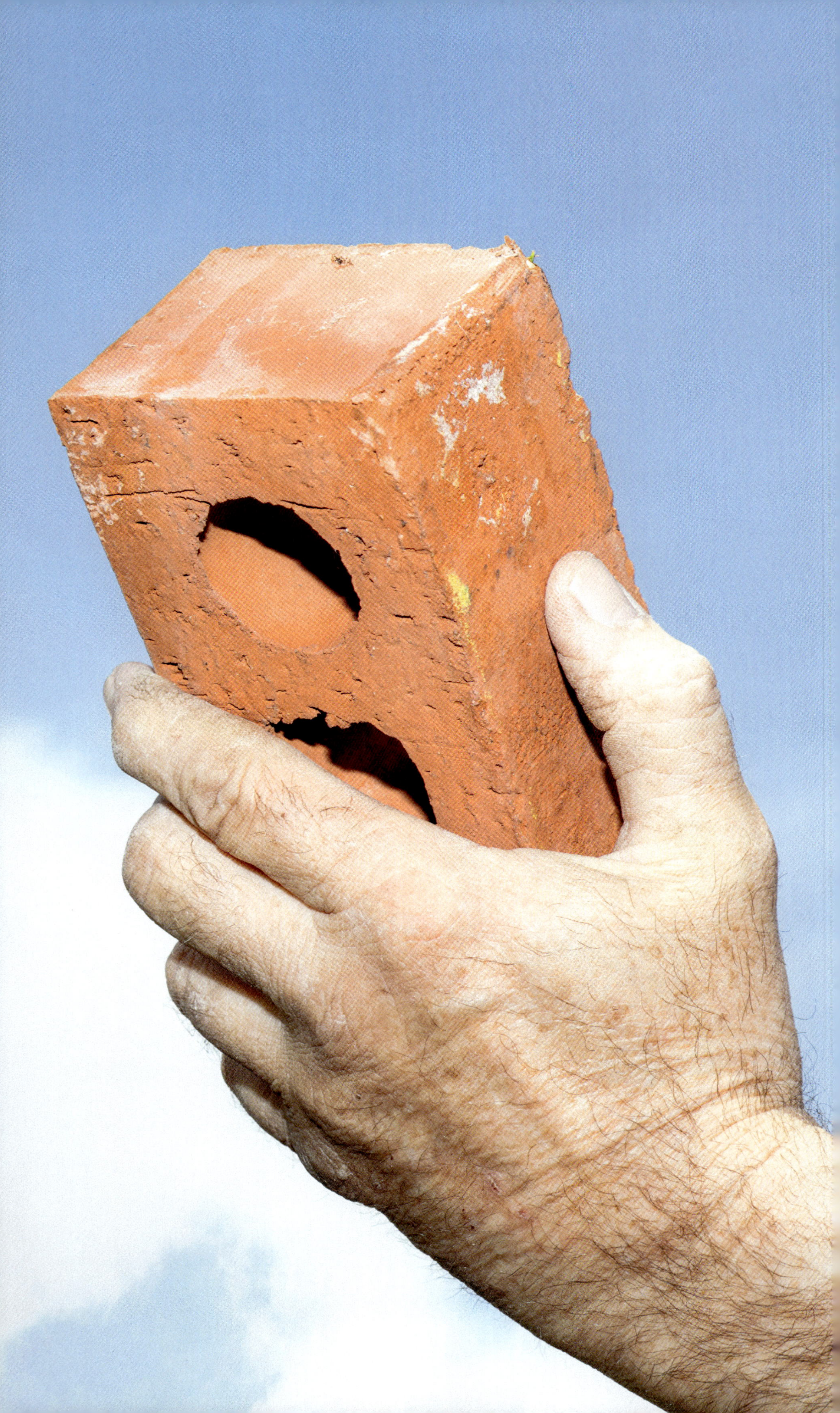

a riot
of masons, structural engineers
and project developers

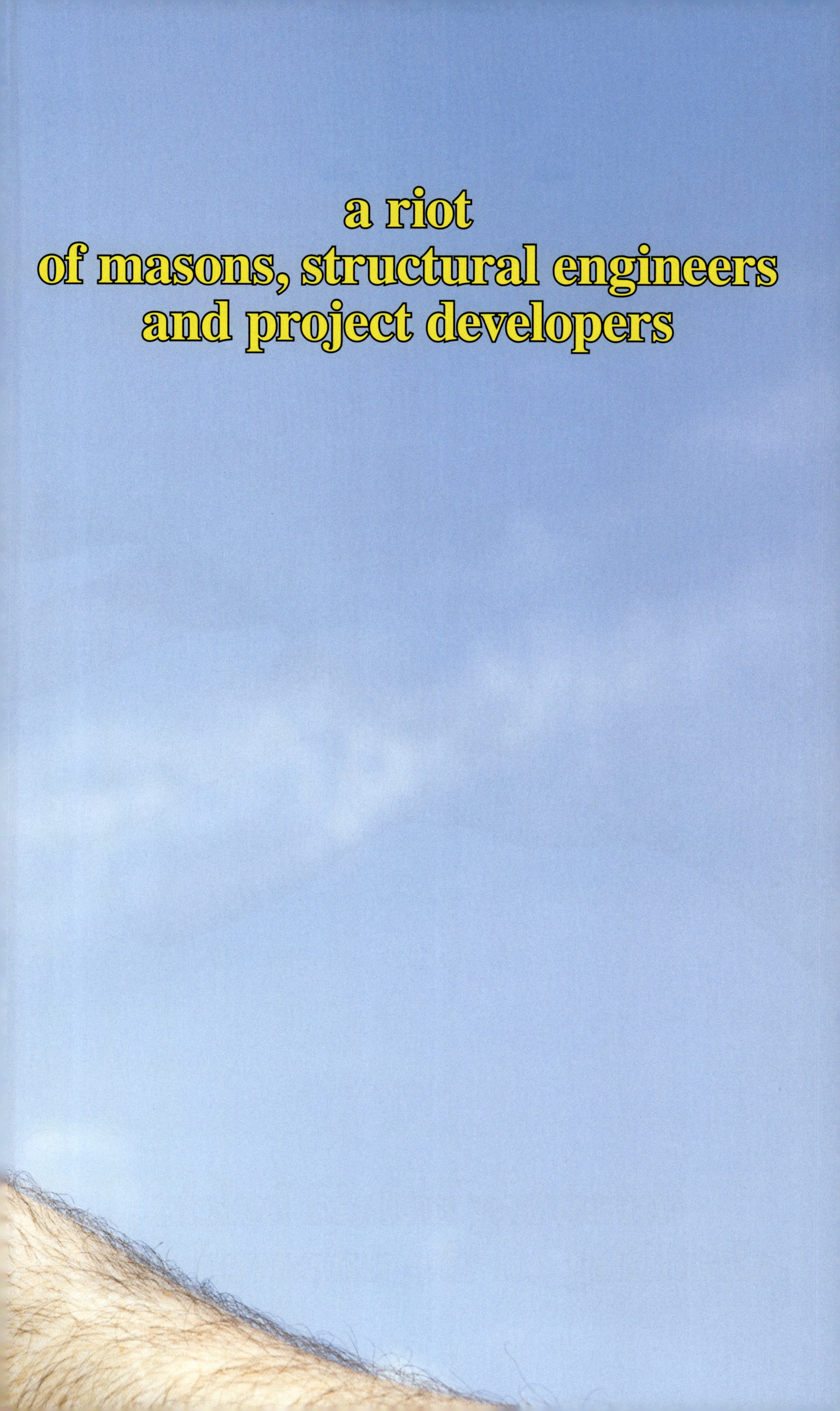

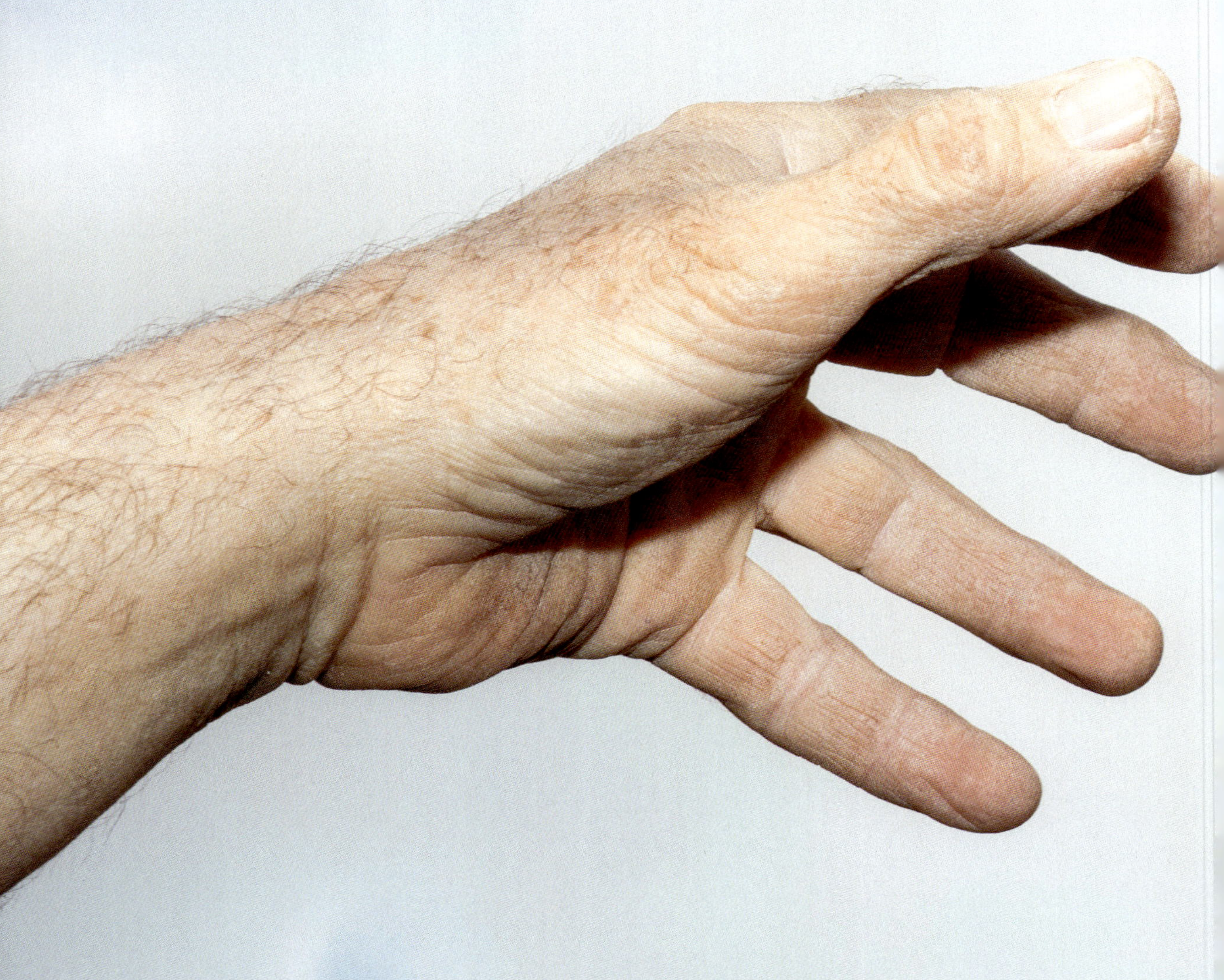

throwing unlaid bricks,
chanting on the unpaved roads

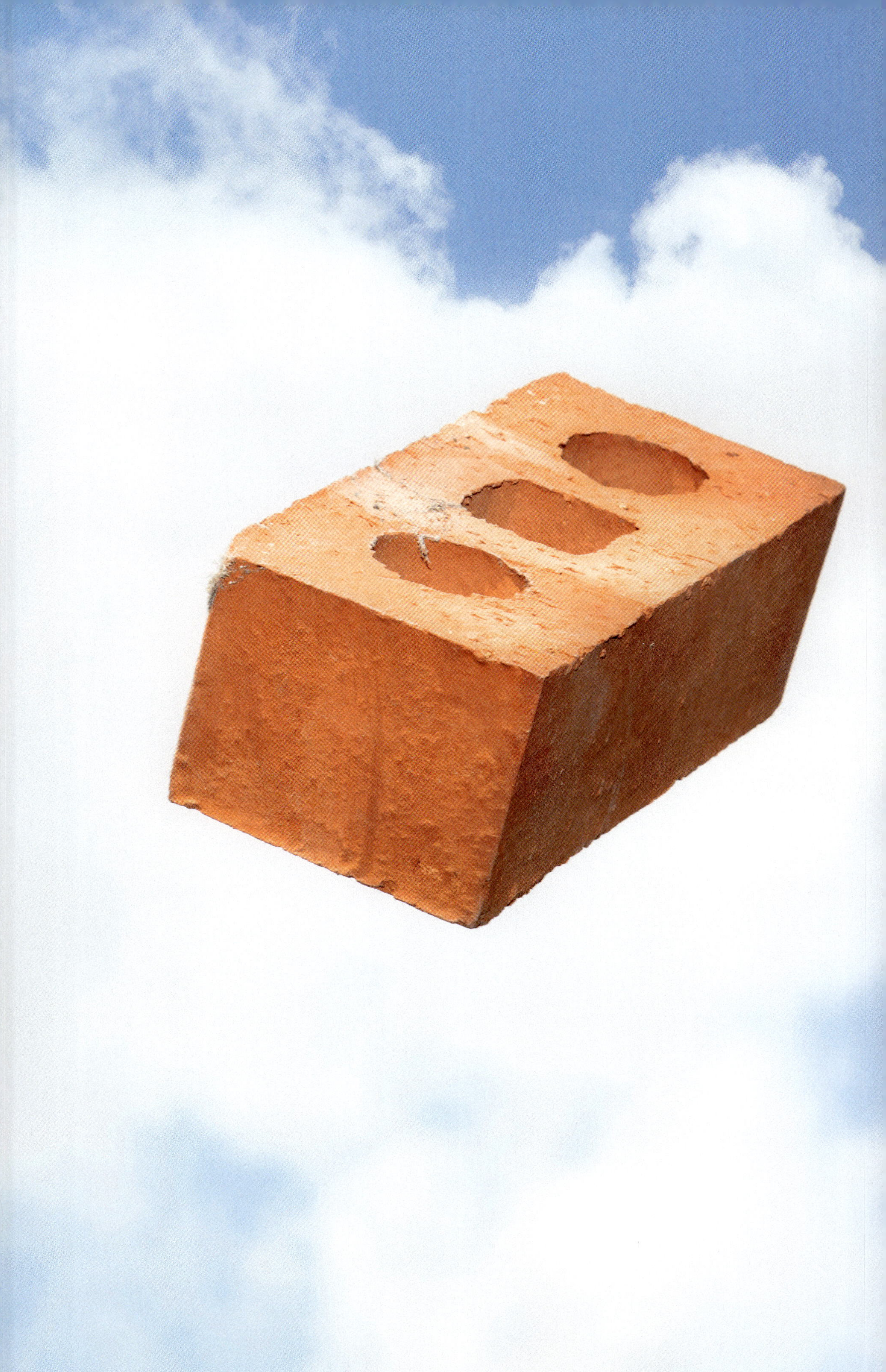

WHAT'S UNCONSTRUCTED WILL RISE AGAIN

a fissure,
it appears

in the plaster

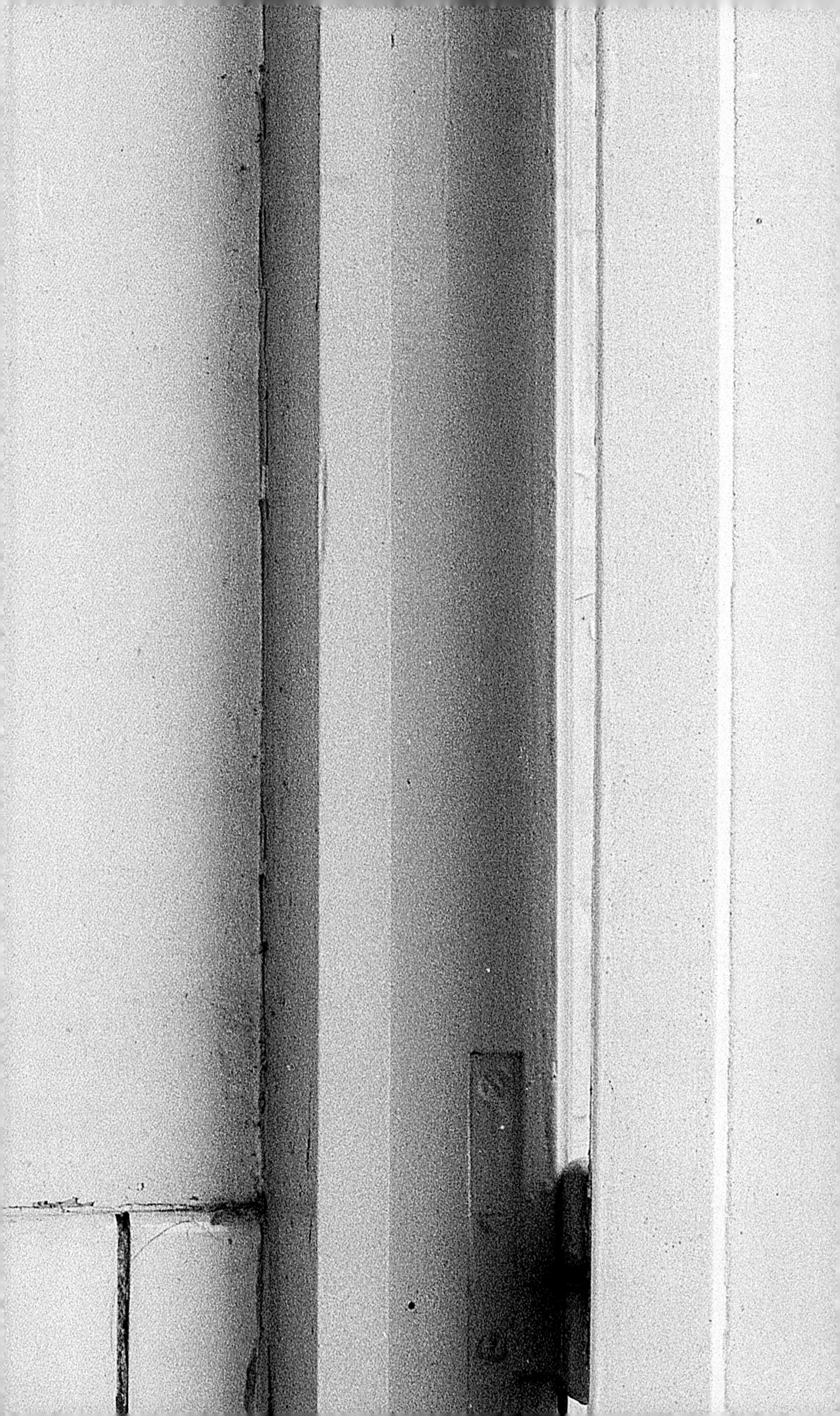

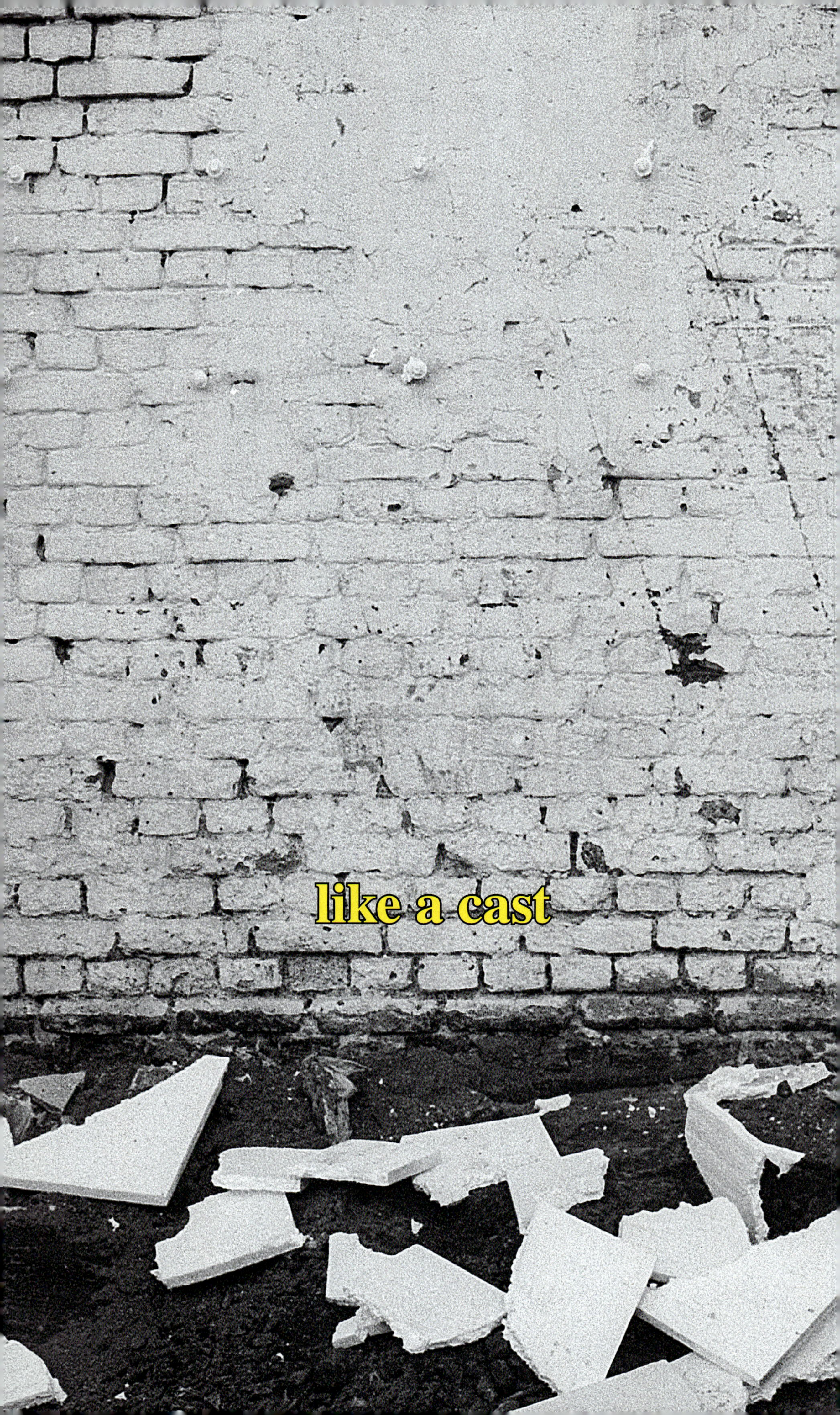
like a cast

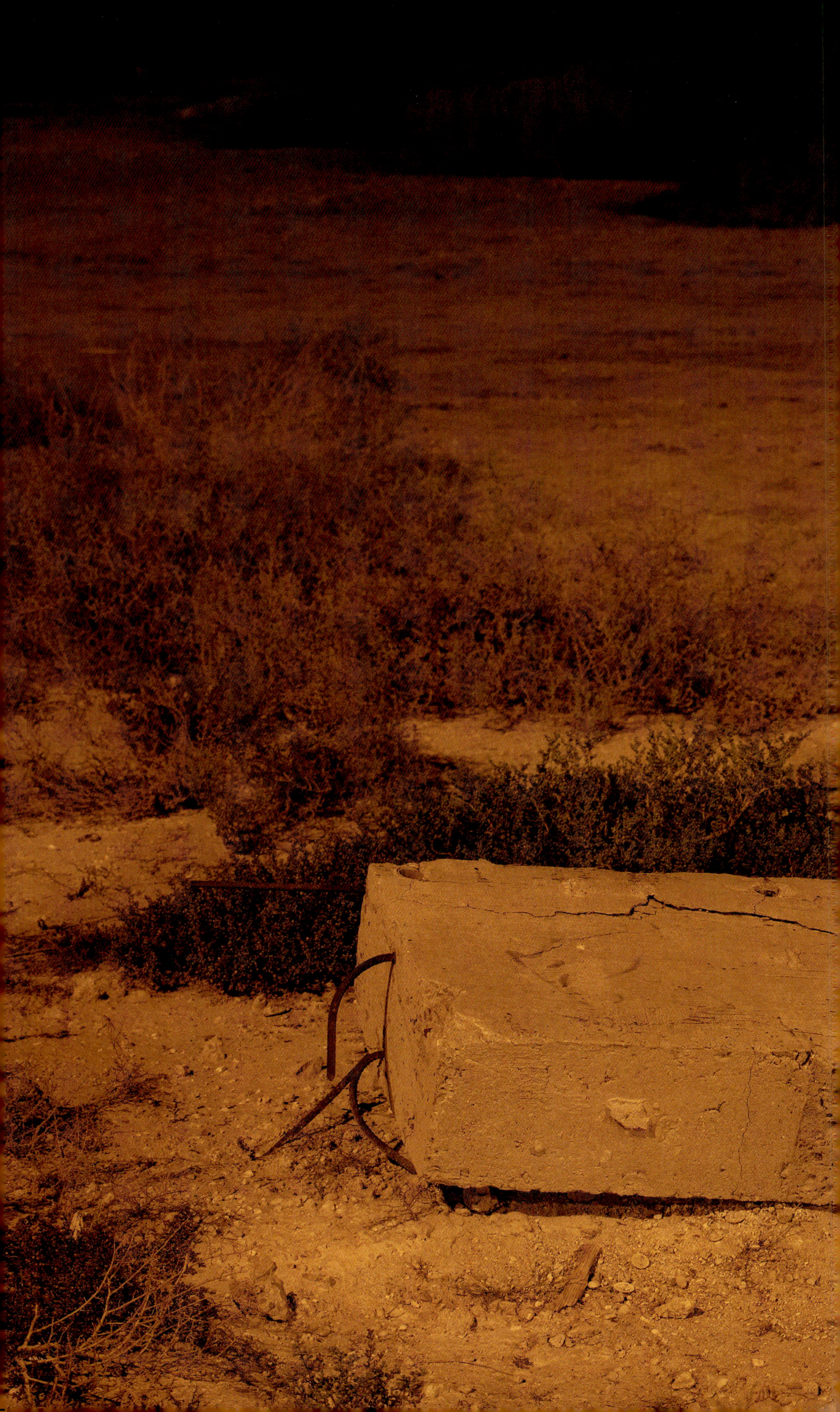

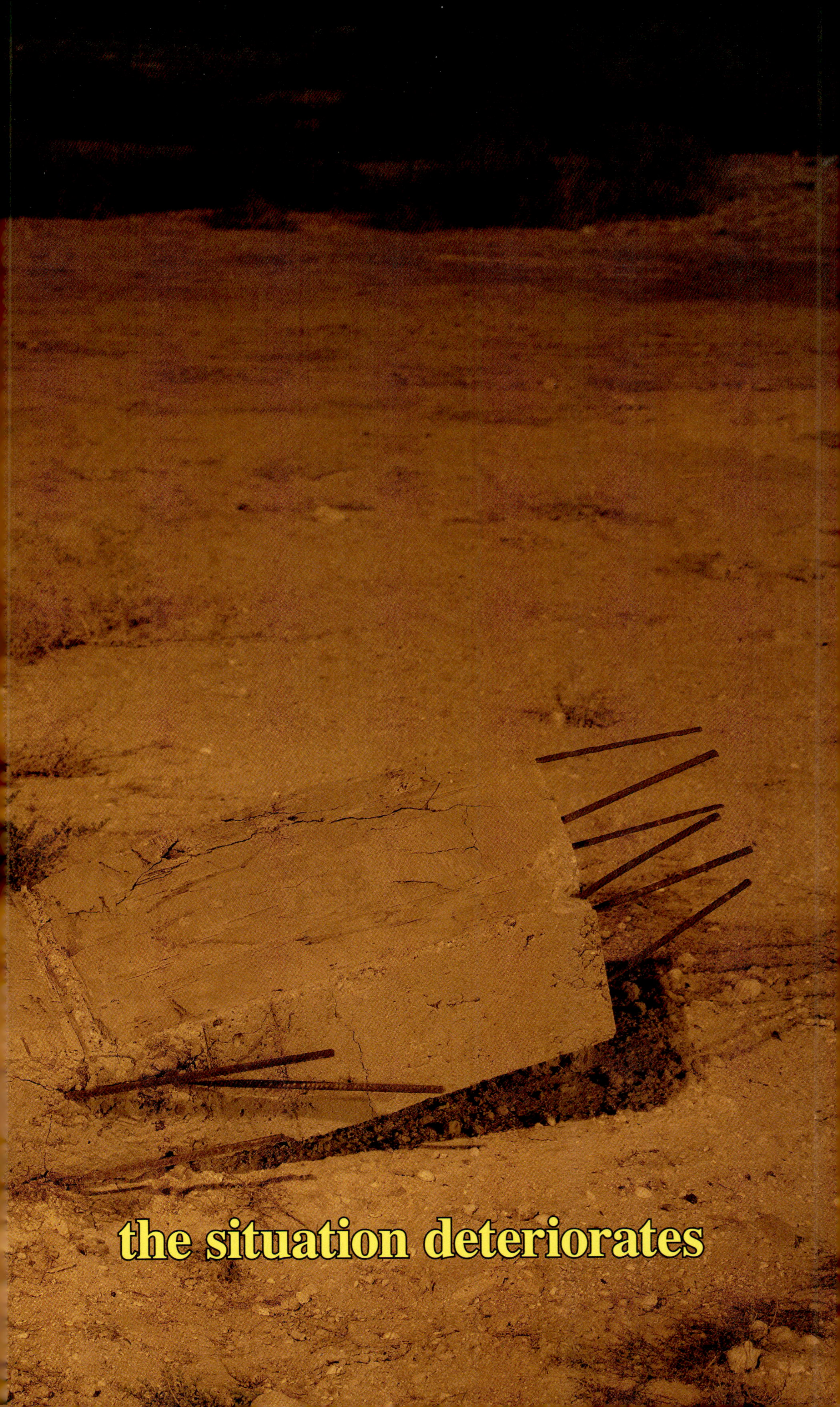
the situation deteriorates

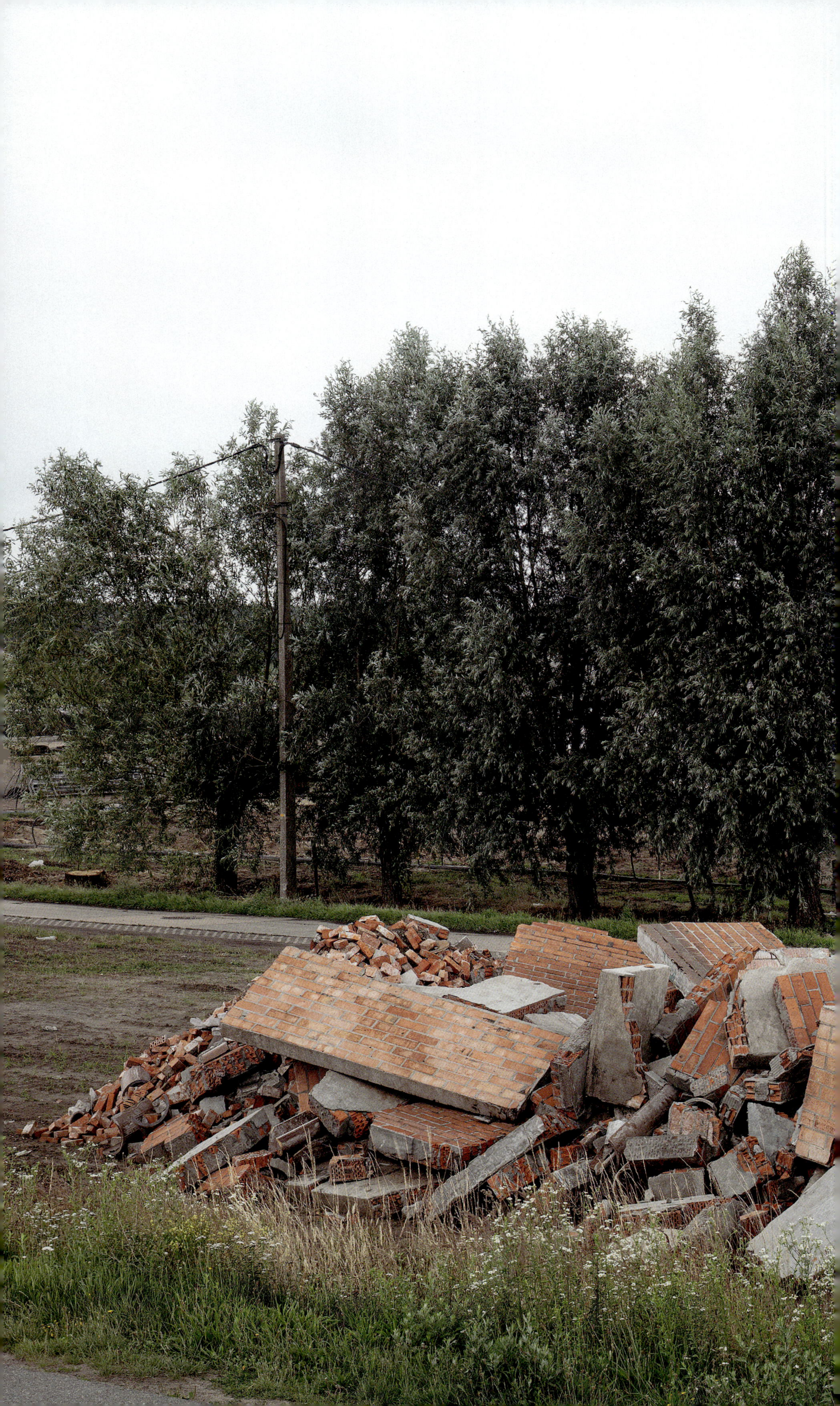

as they start falling, the buildings, they panic

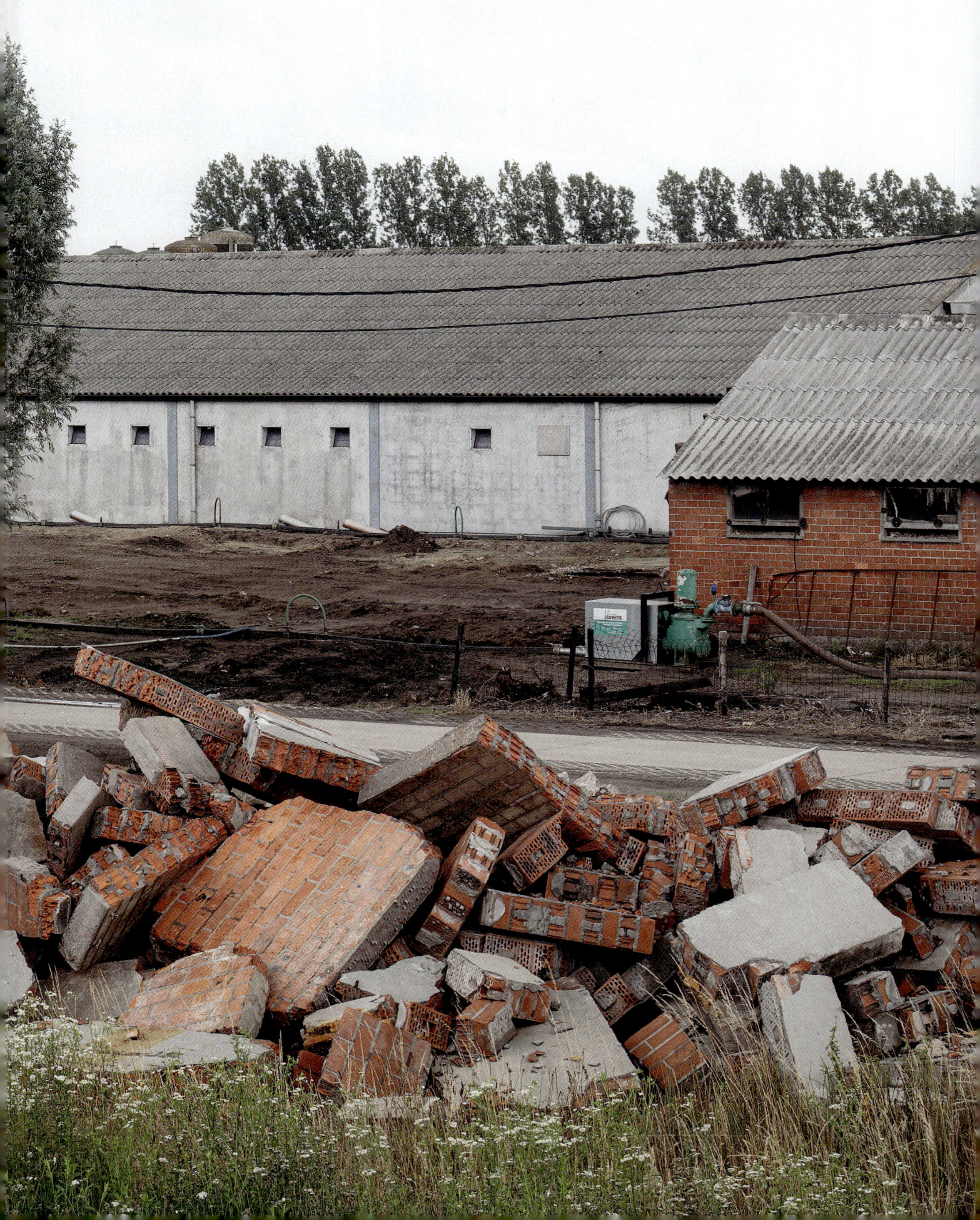

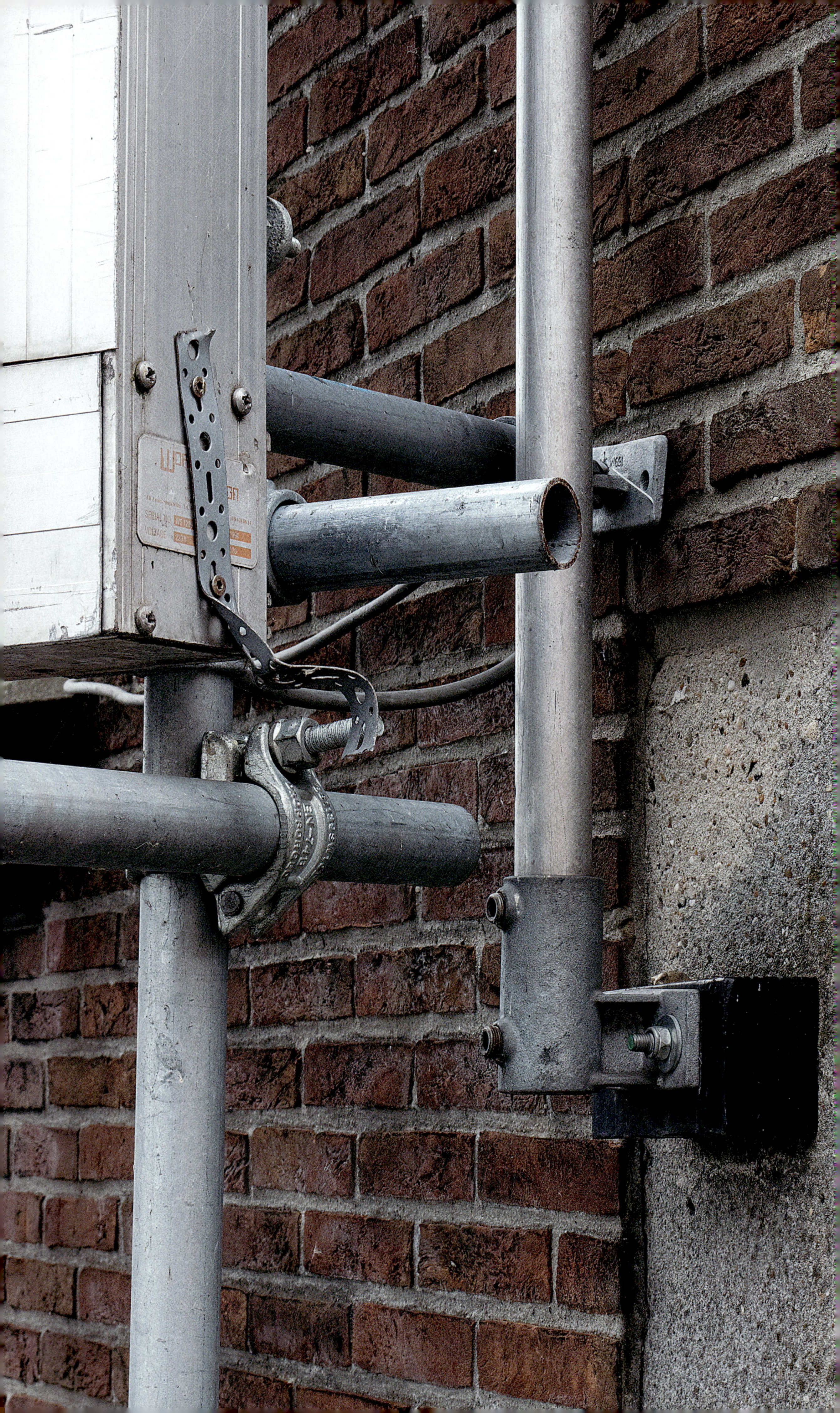

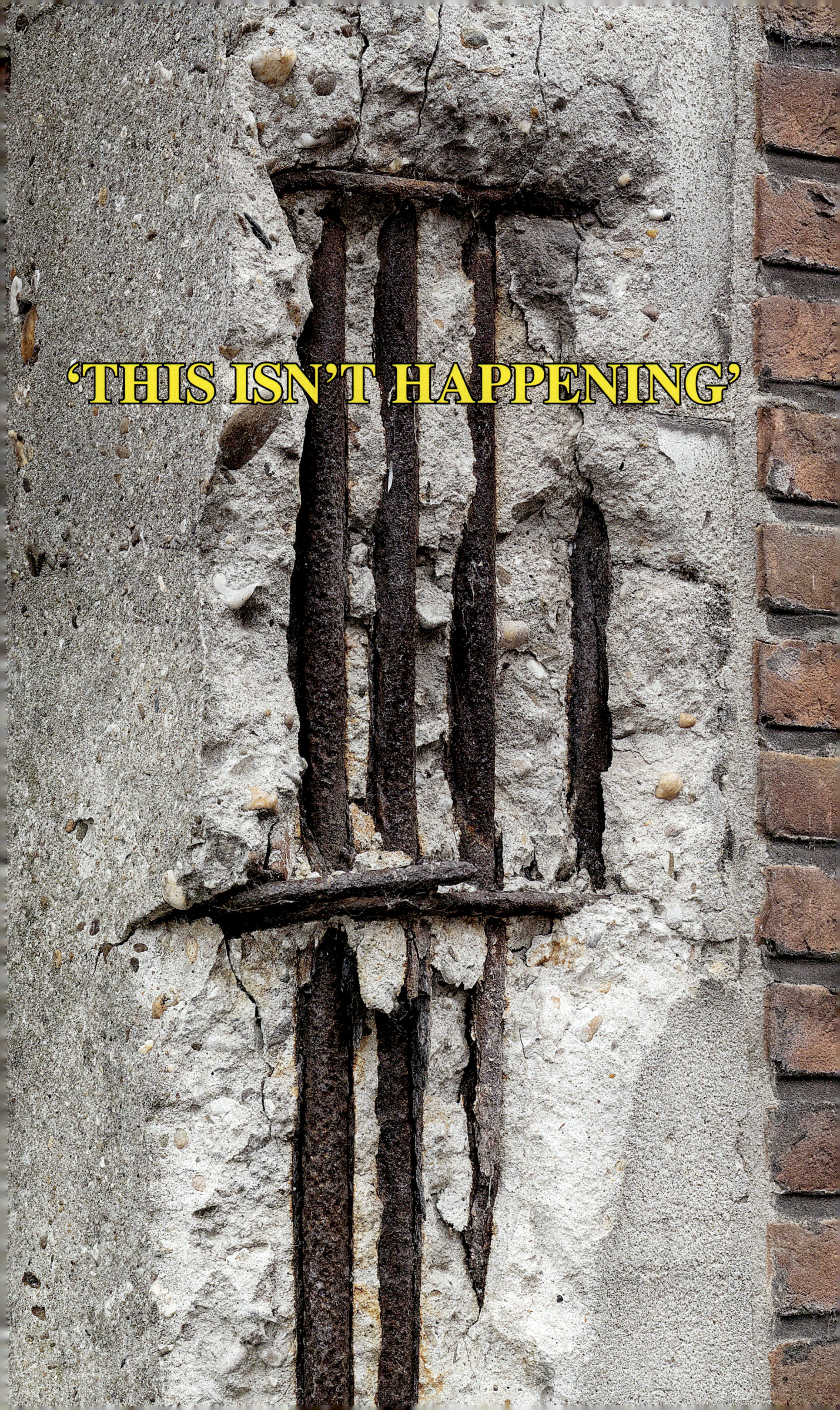

‘THIS ISN’T HAPPENING’

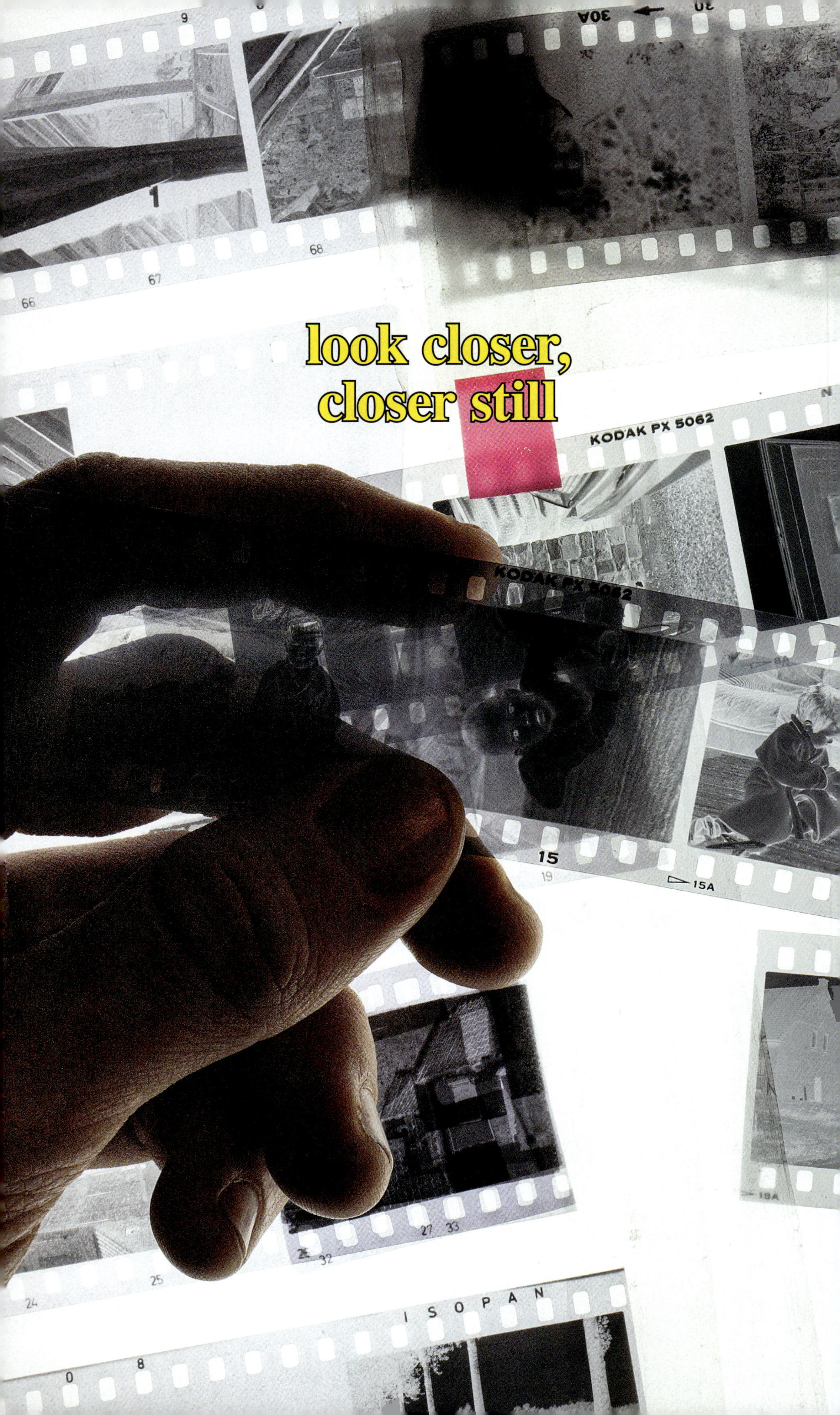

look closer, closer still

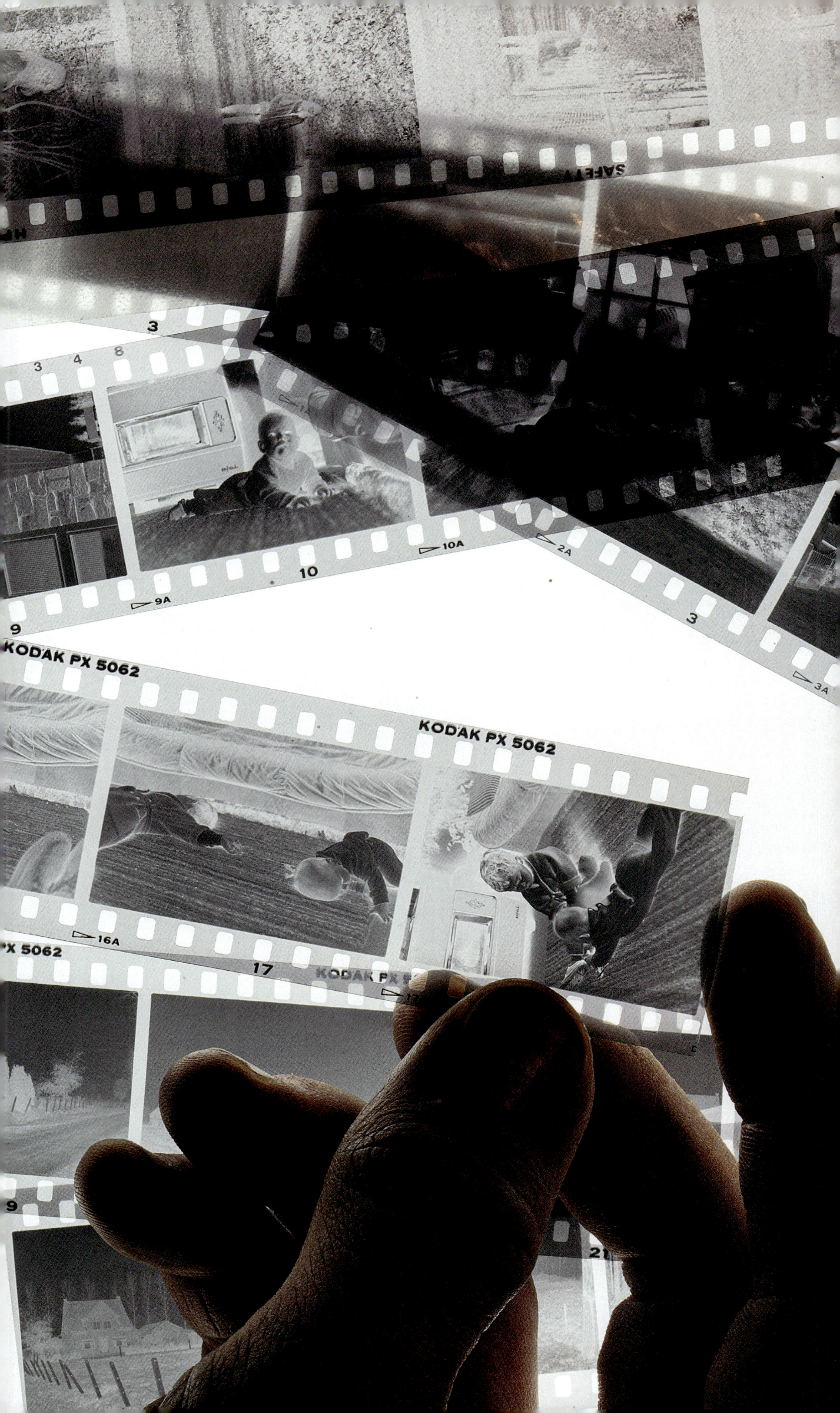
KODAK PX 5062
KODAK PX 5062
PX 5062

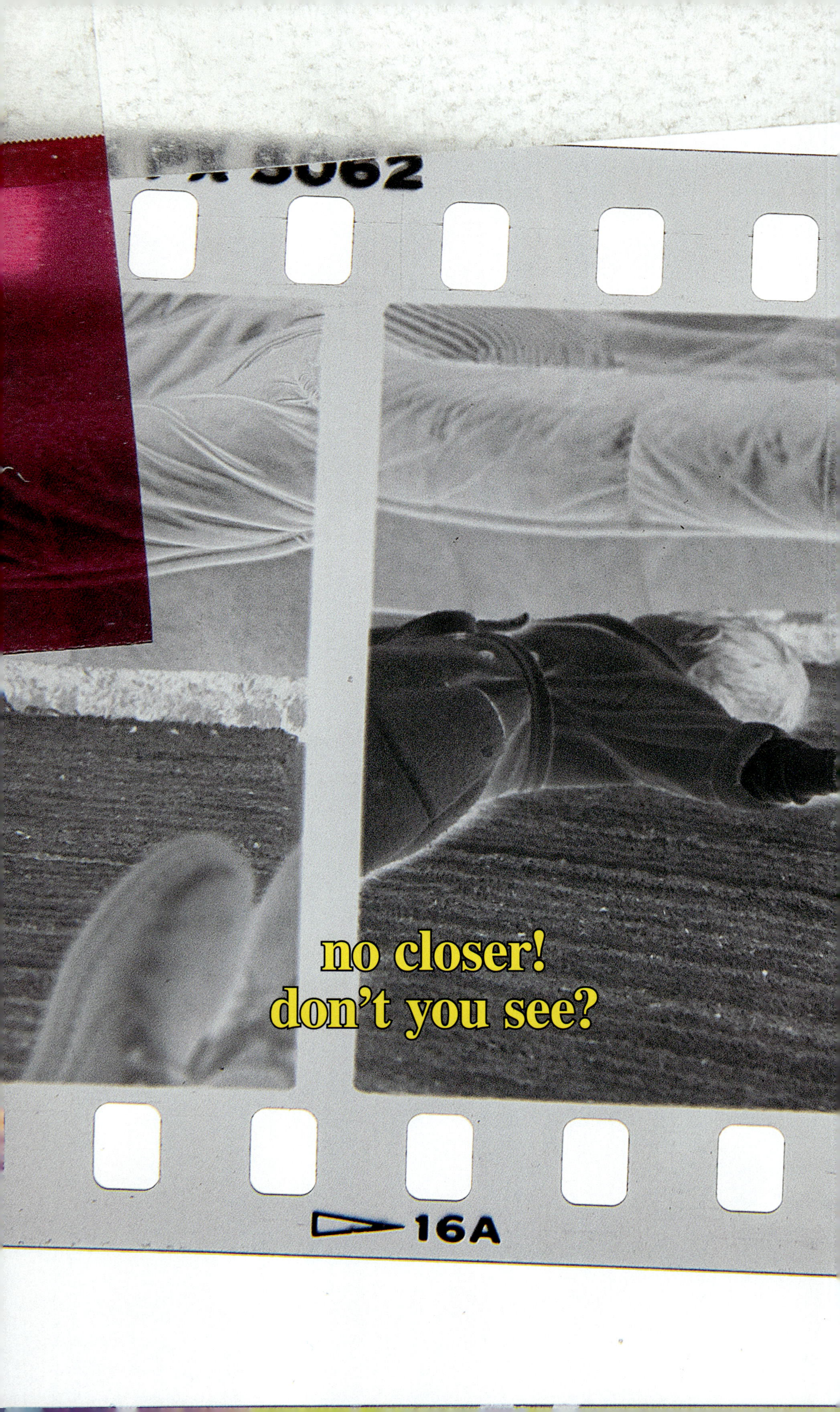

no closer!
don’t you see?

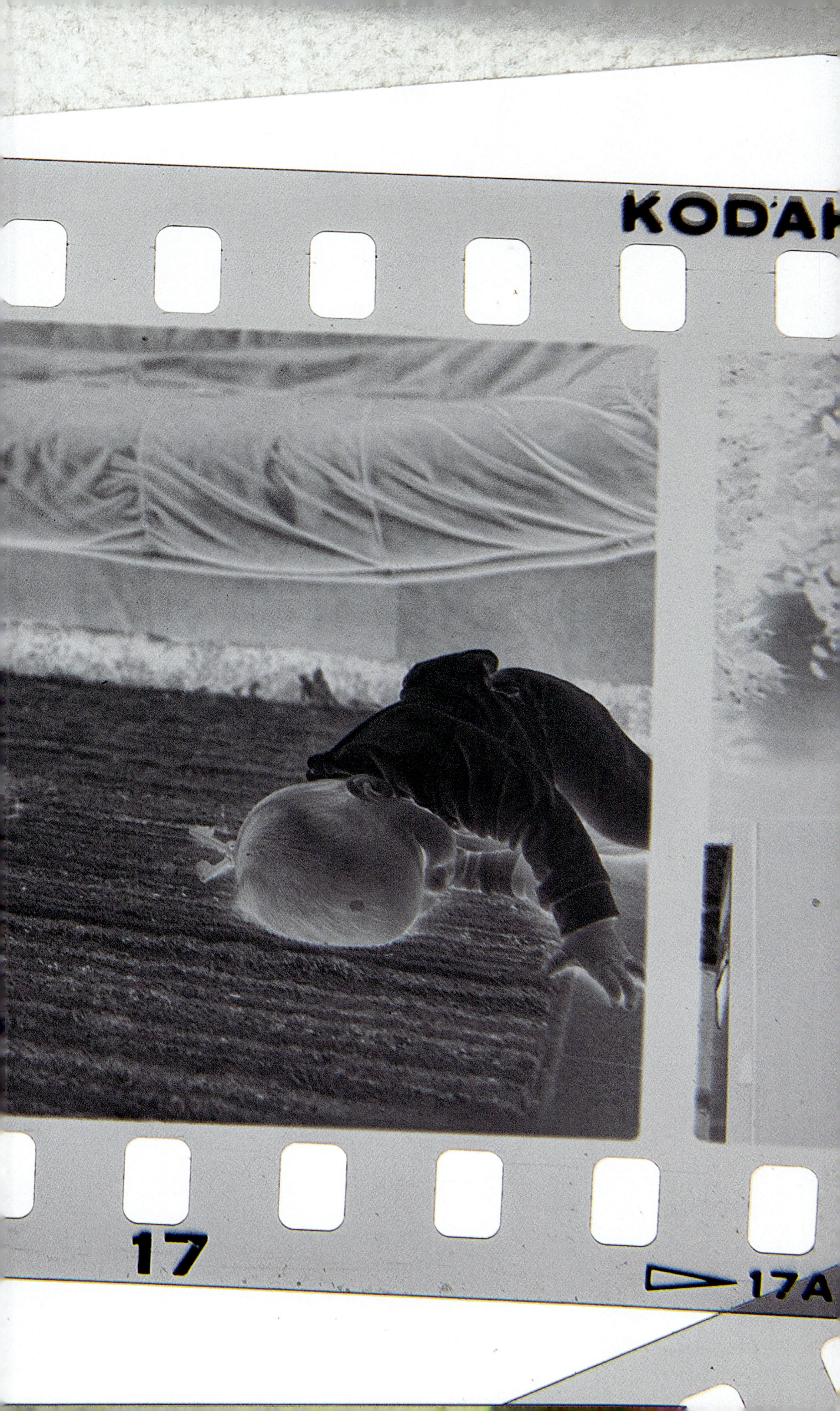

KODAK

17

17A

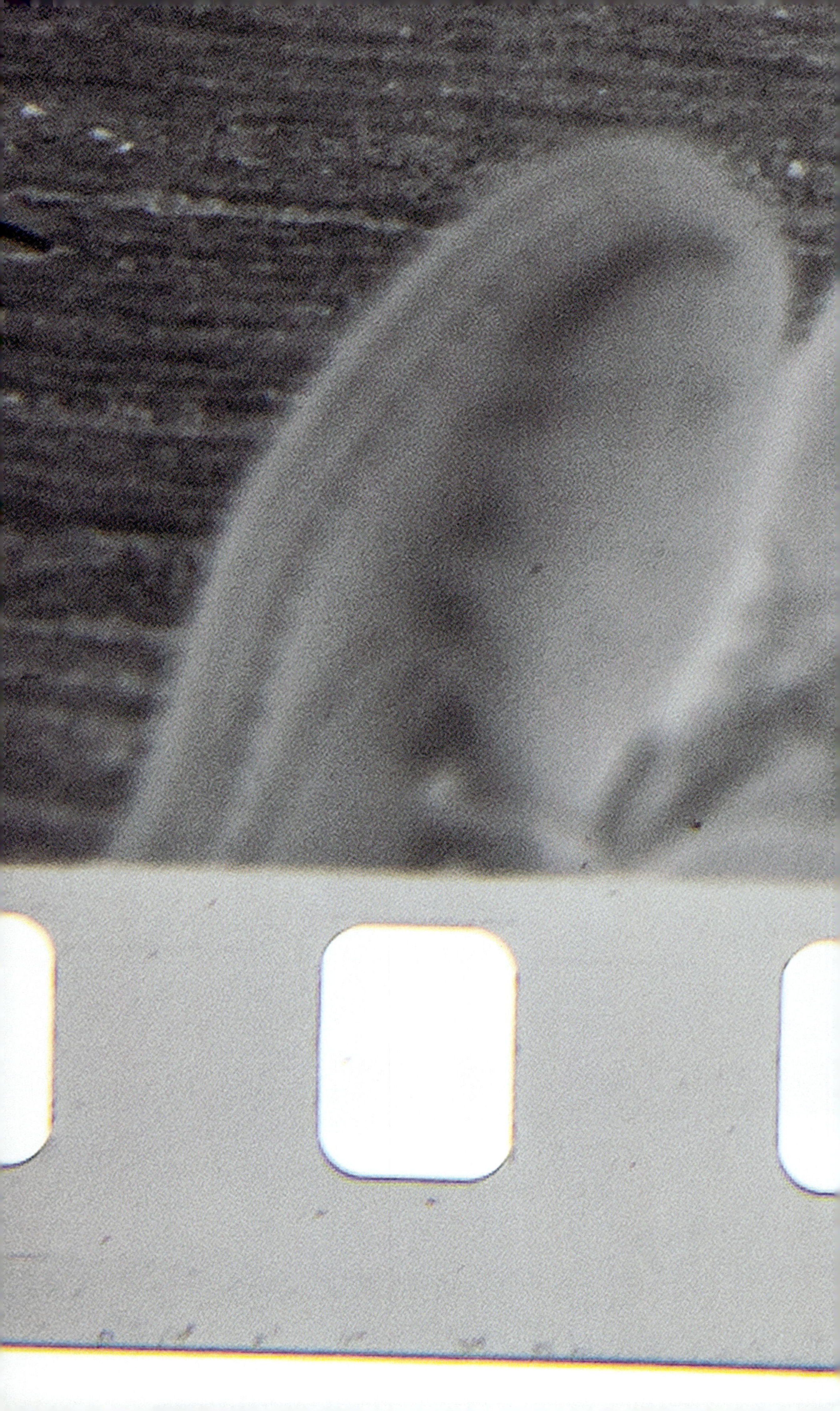

it's right there,
the first trace of the impasse

16A

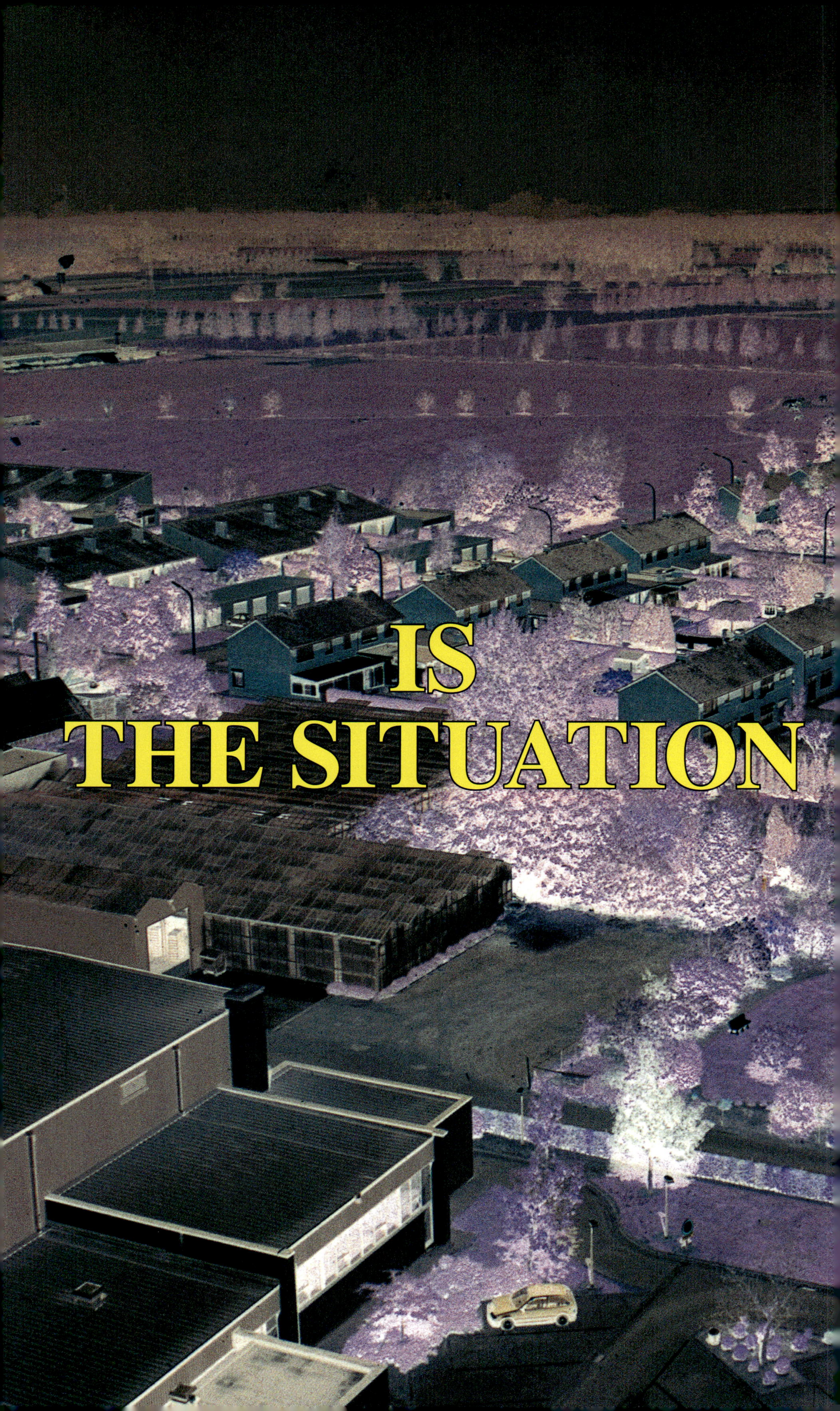
IS
THE SITUATION

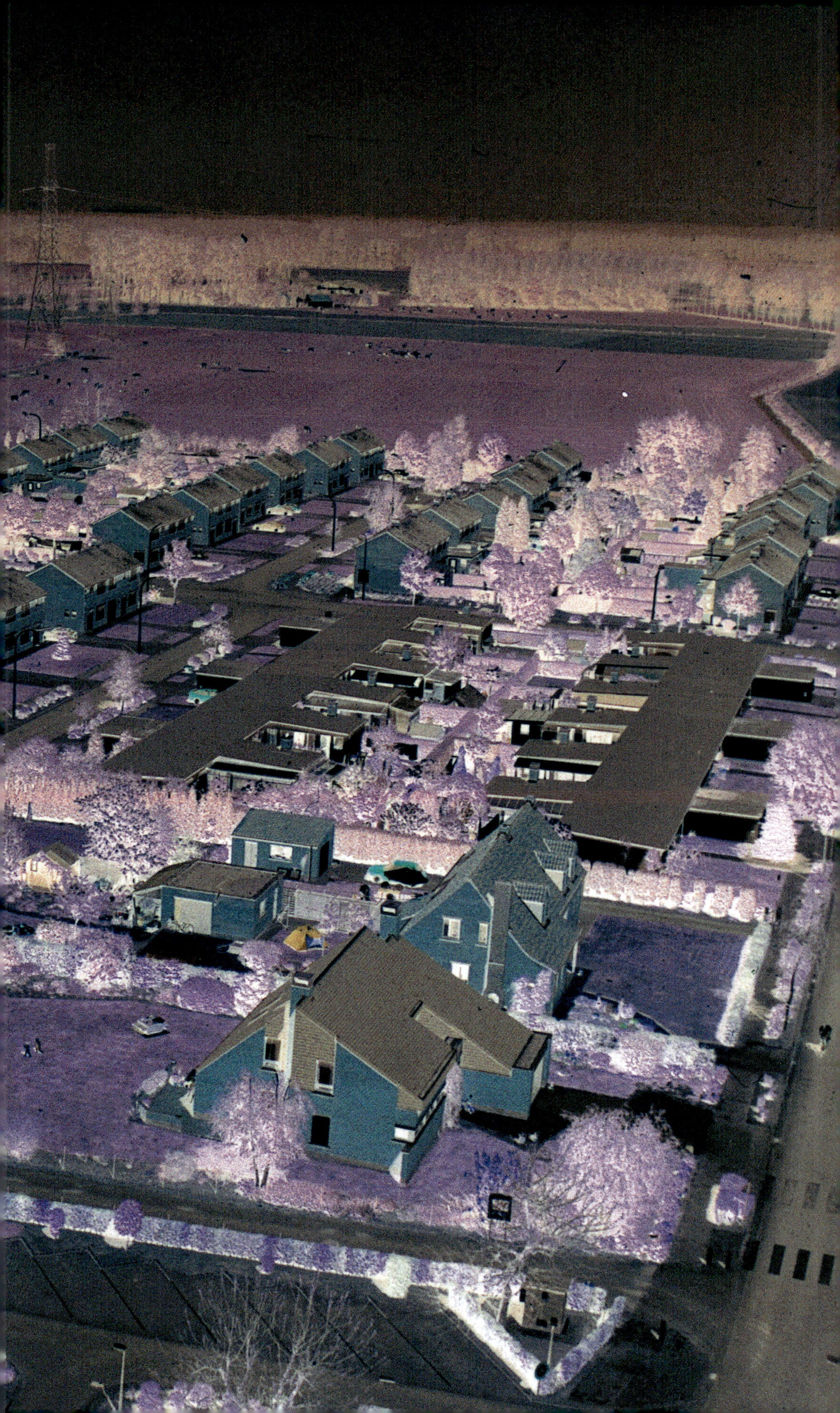

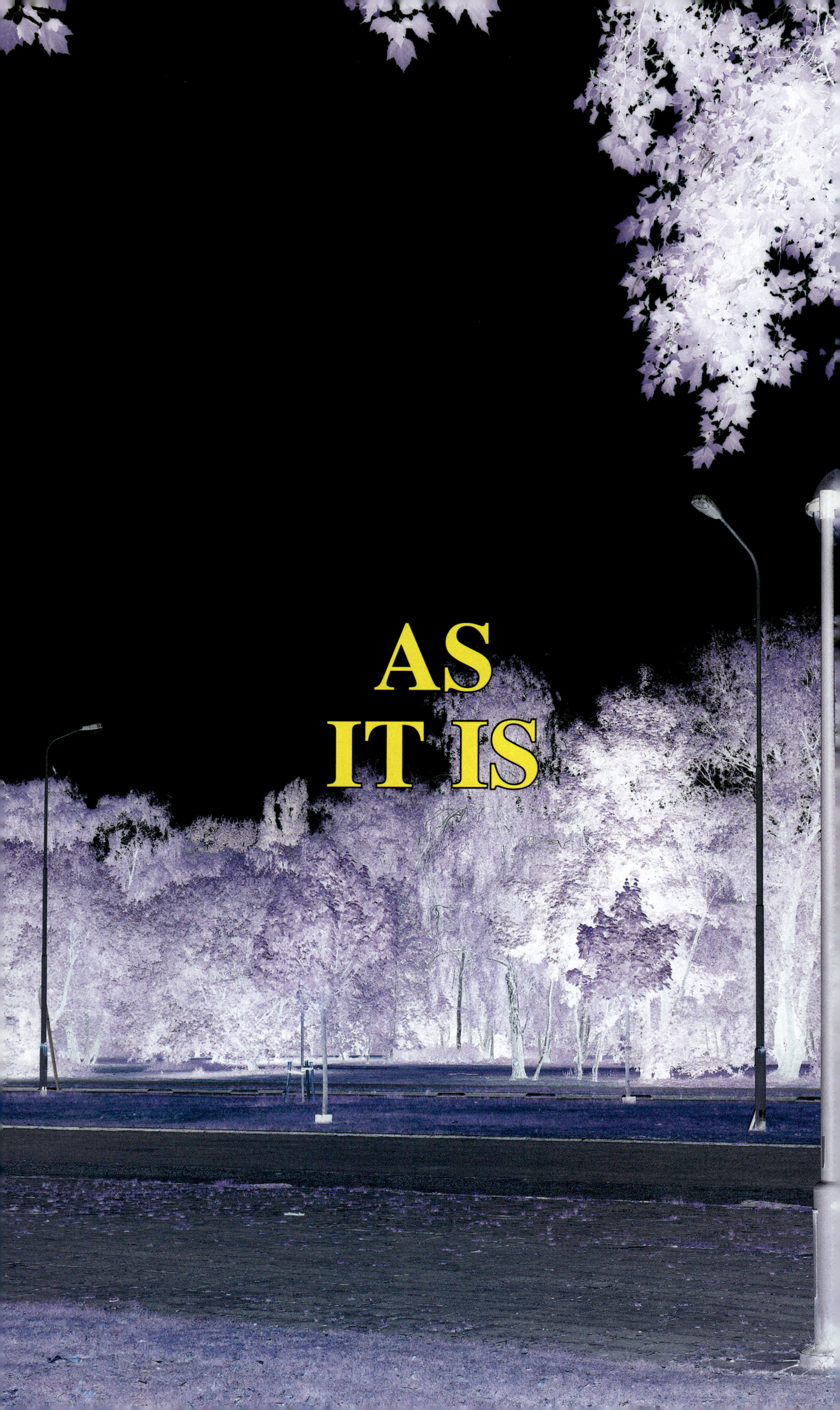
AS
IT IS

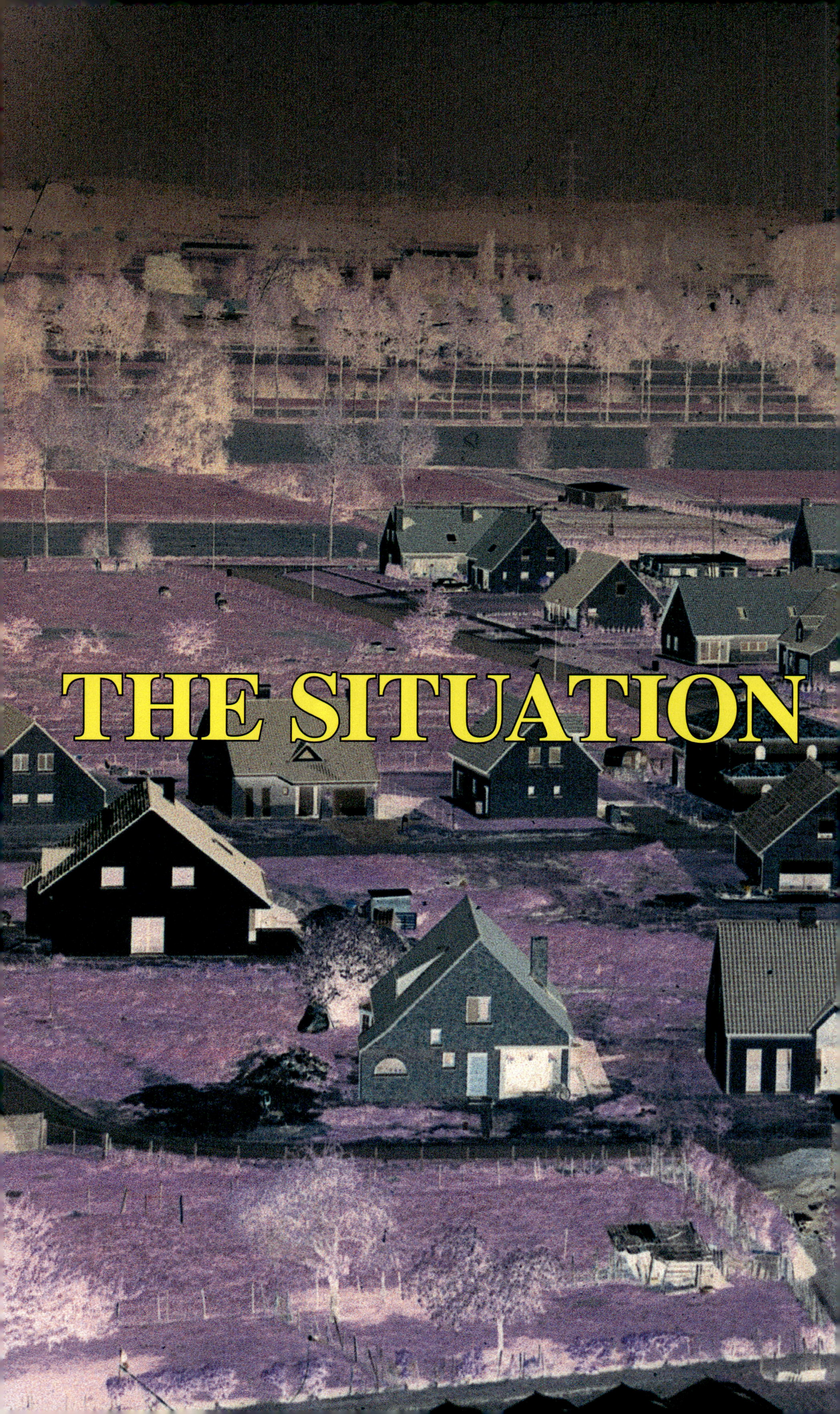
THE SITUATION

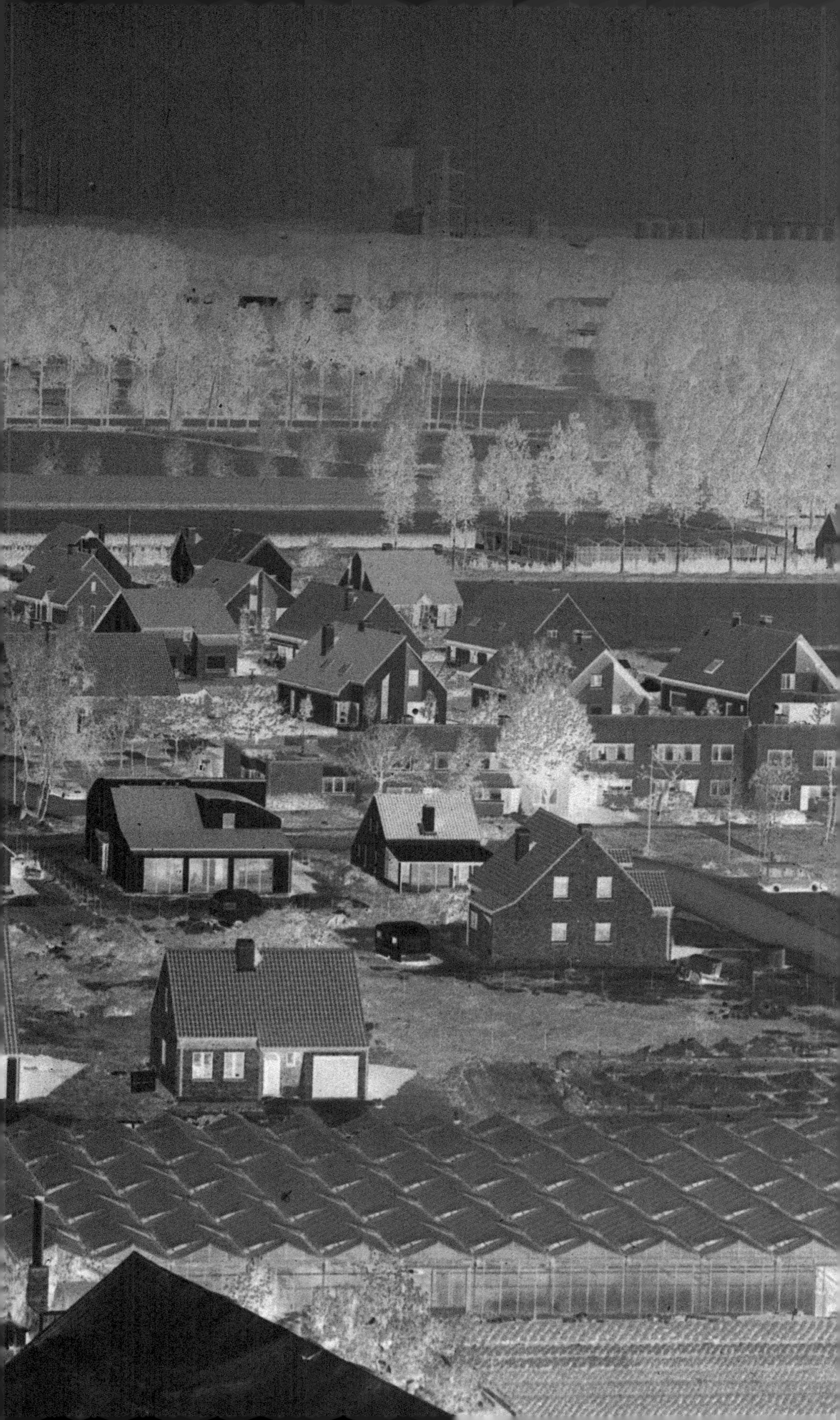

In *La préparation du roman*, one of the seminars Roland Barthes gave at the Collège de France, the literary theorist discusses the possibility of a phantasmatic novel – a novel that is not directed at the past. He asks: how can one write the present? Reconciling the temporal distance inherent in the act of writing with the nearness of the present (the moment written about) seems impossible. There's a fundamental gap between those two instances. Yet, in search of the way life, in all its presence and intensity, can be written, Barthes finds possibilities in the small discursive building block of 'the notation', the haiku serving as his prime example. Provocatively and firmly, Barthes states: 'One can write the Present *by notating it*'.[1]

Transposing Barthes' question to a different medium than writing makes it less vertiginous. It is no coincidence Barthes elucidates the haiku's capturing of the present by referring to photography.[2] To ask what a notation might entail, photographically speaking, seems to be pleonastic, or self-explanatory at the least. A photograph *is* a photographic notation: it proves the present – the *ça-a-été* quality Barthes describes more elaborately in *La chambre claire* as photography's defining trait. A photograph notates in that it reduces the temporal (and spatial) distance to the present to a minimum. There's no need to avert one eye from life unfolding to record it. Both eyes are directed at the same thing: the present, as it is seen and at the same time captured, through the lens.

Following Barthes, that *ça-a-été* quality is photography's *noème* – its defining trait, and therefore present in every photograph. Still, there are photographs that more overtly state and claim their *noème* as such. There is an immense but seldom discussed photographic archive testifying to this: photographs documenting 'the situation as it is', 'the existing state of things' or 'the current state of the property' that are added, as a legal requirement, to every planning application. These photographs, in addition to plans, data, and written statements, are added as attachments to the application, registering what *is*: a building, a neighbourhood, a lot, a landscape. Their goal is important. As part of the application, they serve to justify the alteration of their subject – the demolition, refurbishment or development of the building, neighbourhood, lot or landscape they depict. As such, they are documents that define the way the built landscape changes.

In a suspiciously self-evident way, they are photographs demanded to show the built environment. This seems an altogether fair requirement of a photograph, and it gives them a seemingly clear place in architecture's three-part semiotic system (buildings, images of buildings, and the discourse on architecture)[3] and within 'the overlapping systems of representation' that have shaped modern architecture.[4] Still, as functional photographs – they are photographs made in service of a practical end – of a functional subject – architecture, as an applied art – with a clear discursive description of their use – i.e. describing the situation as it is – it is hard to pinpoint exactly how they function. To what do they refer when they are employed to register the situation as it is? And to what effect? What do they document, and what

[1] Barthes, R. *La préparation du roman I et II. Notes de cours et de séminaires au Collège de France 1978-1979 et 1979-1980* (N. Léger, ed.). Paris: Seuil/IMEC, 2003, 45 (our translation).

[2] 'Cependant, la proximité de la photo et du haïku reste très grande. Certes, la photo est pleine, saturée de détails *inévitables* – et non le haïku; mais dans l'une et l'autre, *tout est donné tout de suite*' (Barthes, 2003, 117).

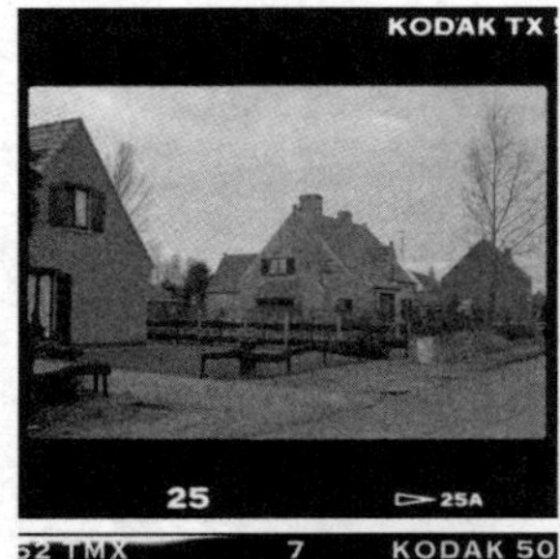

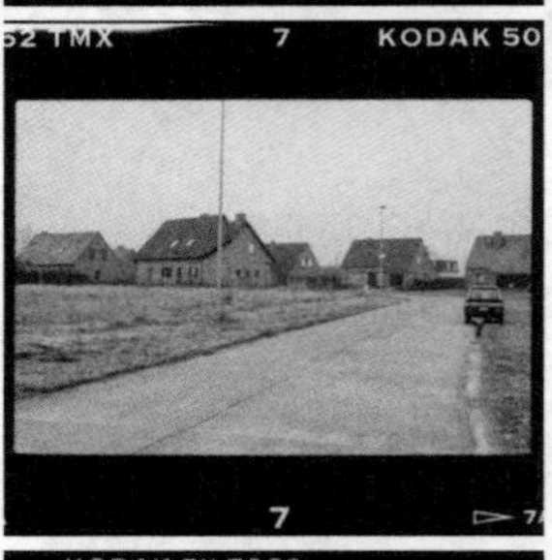

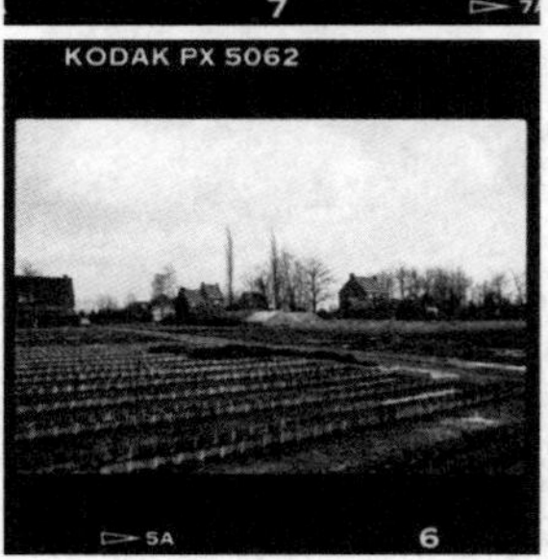

[3] Forty, A. *Words and Buildings. A Vocabulary of Modern Architecture*. London: Thames & Hudson, 2004, 13.

[4] Colomina, B. *Privacy and Publicity. Modern Architecture and Mass Media*. Cambrigde, Mass.: The MIT Press, 1996, 13.

conventions make it possible for them to be read as documents? In short, what do these photographs *do* when they are said to be showing the built present?

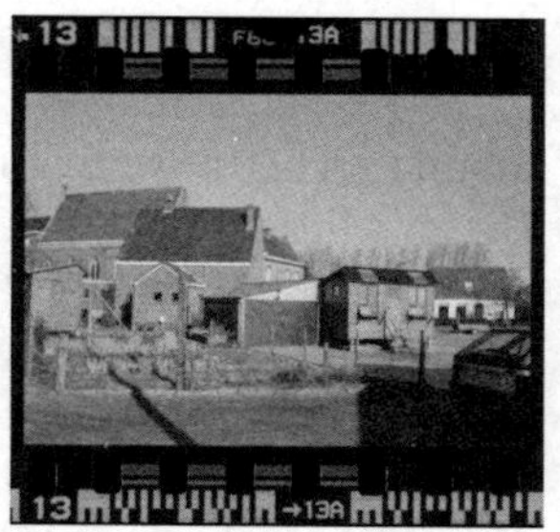

*

The following are the guidelines for the photographs that must be attached to a planning application in Flanders.[5] The Flemish Government states that at least six different recent and numbered photos must be provided, three of which showing the place where the planned works will take place, and three of which showing the building itself and the parcels adjacent to the building lot. In the case of a demolition application, three photographs are sufficient. Format: JPG, JPEG, PNG, GIF or PDF. The numbering or naming of the photographs must be in accordance with the way they are marked on the plan. If the application deals with the removal of a listed building or landscape, the number and type of photographs must be adjusted so that they visualise the current state of every side of the property that is to be demolished, as well as the wider context in which the building or landscape is situated.

[5] Departement Omgeving. *Normen voor digitale aanvragen voor een Omgevingsvergunning. Stedenbouwkundige handelingen met architect* (version 3 November 2020, https://www.omgevingsloketvlaanderen.be/sites/default/files/atoms/files/Normenboek%20digitale%20OMV%20aanvragen%20met%20architect_20201103.pdf, accessed on 3 January 2022).

The guidelines are concise and straightforward, but there's also a set of ideas that are taken for granted and left unsaid. Implicit in these guidelines, and in the general demand to supply photographs of the situation as it is, is a reliance on photography as a means of representation, as a 'realistic' medium: drawn plans are there to indicate the intended future of the lot, building, or landscape, but when it comes to registering the current state of affairs, there have to be floor plans, zoning plans, cross sections, front, side and back elevations *and* photographs. What do these photographs have to show, exactly? One could say the photographs add proof, an element of trustworthiness, to the other documents in the application. But the 'realism' is not inherent to the photographs. The photographs could have been tampered with. They could depict a building in a different place or could have been made on a different occasion. The claim that a photograph shows the (present) situation as it is, can only be made, because the photograph is embedded in the application and tied to the other files in it. There are cross-references in the plans and photographs that link the photographs to the application – filenames, lists, marks on the plans that indicate the location from which the photographs are taken – and as such these references dictate how the photographs can be interpreted as representational. The photographs aren't only there to add an element of realism to the plans. It's also the other way round: the plans corroborate the veracity of the photographs.[6]

In addition to the cross-referential system, the photographs themselves rely on a tradition of photographic realism and a 'documentary style'[7] to be able to function as realistic depictions of the built environment. The guidelines have limited formal constraints, but a clear visual language is implicitly demanded. They push the photographs to a certain stylistic neutrality and objectivity. The photographs are usually made with a wide angle lens, so they can frame the building and its surroundings. There's a level horizon slightly above the middle of the frame. There is a preference for a 'descriptive' kind of light; both cloudy and partly sunny circumstances are acceptable. Two complementary approaches are common: the camera is positioned parallel to the (future) façade (often framing a part of the front-facing garden or street), offering a frontal view (a key characteristic of the documentary style[8]), which is complemented by a camera position at an angle of approximately 45° to the façade, so that the wider surroundings are captured as well.[9]

[6] Baetens, J. *Pour le roman-photo*. Brussels: Les Impressions Nouvelles, 2010, 97. In many ways, Baetens' essay on the photonovel has been a key text in the writing of this essay and in the creation of this project as a whole.

[7] Lugon, O. *Le Style documentaire. D'August Sander à Walker Evans. 1920-1945*. Paris: Macula, 2011.

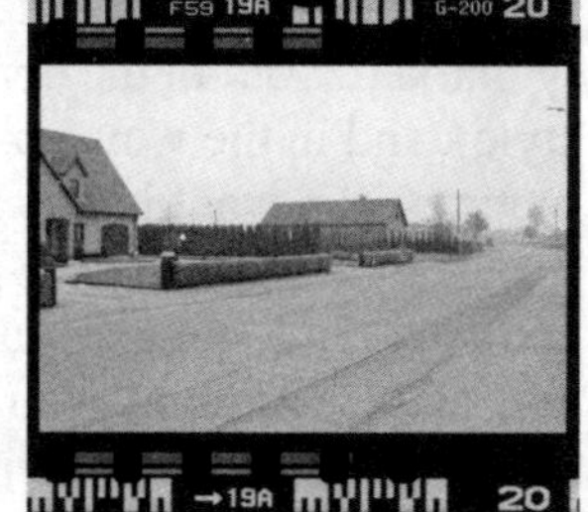

The fact that at least three and often six or more photographs must be added to the application results in a *series* of photographs. All photographs depict the same subject but from a different vantage point. As such, they reinforce each other's representational value: in a relational way, by recognising the same building in the different pictures, the claim that they are each depicting the exact same construction or lot is strengthened. In addition to that, as a series, they also undermine an interpretation as a sequence: recognising identical contextual aspects, such as the type of light, or the weather, indicates these photographs were not only taken on the same spot, but also

[8] Lugon designates 'frontality' as one of the main characteristics of the 'clarity' that defines the documentary style. Besides clarity, documentary photography's reliance on photographic series is another key trait (Lugon, 2011, 147).

[9] From that perspective, they provide the material to ask a crucial question: how does the way the existing situation is pictured photographically, how do the changing requirements and styles, influence the decision that is made, and, via that decision, the built landscape in which we dwell?

at the same instant. After all, they must show the situation as it is, not how it evolves. There is no developing action or a narrative that unfolds. There is little to no change. There is only the claim that the situation depicted at *that* instant (the moment when the series was made), is the situation as it is at *this* instant (the moment when the series is evaluated). As separate photographs, and as a series, they claim instantaneous duration and enduring instantaneity.[10, 11]

[10] In the architectural process, visual sequences are present in other forms, during other stages of the process, and with different ends: drawn storyboards pitching a project to a client and as such relying on techniques stemming from comics (Le Corbusier's storyboard for Villa Meyer is a famous early example), or 3D renders that make it possible to digitally walk through a designed building. For different perspectives on historical and present narrative approaches to the built landscape, see Havik, K., Notteboom, B. & de Wit, S. (eds.). *Oase 98: Narrating Urban Landscapes*. Rotterdam: nai010, 2017.

[11] As a way of describing these photographs, 'the situation as it is', as a formulation, designates the paradoxical characteristics of the photographs as a form of instantaneous ('as it is') duration ('the situation').

That someone must take photographs is a logical result of the seemingly simple requirement to attach photographs to the application. However, upon closer investigation, this entails a complex set of ideas on what an architect is. Except for major construction applications by large firms or the government, employing the services of a (named) professional photographer, the architect and the photographer will, in most other cases, be one and the same individual. While he must legally be mentioned as the architect filing the application, he will nowhere be mentioned as the photographer. To an extent, these photographs are made anonymously, and the anonymity reinforces their status. As anonymous photographs, the objectivity of the photographs is discursively emphasised: there's no need to mention who made them, the anonymity suggests, as the camera (itself) captured, in a neutral way and without a personal touch, what is there. Still, supplying the photographs (anonymously), the architect becomes, as part of his professional activities, an architect-photographer. He will have little to no education as a photographer: an amateur photographer of sorts, producing an instance of vernacular photography. For an amateur photographer, the burden he must carry is enormous. His is a seldom acknowledged but defining role: he is the one who, *as a photographer*, registers, and thus defines, the current and actual landscape. Whatever decision will be made on the intended future of the landscape or building, in part it will always be based on an interpretation of the landscape the way he, literally, envisioned it.

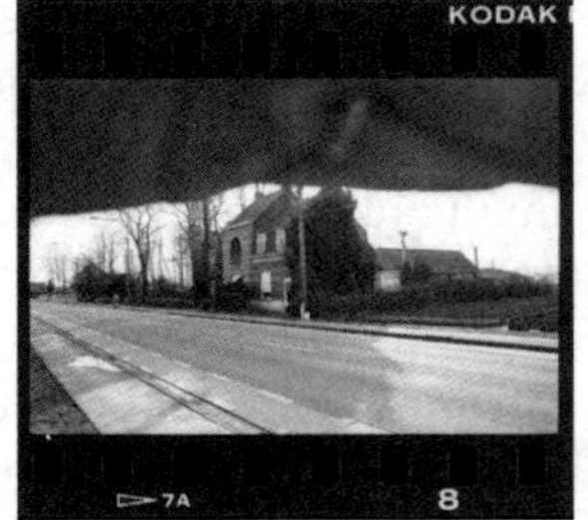

This has formal – stylistic – consequences. For even if these state-ordered photographic guidelines push towards a 'neutral' registering style, there is ample room for choice. However objective his photographs might seem, and however constraining the context within which they appear, these photographs bear the imprint of the architect holding the camera: the type of camera and film he uses, the width of the framing, the persons or objects he depicts although they are not strictly speaking necessary to depict, the time when he visits the lot, the number of photographs he takes, the number of photographs he selects and submits ('*at least* six photographs'), etc. Choices – however trivial – have to be made: whether he parks his car further on (so as not to have the same vehicle in all of his planning applications), whether he shields the lens with his hand in the case of a backlit building, whether the morning fog is too picturesque, whether he should return when the corn is harvested. In short, the photographs are stylistically marked, both in the context of photographic history (the documentary style), and in the way a particular architect-photographer 'stylizes' his pictures. Relevant in this regard, on a more general level, is the question to what extent the architect-photographer's photographic style aligns with the architect-photographer's architectural style. They mustn't necessarily correlate, and there might even be reasons for them to have opposed stylistic characteristics, because of their strategic use (a photograph convincing the viewer of what needs to be changed as opposed to a plan convincing the viewer of what that change will look like), and because of the different (and changing) conventions at play with each medium (photography and drawing).

The relation between the photograph and its maker is marked, but so is the relation between the photograph and its subject. Unlike professional photographs of buildings, which tend to show them in a pristine state, shortly after the last contractor has left and moments before the first dweller sets foot in the building, these are photographs in which context is more clearly present. Not only the context of the landscape in which the building is situated (the adjacent buildings that are required to be present in the pictures), but also traces of life happening in and around them. These pictures add an important aspect to the plans: they show the buildings in use and offer a glimpse of how they are experienced. A courier's van on the driveway, a trampoline in the front garden, the neighbour who comes to see what is happening, the horizon which is slightly askew, a crack in the wall, frost on the veranda door, etc. As a result of photography's characteristics as a medium, the pictures document the surroundings at the time they are framed. In comparison to the plans that also depict the situation as it is, these photographs do not stop registering where the building ends. As such, 'the situation as it is' not only refers to the state the building is in, but also to the time-specific context and surroundings at the moment when the photograph is taken. The photograph documents the situation the situation is in.[12]

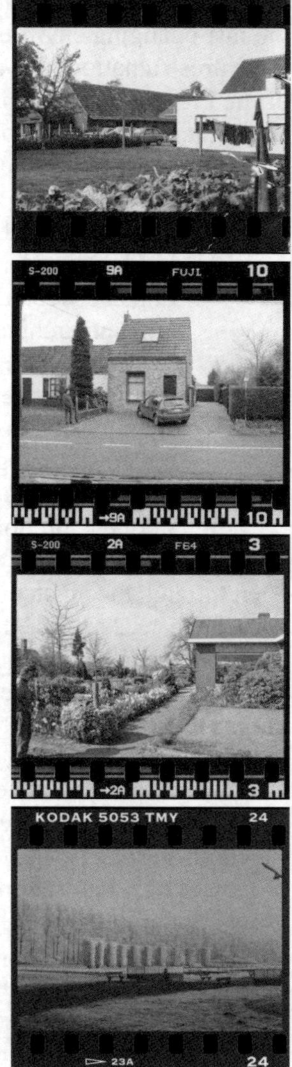

*

The photographic descriptions of the state buildings are in are present in ambitious, public architectural projects, as well as in small-scale, private projects. But even though they are abundantly present in the architectural process, and part of the architectural system, the photographic documentation of the situation as it is lacks critical or public attention. It's not found in stately magazines, portfolios, museum catalogues or art galleries – places where one can come across architecture photography. When architecture is discussed publicly, attention is given mainly to other aspects and other media: renders and scale models that show what will be realised; professional photographs showing a recently finished building without the slightest trace of it being used; a nostalgic and romantic look at architectural heritage, or a virulent attack on the building policy's failure. In planning applications, one will naturally find the plans themselves: documents with an artistic aura, a close translation of a creative idea unhindered by circumstantial limitations, craftmanship in the process of drawing, the visible hand of the author-artist-architect. Within the applications, the photographic documents, however, seem to be neglectable. When it comes to the photographs, in most cases, only the public officer assessing the application, the client, the architect and the photographer (most likely the architect himself) will see them.

[12] On the other hand, while photographs are to an extent exhaustive – they record everything visible within the frame – they also have the possibility to exclude or conceal parts of the building or the environment by framing strategically.

Still, these photographs exist and are preserved. Because of the legal requirement to add photographic documents to a planning application, an immense archive of photographs of the built landscape has formed over the years. As such, they offer a historical architectural overview. Historical, as a consequence of the fact that, from the outset, they cannot live up to the task they have to perform: by the time the administration will assess the planning application and the photographs that are part of it, the photographs will show the situation no longer as it is, but as it was (a couple of days, weeks, a month ago – depending on the architect's and the administration's swiftness). But apart from that intrinsic historicity, they also constitute a historical archive showing past landscapes, and as such this archive, and the photographs in it have a lot in common with other and more famous projects and archives in photographic history. Extensive projects such as the Mission Héliographique in France in the mid-nineteenth century and the Mission Dhuicque in Belgium during World War I relied on photography's capacities to register and safeguard the built environment; contemporary projects such as the New Palmyra Project build on photography to reconstruct destructed built heritage. Within the context of the research group Forensic Architecture, photography (among other 'sensors') is relied upon as an aid to document buildings, themselves conceptualised and investigated as a documentary medium on and within which traces of force fields are stored.

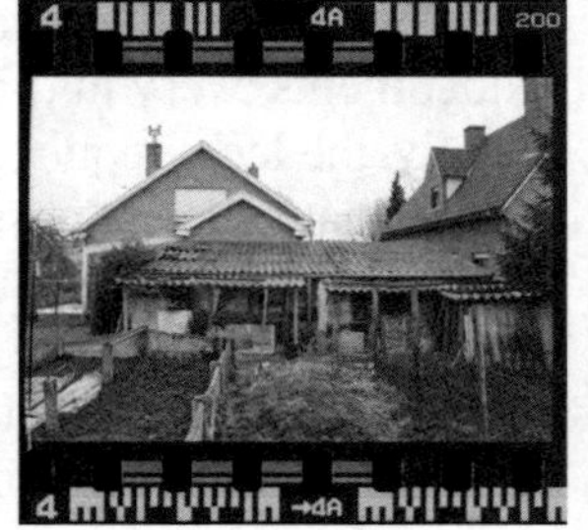

The photographic surveys of the Survey Movement in Great Britain at the end of the nineteenth and the beginning of the twentieth century are another case in point. As Elisabeth Edwards describes it in *The Camera as Historian*, a myriad of amateur photographers recorded 'the English past so that it might be preserved for future generations'. In the context of the widespread availability and popularity of cameras on the one hand, and the fast-changing environment at the turn of the century on the other hand, there arose a nationwide project 'to constitute a "True Pictorial History of the Present Day"'.[13] Nationalistic, romantic and nostalgic longings and ideas intertwined with epistemological beliefs concerning the power of photography to hold time:

[13] Edwards, E. *The Camera as Historian. Amateur Photographers and Historical Imagination, 1885-1918*. Durham/London: Duke University Press, 2012, 2.

> The promise of photographs was to grasp time and rematerialise it. Photographs extended the reach of the temporal beyond relations between the present and the past to the future as well, creating an archival grid through which the past might be accessible in an imagined future. [...] In this way, time, as an indissoluble relation between historical past, present, and future visibilities, saturates the discourse of the amateur surveys and formed one of the epistemological bases for the endeavours in which the very act of photography and the experience of taking a photograph implies duration.[14]

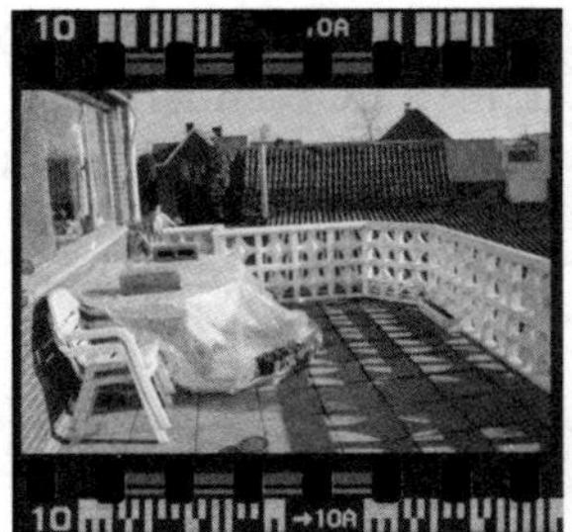

[14] Edwards, *The Camera as Historian*, 7.

Seen through the amateurs' lenses, the duration of the built landscape was at once laid bare, established, and longed for. In the context of the Survey Movement, photography, archive and landscape all became sites of temporal density.[15]

[15] Edwards, *The Camera as Historian*, 166.

Without being intended or preserved as such, the archive of photographs depicting the (once) current state of the built environment, as added to planning applications, came into being. These documents are tucked away in seldom consulted stacks but, like the photographs of the Survey Movement, have the potential to reveal the way the built environment functions in society, by means of amateur photographs, and to show how processes of urbanisation tend to proceed. The archive has grown and still grows, and photographs have been and still get added, relentlessly and continuously – almost like an archived, photographical livestream of the landscape, day in, day out, file upon file, lot after lot, building after building. The archive's extent is unfathomable, as is its rigour. What these pictures present is an extensive visual registration of landscapes and buildings that, in most cases, no longer exist (or no longer exist as such). They show high-end, prestigious public buildings, state-of-the-art bridges and dams. But for every prize-winning school or library, there are also thousands of pictures of houses, sheds and carports. In contrast to the public image and imagery of architecture, this archive reflects architecture's presence in all its variety and ordinariness, throughout all layers of society, and without concerns of prestige. It avoids selecting and tends towards exhaustivity. It's not content with providing a representational image: it doesn't state, 'This can be regarded as a photograph of a mid-1980s garage that needs to be extended'. It documents every mid-1980s garage that needs to be extended. Unintentionally, the legal requirement to register the situation as it is has led to an archive that makes it possible to analyse changing architectural tastes, cutting across the whole of society and the dwellings in which we live (except for the dwellings that are erected illegally and that do not end up in applications). It is an archive full of uneventful, day-to-day views of architecture being used and lived in, but it is precisely in that respect that the archive is unique: the images show an unspectacular historical landscape, likely on the verge of being changed.

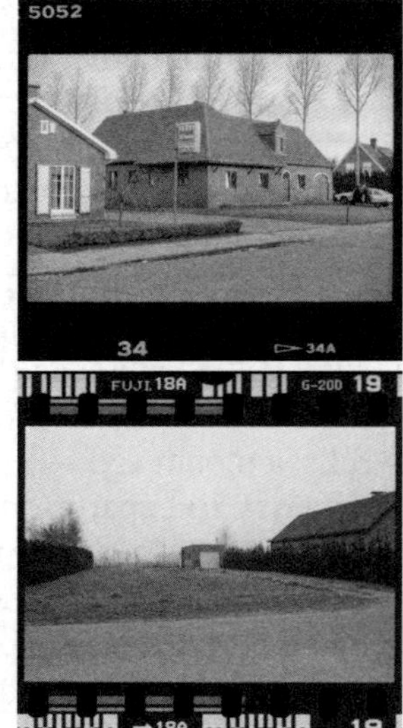

*

While this archive can be compared to and interpreted much like other photographical surveys, containing thousands of photographic documents recording the architectural present as the past, the system and discourse in and for which they were produced give them a diametrically opposed function. For as the photographs in archives such as the Survey Movement recorded the present – which was changing by an external force – in order to preserve it for posterity, the photographs in the planning applications we are considering here record the present in order to change it, paving the way for a different future.

As a consequence, while the archive presents an extensive, cross-sectional view of the built environment, it does so partially, *depicting only that which was thought of as something in need of change*. As such, it not only shows a fragment of the landscape as it existed, it also shows, from the architect-photographer's present, yesterday's outdated architecture. These photographs are inherently critical and, despite their superficial neutrality, they are ideologically loaded. When they register, they also interpret and convey an opinion, and as such testify to the way a society decides to organise itself spatially. The archive demonstrates what taste, society, aesthetics, economy do to the landscape (and undo). Even if the application did not receive a positive evaluation, and the buildings which it depicted and wanted to change are still there, unchanged, its criticism remains intact. The photographs keep showing what was deemed in need of change by the community, the architect, the clients. As such, every photograph of the situation as it is, is tainted, influenced and, to an extent, created by a second image of what the situation is desired to be: a second image that is present in the application as a drawing. In a way, the architect photographs the situation as it is, informed and instructed beforehand by a different medium: the drawing in which he shows that situation, differently. In a way, the drawn image of the uncertain future, informs the composition of the photograph of the architectural present.

In that regard, it's a photographic archive of the unfashionable, the unstable, the inconvenient, with the fashionable, the stable, and the convenient being photographically absent (but implicitly present via the drawn image that informs the photographs of the present). The motivations for that change are not explicit, and the photographs are therefore suggestive with regard to the reason for their existence.[16] These photographs inform, albeit vaguely. There are implicit constructional and aesthetic motives – photographs showing a wall that's askew, or a vertical window. There are ecological and economic evolutions pointing at the need to change what is there – shops with empty vitrines, a petrol station besides the school yard. There are sociological factors – houses with too few bedrooms. Often, the photographs suggest a bourgeois tendency – the empty lots besides the cul-de-sac, with the corn roots still pushing the earth in heaps. Above all, they undeniably show a mesmerising urge to build.

[16] A written statement by the architect can be added to the planning application. In it, he can expand on the motivations. The written statement is not compulsory.

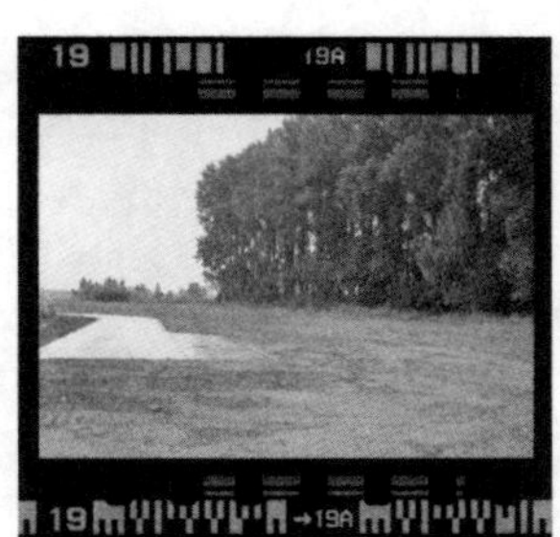

As photographs depicting the present to alter it, they testify to a crucial aspect of their functioning. Documenting the present to alter it, by relying (specifically) on a premise of realism, is of course not a unique feature of the architectural photographs under consideration. Still, it is hard to find a comparable set of photographs in the history of architectural photography. Berenice Abbott's renowned series *Changing New York* comes to mind, a series in which she depicted the fast-evolving city in the 1930s. The 'realism' on which she drew is, according to Terri Weissman, a critical realism, with photography functioning as a means to open up a space of civil discourse on the topic of the city's architectural future.[17] It's the double interpretation the title of her work implies. It's what her photographs show, but also do: changing New York.

[17] Weissman, T. *The Realisms of Berenic Abbott. Documentary Photography and Political Action.* Berkeley: University of California Press, 2011.

In the broader history of photography, there is socio-critical documentary photography and photojournalism that accuses and denounces practices with a view to changing them for the better by depicting them (such as Jacob Riis' famous 1890 publication *How the Other Half Lives: Studies among the Tenements of New York*). Yet, in comparison to that kind of photography, the architectural images of the situation as it is are different because the witnessing function of societally-engaged photography is absent. This is not photography after the fact, but photography before the fact. These photographs are all but intended to preserve an image of the present as it is bound to disappear in the face of change. They survey meticulously, not to preserve, but to alter. In a way, what these photographs are intended to do is not only to denounce, but to draw attention away from what they show, and even from themselves. In other words, these pictures are not intended to memorialise, but are a vehicle to get from the present to the future, by erasing what they depict and, if successful, undermining their status as pictures of the situation as it is.

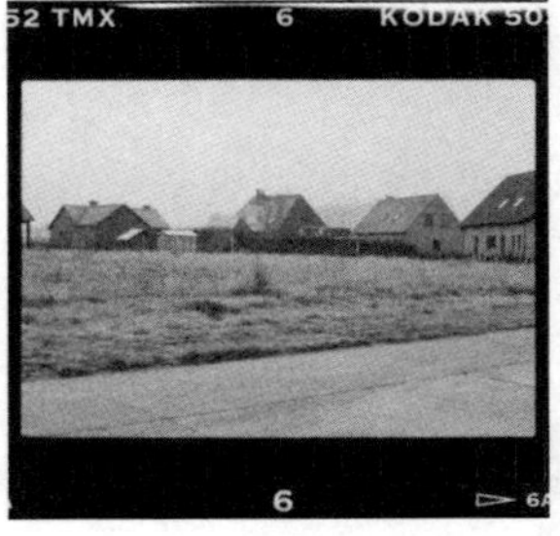

An apt correlate can be found in an utterly different context. The functioning of the photographs is reminiscent of what Harun Farocki in 'Reality would have to begin' wrote about the civil engineer Albrecht Meydenbauer, who in the nineteenth century discovered a way to use photography to take scale measurements of buildings. His discovery got picked up by different organisations with different aims: 'The military took up the idea of measuring from photographs, as did the historic preservationists of monuments – the former destroy, and the latter preserve. [...] Using these archived photographs, one ought to be able to read and calculate the building's plan, in the case of its destruction – a destruction already conceived in these protective measures.'[18] It is within the military system, and the way in which photography, buildings and discourse interact in that context, that photographs of the situation as it is find a strange and unsettling comparison. In both cases, photography doesn't document change, it exacts it.

[18] Farocki, H. *Nachdruck/Imprint. Texte/Writings* (S. Gaensheimer & N. Schafhause, eds.). New York: Lukas & Sternberg / Berlin: Vorwerk 8, 2002, 196-198.

These are, in short, not mere 'documents', registering passively what is there. These photographs have agency. In a way that harks back to early superstitions surrounding the medium, a lot of these buildings disappeared when they got photographed. They got photographed *away*. The building can be said to whither, not because, as Walter Benjamin famously stated, the photograph, as a technological reproduction of an artwork, devaluates the here and now of a building, and as such, its auratic authenticity,[19] but because the photograph, by proving the here and now, precisely *refuses* to function as a reproduction. It functions instead as reproduction's opposite. It is by taking a photograph that the architect not only makes a statement about the built environment, but also alters it. The architect is the one who, by profession, designs to construct. When he's holding a camera, however, destruction is imminent.

[19] Benjamin, W. 'The Work of Art in the Age of Its Technological Reproducibility. Third version', in: *Selected Writings. Volume 4: 1938-1940* (H. Eiland & M.W. Jennings, eds.). Cambridge, Mass./London: The Belknap Press of Harvard University Press, 2003, 254.

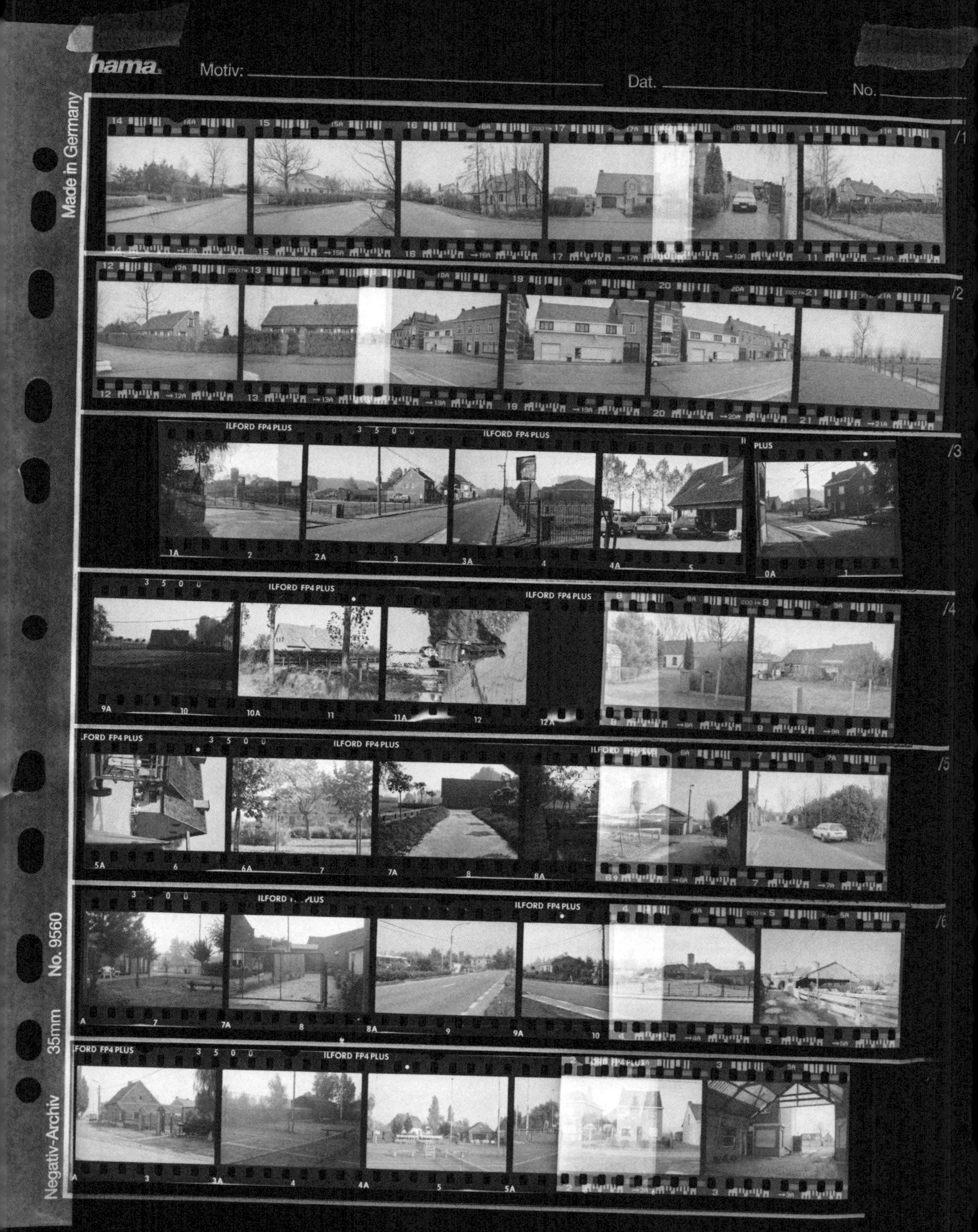

hama

Motiv: ______ Dat. ______ No. ______

Made in Germany

Negativ-Archiv 35mm No. 9560

Episode 1 — Prologue

<table>
<tr><td>we find ourselves in taupe ring binders</td><td>among construction sites, birthdays,
scaffolding, his Citroën BX, zinc
gutters, greenhouses, our dog,
the dead-end street for an unbuilt
neighbourhood</td><td>until the documents turn into
something else</td></tr>
<tr><td>among construction sites, birthdays,
scaffolding, his Citroën BX, zinc
gutters, greenhouses, our dog,
the dead-end street for an unbuilt
neighbourhood</td><td>until the documents turn into
something else</td><td>we find ourselves in taupe ring binders</td></tr>
<tr><td>until the documents turn into
something else</td><td>we find ourselves in taupe ring binders</td><td>among construction sites, birthdays,
scaffolding, his Citroën BX, zinc
gutters, greenhouses, our dog,
the dead-end street for an unbuilt
neighbourhood</td></tr>
</table>

A kid blows out three candles on a whipped cream covered cake. Smoke fills the living room.

ARCHIVE (1)
The photographic archive of the architect consists of negatives, stored in two ring binders and a cardboard box filled with Fujiprint envelopes. Most of the photographs were made by the architect for professional purposes, as a planning application requires the inclusion of photographs of 'the situation as it is' (buildings, empty lots, greenery, streets, etc.). The archive also includes photographs of cracks in ceilings, a construction prop holding up a beam or a sagging roof ridge: photographs that attest to either shortcomings and problems or important phases during construction. Among those photographs are family pictures. We see our uncles and aunts, ourselves, the dogs we had. The archive consists of 2,583 photographic negatives and covers a period ranging from the beginning of the 1980s until the end of the 1990s, when digital photography was introduced.

BILLBOARD (1)
The Situation As It Is was conceived as a visual story of fifteen episodes of three frames each. During the course of a year and a half, those three-part episodes were presented on a rotating, three-sided billboard, mounted on the facade of art space 019 in Ghent, Belgium, along the R40, the inner city ringway. As a consequence of the characteristics of the billboard, the rhythmically alternating episodes had to be made following these constraints:

- Each episode must consist of three frames.
- Each frame must consist of a photograph and text.
- Each frame must be able to be seen and read as the first (or second, or third) in that episode.
- Each episode of three frames must tell a narrative of its own.
- All fifteen episodes must together tell a grander narrative.

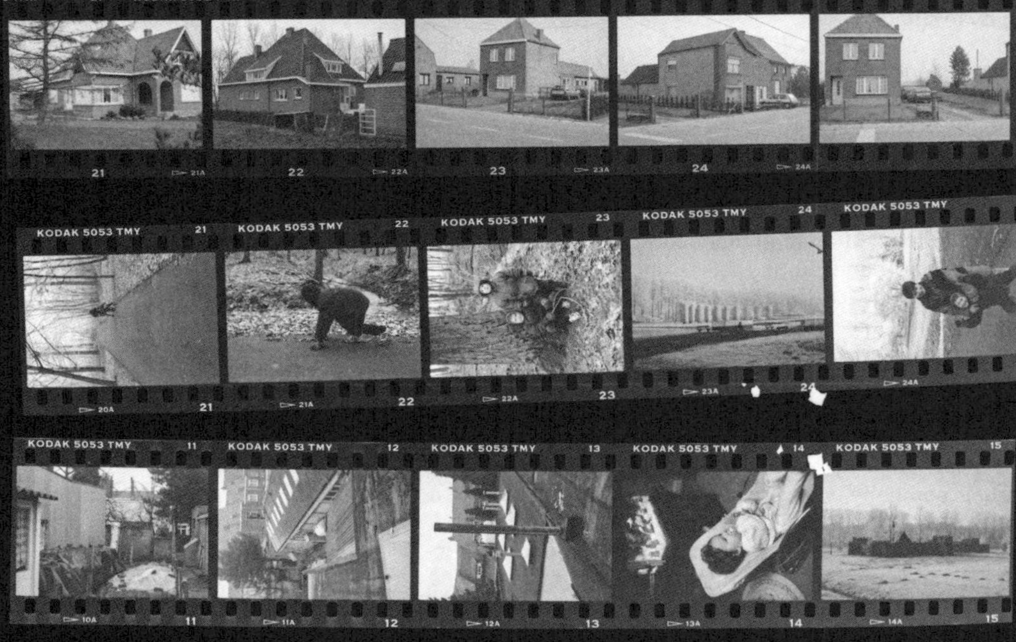

hama negativ-ablage typ 357 as · no. 9055 made in germany

Episode 2 — Title

THE SITUATION	AS IT	IS
AS IT	IS	THE SITUATION
IS	THE SITUATION	AS IT

The church tower is in scaffolding. The architect climbs the 51 metre high structure to follow up on the details of the restoration and, if necessary, take photographic records of shortcomings on the part of the contractor. Earlier that day, he loaded a roll of colour negative film in his camera. He turns away from the lead and zinc, focuses on infinity and captures the village sprawling. Two children are running towards a white bench in the day care's garden.

LANDSCAPE (1)
On the horizon industry looms. There were a few situations when we were keenly aware that we didn't live on the edge of a remote village, but a stone's throw from the city and its industry. A westerly wind brings thick, sweet air. Along the canal, in silos, the grain ferments. It's winter and the bare trees no longer shield the view. Through the poplars we see the flaming flare stack that lights up the edge of the cooling tower.

Once, during a balloon flight, the pilot said that the milk produced within a fifteen kilometre radius of the steel factory was purchased by the factory and then poured away. The story was never confirmed but was passed on and gained momentum when the effects of the ruling were becoming visible.

With a westerly wind in January, we lived in a suburb, fleetingly.

CAR (4)
We remember sitting in the back seat of the grey Citroën BX (the architect's fourth car) on a Wednesday afternoon after school, with a folding ruler in our lap, being driven to a construction site to help set out the dimensions of what would become the foundations of another house. The car appears forty times in the archive (ten in black and white, thirty in colour).

CAMERA (1)
At first, the architect used a Canon AE-1 camera with a 50mm (1.4) prime lens.

BILLBOARD (2)
A Trivision is a billboard that can change due to the fact that it consists of rotating triangular prisms. They do so in 120° increments around their axes. Each vertical face of a prism shows a segment of another image or message. There's a three-fold benefit to this system. First, the real estate, hosting the billboard, is capable of showing three ads instead of one (or one ad with three faces). Second, a rotating billboard broadens and strengthens the narrative potential of the static billboard. As one of advertising's pre-eminent forms, a billboard addresses you as someone who is missing something (a product, a service), a lack the company speaking to you via the ad can remedy. It bridges the gap between the longing (it installs) and the fulfilment of that longing (it promises), via a story. A Trivision taps into the narrative requirements: a static roadside picture turns into another image, and another image, after which it automatically returns to the first one (although 'first' is irrelevant in this context). Third, the movement of the turning prism attracts the attention of the passer-by and increases the billboard's impact. It's a film of sorts, made up of three separate images (without it being an actual film, which would not be allowed by the Belgian Highway Code). Other common names for a Trivision are Tri-Face, three-message sign, Prismavision, prismatic display, Rotapanel or Prismatron. The Trivision's technique can be said to go back to ancient Greek theatre, in which a *periaktos* was a three-sided revolving apparatus used on stage. Each side of the apparatus presented a different scene. The rotation of the prisms of the apparatus resulted in a different landscape.

BILLBOARD (3)
The Trivision mounted to the facade of 019 consists of 29 prisms, each measuring 80mm in width and 2,000mm in height. The space between the prisms (necessary to allow fluid movement of the mechanism) averages at 6mm. The total size of one combined face is 2,488mm in width and 2,000mm in height. The total surface of the rectangle is 4,976,000mm^2. However, the actual surface taken up by the image only amounts to 4,640,000mm^2. The missing 336,000 mm^2 that the 28 gaps of 6mm amount to are filled in by the viewer.

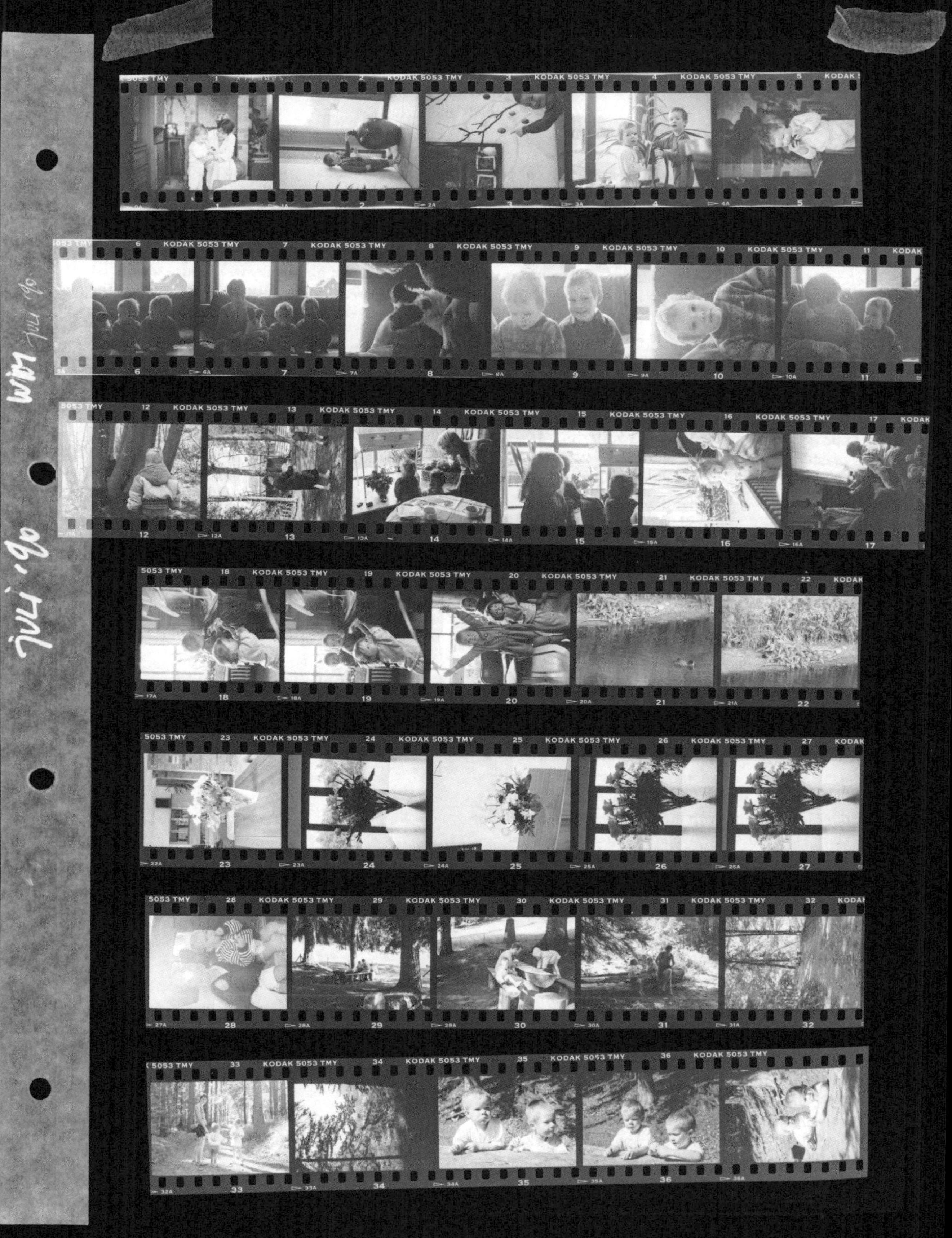

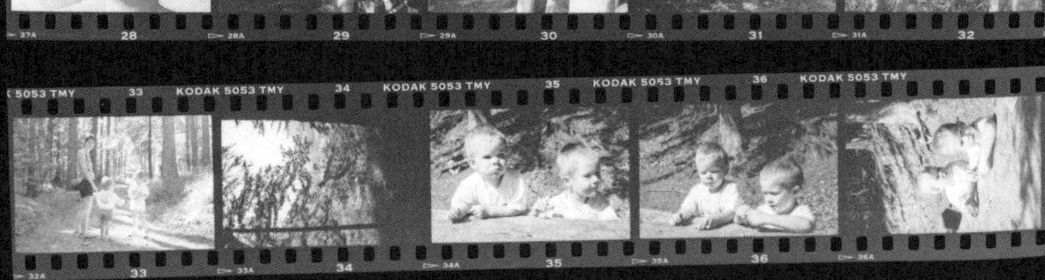

Episode 3 — Setting

for the houses he builds for florists, newlyweds and farmers	the local planning authority requires the architect to photograph what is there	now
the local planning authority requires the architect to photograph what is there	now	for the houses he builds for florists, newlyweds and farmers
now	for the houses he builds for florists, newlyweds and farmers	the local planning authority requires the architect to photograph what is there

A nondescript dwelling. Flowers in front of a greenhouse's chalked glass. A muddy bend in the road among newly built houses and empty lots. The protagonist, an architect, is introduced.

ARCHIVE (2)
Sometime around 1992, colour photography is introduced to the archive. The architect documents the situation as it is, but no longer in grey tones. The flowers next to the greenhouses are blooming. In the archive, 1,466 of the 2,583 negatives are in colour.

LANDSCAPE (2)
As a verb, 'to sprawl' may describe a person sitting, lying or falling with arms and legs spread out in an awkward, clumsy fashion. When it applies to urban development, it means that the built environment spreads out over a large area in an untidy or irregular way. 'Sprawl' has its roots in the Old English *spreawlian:* to move the limbs convulsively.

CAR (5)
The Citroën BX was replaced by a Volkswagen Golf. After a while, when you locked the doors by pushing a button on the car's key fob, the automatic roof would open. The dark grey car appears thirteen times in the archive.

BILLBOARD (4)
In *Radical Artifice*, literary scholar Marjorie Perloff invokes *Learning from Las Vegas*, the 1972 book by Robert Venturi, Denise Scott Brown and Steven Izenour that caused upheaval due to its postmodern take on the built environment. Billboards, as seen on the Las Vegas strip, are one of the authors' examples. They are signs combining maximum information with high-speed communication. Perloff writes: 'According to *Learning from Las Vegas* – and the Venturis' argument is a powerful one – no artist (in their case, architect) can afford not to learn from the "existing landscape," not to study its semiotic' (Perloff, 1991, 96-97). The architects' notorious text starts out with a quote on T.S. Eliot's use of citations of existing discourses, to continue to architecture: 'Learning from the existing landscape is a way of being revolutionary for an architect. Not the obvious way, which is to tear down Paris and begin again, as Le Corbusier suggested in the 1920s, but another, more tolerant way; that is, to question how we look at things' (Venturi, Scott Brown & Izenour, 1977, 3).

MONTAGE (1)
In *The Arcades Project*'s 'Convolute N', Walter Benjamin develops a historical materialist approach of his subject, nineteenth century Paris. *The Arcades Project* contains a mass of citations, sometimes commented upon by Benjamin, and fragments written by the author himself. Benjamin famously defined it as follows: 'Method of this project: literary montage. I needn't *say* anything. Merely show. I shall purloin no valuables, appropriate no ingenious formulations. But the rags, the refuse – these I will not inventory but allow, in the only way possible, to come into their own: by making use of them' (Benjamin, 2002, 460). By showing and using those 'rags', Benjamin aims to present a radically new approach of history, in which its revolutionary potential is laid bare. The historical materialist recognises and constructs 'dialectic images', in which 'what has been' and the 'now' act upon each other: 'It is not that what is past casts its light on what is present, or what is present its light on what is past; rather, image is that wherein what has been comes together in a flash with the now to form a constellation. In other words: image is dialectics at a standstill. For while the relation of the present to the past is purely temporal, the relation of what-has-been to the now is dialectical: not temporal in nature but figural <*bildlich*>. Only dialectical images are genuinely historical – that is, not archaic – images. The image that is read – which is to say, the image in the now of its recognizability – bears to the highest degree the imprint of the perilous critical moment on which all reading is founded' (Benjamin, 463). Benjamin does not reconstruct a historical state of affairs, but constructs it: '"Construction" presupposes "destruction"' (Benjamin, 470).

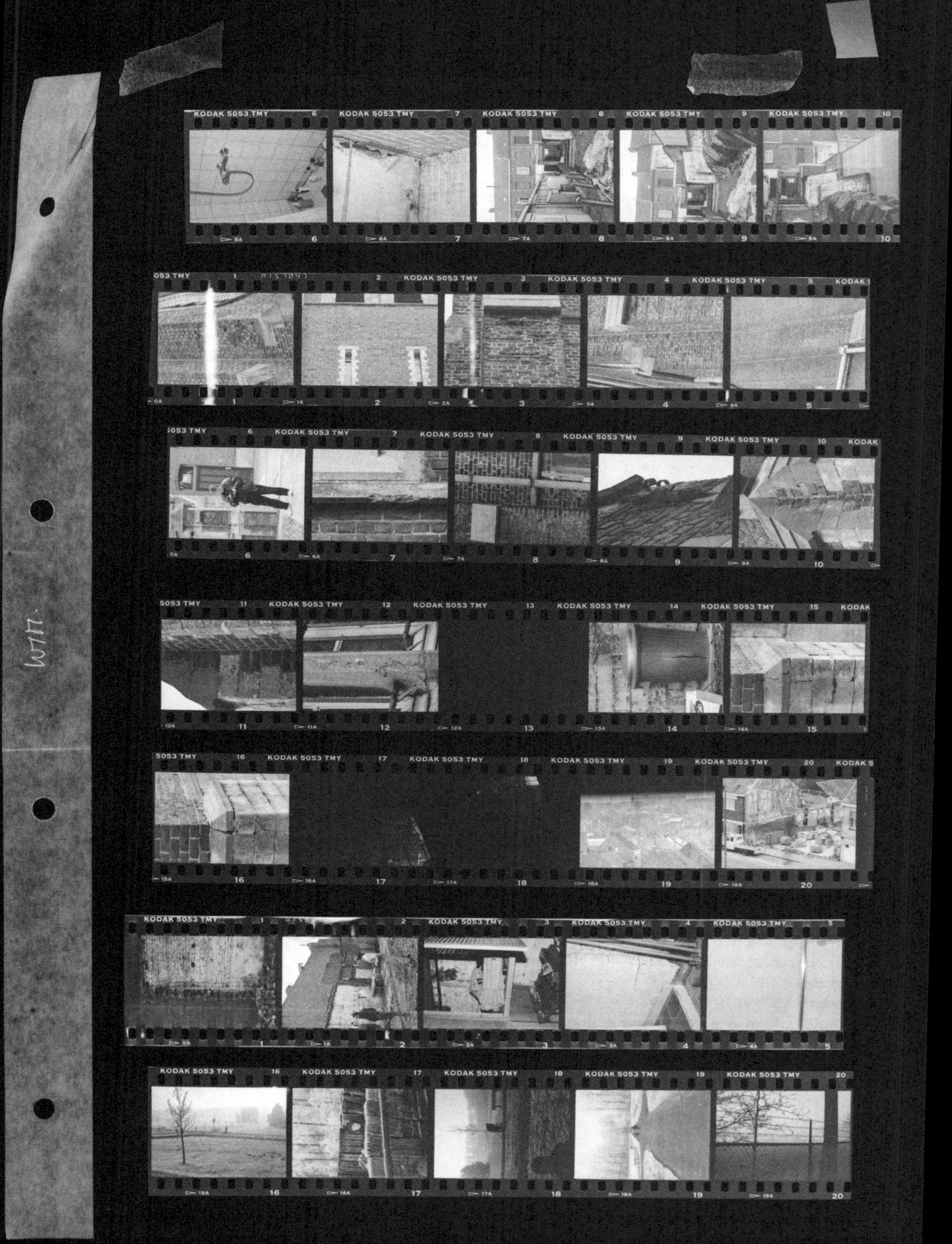

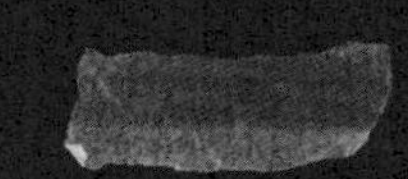

Episode 4 — The narrators' perspective

little did we know	then	things would stagnate
then	things would stagnate	little did we know
things would stagnate	little did we know	then

In those thirty odd years between then and now, time created hindsight. A post factum point of view on what was, then, barely recognisable as a fact.

ARCHIVE (3)
In addition to the architect's photographic archive, *The Situation As It Is* shows six photographs from the archive of documentary photographer M. De Cleene, made between 2017 and 2022. Seven photographs were made, based on the photonovel's script. In episodes 7 and 9, the office clerk's hand, the telephone and the telephone cord, the structural engineer's hand and the (flying) brick were framed in such a way as to make it possible to include captions at the bottom of the billboard without them interfering with the photograph's subject. We had to wait for an apt configuration of clouds to be able to state 'what's unconstructed will rise again' against a whitish background. There was a strong, cold wind, but the clouds seemed to be static.

LANDSCAPE (3)
What is open space in 2040 will remain as such. Any lot that isn't built upon by then will never be occupied by buildings. Only the space that has already been taken up by buildings could then be repurposed. The rest of the landscape must remain untouched. The policy that the Flemish Government developed concerning this issue was formerly called *betonstop* (lit. 'concrete stop'), now toned down to *bouwshift* ('building shift'). It is an attempt to change the way the people of Flanders build and reside in the landscape. The policy stems from the intention to get people to live in well-situated places – close to public transport and communal facilities – and to get them to do so in less fragmented ways. The cost to realise this will be astronomical as many citizens invested in plots that were designated as building land by local governments in the past. When the regional plans were drawn up between 1970 and 1980, every square metre was given a destination (residence, industry, recreation, agriculture, greenery or public utility). Determined by royal decree, the land's destiny was anchored by those decisions and, save for a few corrections, was to remain valid indefinitely. The cost of this literal change of plans in 2040 is referred to as *planschade* ('planning damage'), the total cost of which is estimated somewhere between 2.3 and 31 billion euros. An extensive densification of village centres and urban peripheries is expected in the run-up to 2040 and beyond. In the meanwhile, owners of buildable land have been hastily building and filling up snippets of open space.

BILLBOARD (5)
The state has a long history of collecting photographs of the present-day landscape. Documentary photographer Walker Evans spent an important part of his career working for the United States Government. Between 1935 and 1938 he was employed as 'information specialist' within the Resettlement Administration (later Farm Security Administration) of the Department of Agriculture. Every photograph he made within that context 'was government property, available for circulation without further consent' (Tagg, 2003, 30). His photograph 'Houses and Billboards in Atlanta, 1936' appeared in Archibald MacLeish's populist, poetic photographic book *Land of the Free* (1938) without Evans knowing. A few months after the book's publication, Evans sent a note to Roy Stryker, the government official who had been giving him his assignments. The note came with a clipping from an advertisement for the book including one of his photographs. 'Evans insisted that he was sending the cutting to Stryker only "as an item of mild interest and amusement, not as a howl of pain." But the clipping was annotated with the one word: "Gawd!"' (Tagg, 36).

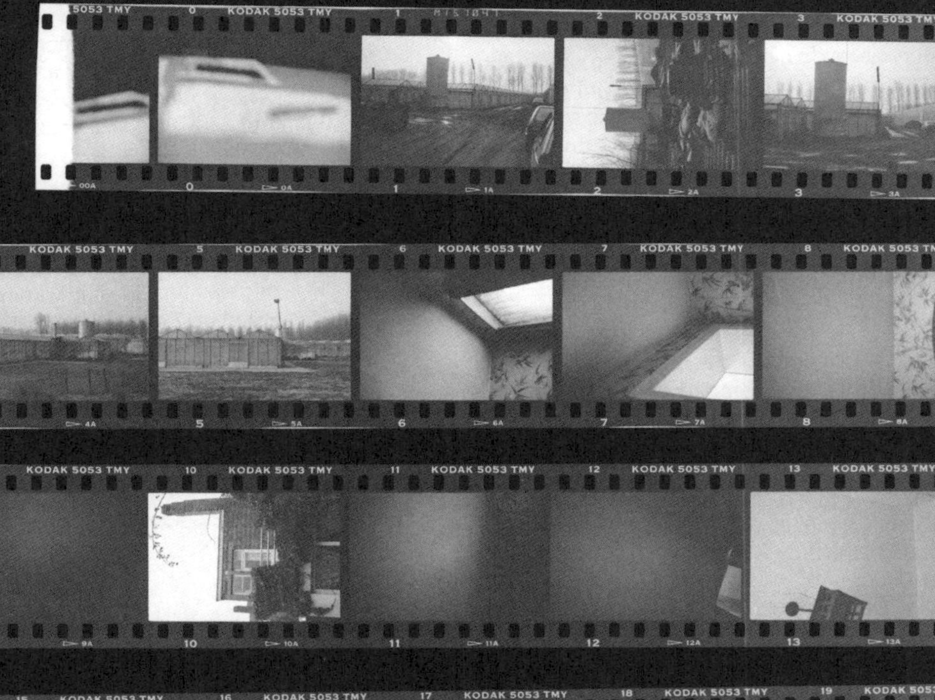

Wim 24/2/92

Episode 5 — Introducing the architect's family

on Sunday	your pyjamas are backwards	she says
your pyjamas are backwards	she says	on Sunday
she says	on Sunday	your pyjamas are backwards

On summer days the brightly coloured bloom of the begonias attracts visitors to the provincial domain's flower garden, an area of approximately 20 hectares, largely arranged as a symmetrical French garden. The hornbeam arcades and large stone pergolas look like they're straight out of a rom-com and give a sense of grandeur as you stroll past them with the mist from the large fountain pond kissing your face. Kids are riding their BMX's. The horns, scattered around the garden, emit a high pitch tone to repel rabbits.

ARCHIVE (4)
There is one contact sheet (39) that has no bearing on the rest of the archive. Twenty-four negatives, shot on Kodak Gold 200-6 colour negative film. They appear to have been shot on another family's holiday. Neither the architect nor our family appear in the pictures. Most photographs are taken on a white yacht. The sun is shining. An older man with a blue shirt, beige trousers and a white cap is steering the boat in negative 16. The same man and boat are seen in a canal lock holding onto a rope in the adjacent negative 17. A woman wearing a white Mickey Mouse sweater is below deck. She is sitting at a wooden table in negative 19, smiling at the camera. She is holding a bun. There are two kinds of cheese on the table, a bowl of sliced tomatoes, a jar of mayonnaise, a salt shaker, a pepper mill and a plate filled with four herrings, three stockfish and four slices of halibut. The boat is called 'Surprise' (negative 14).

CAR (1)
The architect's first car that appears in the archive is a yellow Citroën 2CV. It appears five times in the archive in black and white. He owned a blue one as a student (a period not covered by the archive).

CAR (2)
The architect's second car was a brown Citroën LN. It appears in the archive twice in black and white.

CAR (3)
The architect's third car was a grey Citroën Visa. It appears eight times in the archive in black and white.

BILLBOARD (6)
On Friday, 20 March, 1936, Walker Evans came across this scene: two wooden, artisanal houses with in front of them two large billboards advertising films (*Chatterbox* and *Love Before Breakfast*). According to John Tagg, this photograph ('Houses and Billboards in Atlanta, 1936') is an instance of 'melancholy realism', the appearance of which, he states, in the archives of a government department, is a puzzle in itself. In his doubling of representation (a photograph of a billboard), Evans does not resort to irony. He presents the viewer with an image that can be misread, an image that is, with respect to meaning, not one-dimensional. A photograph taken by Margaret Bourke-White, following a severe flood, of a line of African American people lining up for food underneath a large billboard that reads 'There's no way like the American way' serves as the counterpoint in the argument Tagg is making. In the work of Bourke-White, 'meaning always arrives, guaranteed by the transparency of rhetoric and the finality of photographic truth' (Tagg, 2003, 59). In contrast, he argues that Evans' photograph 'resists the arrival of meaning', it 'does not accommodate itself to instrumental communication, but is encrypted, locked away in layers of representation like an infinite series of Russian dolls' (Tagg, 59). The real, Tagg says, is unencounterable and does not lend itself to representation.

CAMERA (2)
From time to time the film would jam inside the Canon AE-1. By exerting force onto the lever, the architect was able to move the film forward. However, sometimes, the plastic separating the sprocket holes would tear, causing the film to advance less, inadvertently creating a panoramic negative.

BILLBOARD (7)
The Belgian Highway Code of 1 Dec. 1975, decrees that:

- illuminated or luminescent advertising media with red or green tints located within 75 metres of a traffic light, less than 7 metres above the ground, are prohibited;
- illuminated or luminescent advertising materials that dazzle drivers are prohibited;
- publicity media that mislead drivers are prohibited;
- publicity media that partially or completely imitate, might be confused with, or reduce the effectiveness of traffic signs, are prohibited.

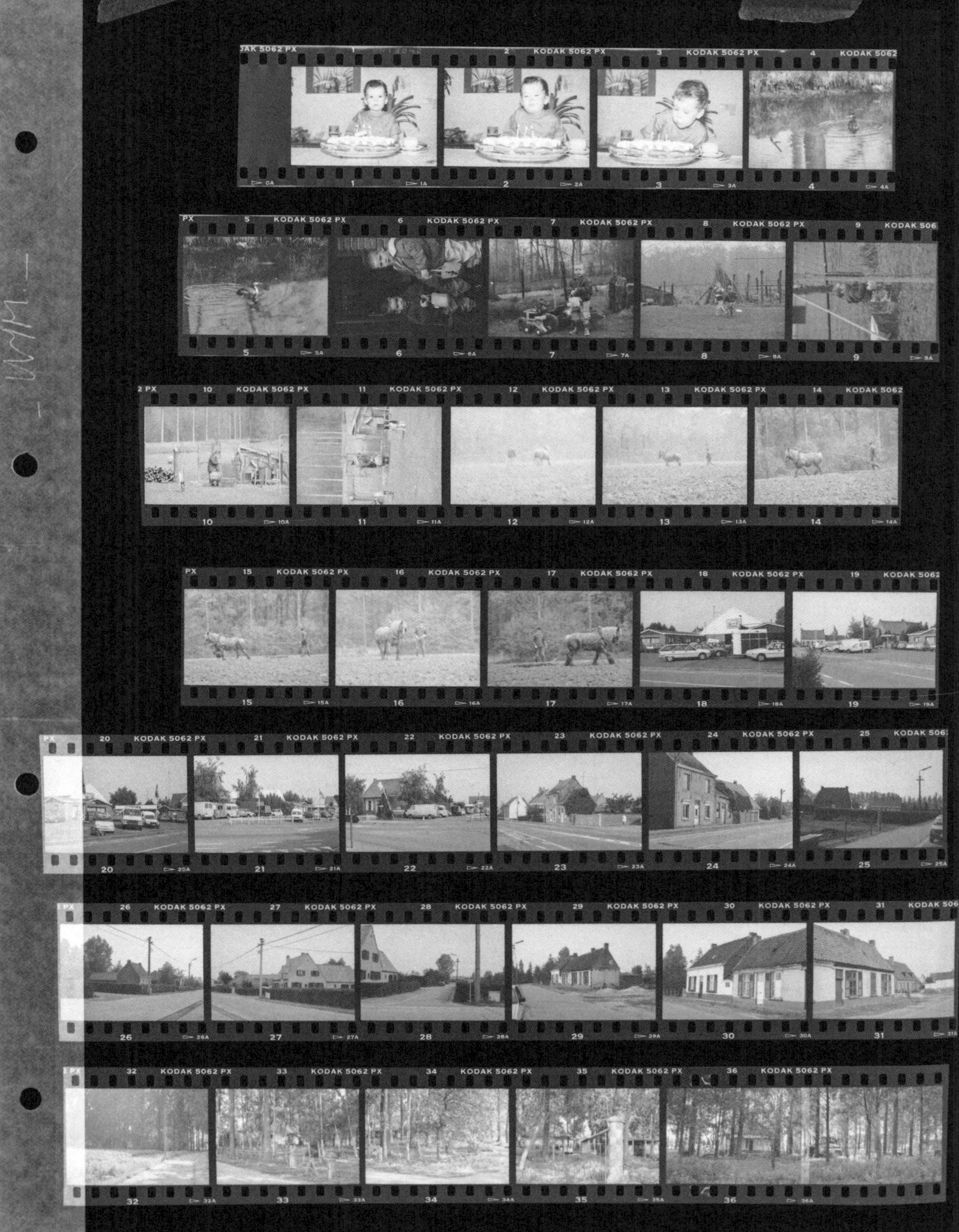

Episode 6 — Interior monologue #1

I'm not	sure	am I seeing this straight?
sure	am I seeing this straight?	I'm not
am I seeing this straight?	I'm not	sure

Half thoughts, impressions, doubts and associations trouble the architect. A roofless house with windows. A pool of grey, viscous sludge that won't cure. An impasse.

ARCHIVE (5)
After scanning all 2,583 negatives, keywords were assigned to a selection of them.

demolition/fire (26)
fence (24)
antenna (7)
car (106)
forest (32)
fallow land (41)
roof (5)
family (67)
flash (3)
glitch (11)
greenery (41)
dog (13)
interior (2)
landscape (40)
aerial photograph (14)
finger in front of lens (4)
soccer (11)
construction site (24)
allotment (74)
fog (11)
panorama (7)
dad (11)
person (86)
plastic (17)
pylon (20)
rain (13)
red ribbon (5)
crack/detail (100)
farm/barn (45)
greenhouse (21)
snow (8)
mirror (3)
prop (1)
tennis (7)
garden furniture (10)
barrel (5)
birthday (16)

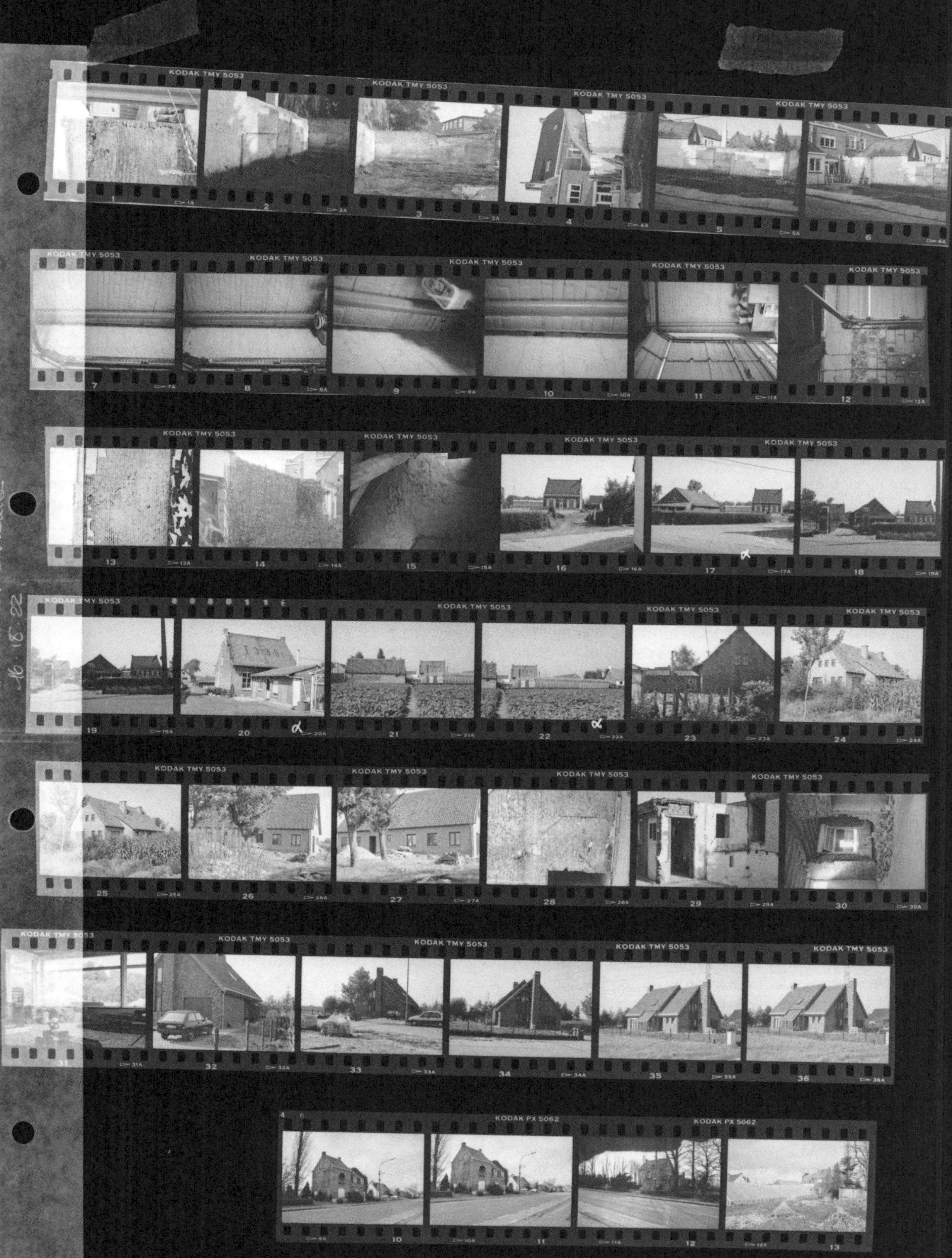
KODAK TMY 5053
KODAK PX 5062

Episode 7 — The conversation

inquiring on behalf of client W.V.P.
'... a decision was made on the top floor...'

with regards to the refusal of the building application
'... we no longer accept change...'

the planning authority's office clerk responds
'... the photographs you and your colleagues filed are now considered as blueprint for landscape conservation...'

with regards to the refusal of the building application
'... we no longer accept change...'

the planning authority's office clerk responds
'... the photographs you and your colleagues filed are now considered as blueprint for landscape conservation...'

inquiring on behalf of client W.V.P.
'... a decision was made on the top floor...'

the planning authority's office clerk responds
'... the photographs you and your colleagues filed are now considered as blueprint for landscape conservation...'

inquiring on behalf of client W.V.P.
'... a decision was made on the top floor...'

with regards to the refusal of the building application
'... we no longer accept change...'

And then, as if out of nowhere, everything built became heritage. Every brick, every beam and pipe, every tile, tap and cavity had to be preserved. The regulation would be confirmed in writing shortly, but on the telephone the office clerk left no room for doubt.

THE OFFICE CLERK

[Thursday, 5:15pm]
The office clerk drove out of the parking garage, up into the dimly lit city centre, with its skyscrapers condescendingly nodding at the red Peugeot, in whose front seat she was pushed back as she hit the gas pedal violently again. The concrete ramp was steep. Normally, leaving at 5pm, she could see the sixth-floor office ceiling of the State Archive building on the other side of the avenue: beige tiles resting on a gridded metal structure with a built-in light every third tile of every second row. But as her meeting had run late, she left late. The Archive's lights were already out. In the sombre glass panels she now could see the reflection of her overzealous twelfth-floor colleagues' office lights, shining, she knew, on documents and rulings she had typed out and that were now being heavily debated above her as they would change the way we would perceive the built landscape she was and would be driving into, for years and years to come.

[Friday, the press conference]
She stood at the back of the room. Despite the fact that the press conference was only communicated about the evening before, there were hardly any empty seats left. She leaned against the beige wall that separated the cafeteria-turned-press-room from the small kitchen with its microwave, the chalked-up kettle and sink. She had already left by the time they had sent out the note the evening before. It must have been in haste. They left a typo in it. The twelfth floor was never big on spelling, but this was basic stuff. The press conference had been going on for more than an hour. There had been some mumbling among the assembled journalists. Her direct superior, Alain, hadn't spoken yet, but went up to the microphone after Veronique – her superior's superior – gave him one of her nods. 'We won't be taking any questions today,' he said as he took a folded A4 page out of his inside pocket (uproar and complaints among the journalists), unfolded it and started reading the printed text, 'but as a final statement in this conference, I would like to shortly and directly address the citizens, the contractors, the architects and the developers.' He coughed. 'To be clear, this is far from a laissez-faire attitude, or a non-intervention policy. We – you – will intervene. It will take energy and commitment, which we will support with subsidies and tax reductions.' Is he looking straight at her? 'But the interventions will only be aimed at preventing the further decay of the present – I mean Thursday's – landscape. We have come to call it "arrested decay".' He looked up from his paper and started folding it again. Even from the back of the room she recognised the department's letterhead.

[Five days later]
The office clerk grew tired of answering the same questions over and over. Every phone call ended with the same cursing, swearing and yelling. Her superior had said it would all blow over in a matter of time. Sure, the first week would be strenuous, he said, but after that, her job would become much easier. The ruling is clear, after all. Not that the rules weren't clear before. No, of course not. But there were a lot of them and that left ample room for negotiation. It used to be a running joke in the department: this country is the only one where clear and simple rules are not the basis for decision, but the basis for negotiation. She didn't think it was that funny. It was almost like a game. But that's over now. Alain is right, the ruling is clear, everything stays the way it was last week. Plain and simple. Of course, Alain isn't on the phone. No, he isn't.

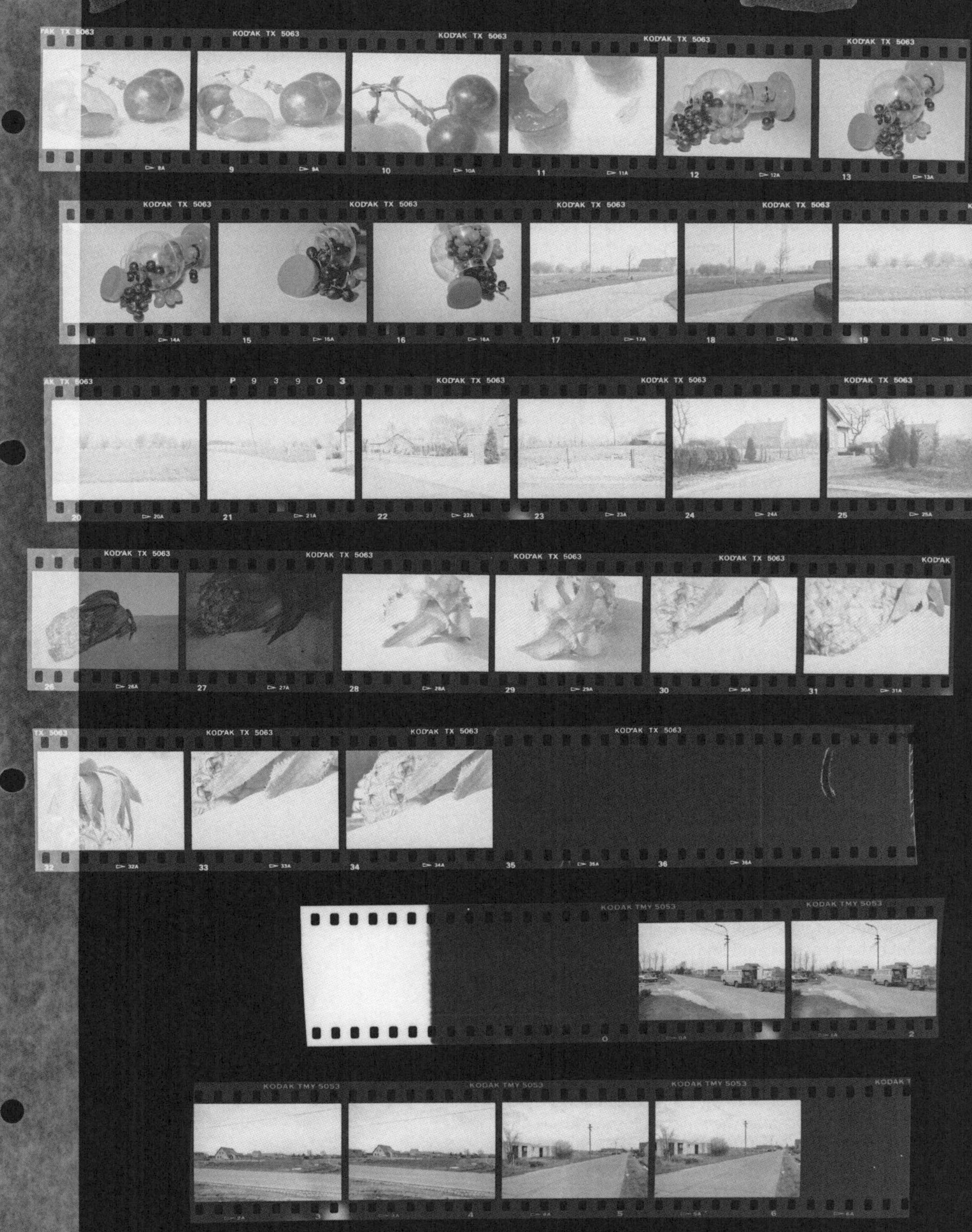

Episode 8 — The decision

the local planning authority took a long lunch break	it had been hectic since the decision was made	at the coffee machine, a note: 'LEAVE IT AS YOU FOUND IT!'
it had been hectic since the decision was made	at the coffee machine, a note: 'LEAVE IT AS YOU FOUND IT!'	the local planning authority took a long lunch break
at the coffee machine, a note: 'LEAVE IT AS YOU FOUND IT!'	the local planning authority took a long lunch break	it had been hectic since the decision was made

A surplus of clay honeycomb blocks, a shortage of white-red ribbons.

ARCHIVE (6)
Who does the photographic archive belong to? 'Archives', Allan Sekula writes in 'Photography between Labour and Capital', 'constitute a *territory of images*; the unity of an archive is first and foremost that imposed by ownership. [...] New owners are invited, new interpretations are promised' (Sekula, 2020, 16). As a consequence, the meaning of photographs in an archive is up for grabs: 'In an archive, the possibility of meaning is "liberated" from the actual contingencies of use. But this liberation is also a loss, an *abstraction* from the complexity and richness of use, a loss of context. [...] So new meanings come to supplant old ones, with the archive serving as a kind of "clearing house" of meaning' (Sekula, 16). The archive makes it possible to interpret the photographs in it as historical documents, or as aesthetic objects. Both interpretative schemes are misleading, Sekula states: 'We need to understand how photography works within everyday life in advanced industrial societies: the problem is one of cultural history rather than art history' (Sekula, 21). Official, functional photography on the one hand, and family pictures, on the other, would be two instances of such everyday use of photography – two categories, Sekula stresses, that are not mutually exclusive.

LANDSCAPE (4)
The construction sites were 'frozen', paused. Scaffolding became something different than what it had been for a long time: not the sign of temporality, behind which a different building waited to be unveiled, but temporality turned permanent. But, as years went by and materials deteriorated, expanded or shrunk, public safety, on the one hand, and the unwanted, pending change of scenery on the other, compelled the restoration of the scaffolding into the state it was at the time of the ruling. An addendum was added to the ruling, stating that, for a limited amount of time, new scaffolding could be erected to restore the existing scaffolding.

ARCHIVE (7)
The Flemish Government states that at least six different recent and numbered photos must be provided, three of which showing the place where the planned works will take place, and three of which showing the building itself and the parcels adjacent to the building lot. In the case of a demolition application, three photographs are sufficient. Format: JPG, JPEG, PNG, GIF or PDF. The numbering or naming of the photographs must be in accordance with the way they are marked on the plan. If the application deals with the removal of a listed building or landscape, the number and type of photographs must be adjusted so that they visualise the current state of every side of the property that is to be demolished, as well as the wider context in which the building or landscape is situated.

CAMERA (3)
The light baffle in the Canon AE-1 became brittle and crumbled, the archive shows. Minor light leaks occurred.

LANDSCAPE (5)
In *Court traité du paysage* (1997) Alain Roger talks about the reinforcements that were built in the 1980s to try and halt the effects of erosion on the iconic, conical shape of Mount Fuji. He says that in an attempt to ensure the mountain would conform to its image, concrete structures were built. A 1984 New York Times article speaks of a 'cement band aid' to slow down the erosion in the Osawa failure at a height of 2,195 metres.

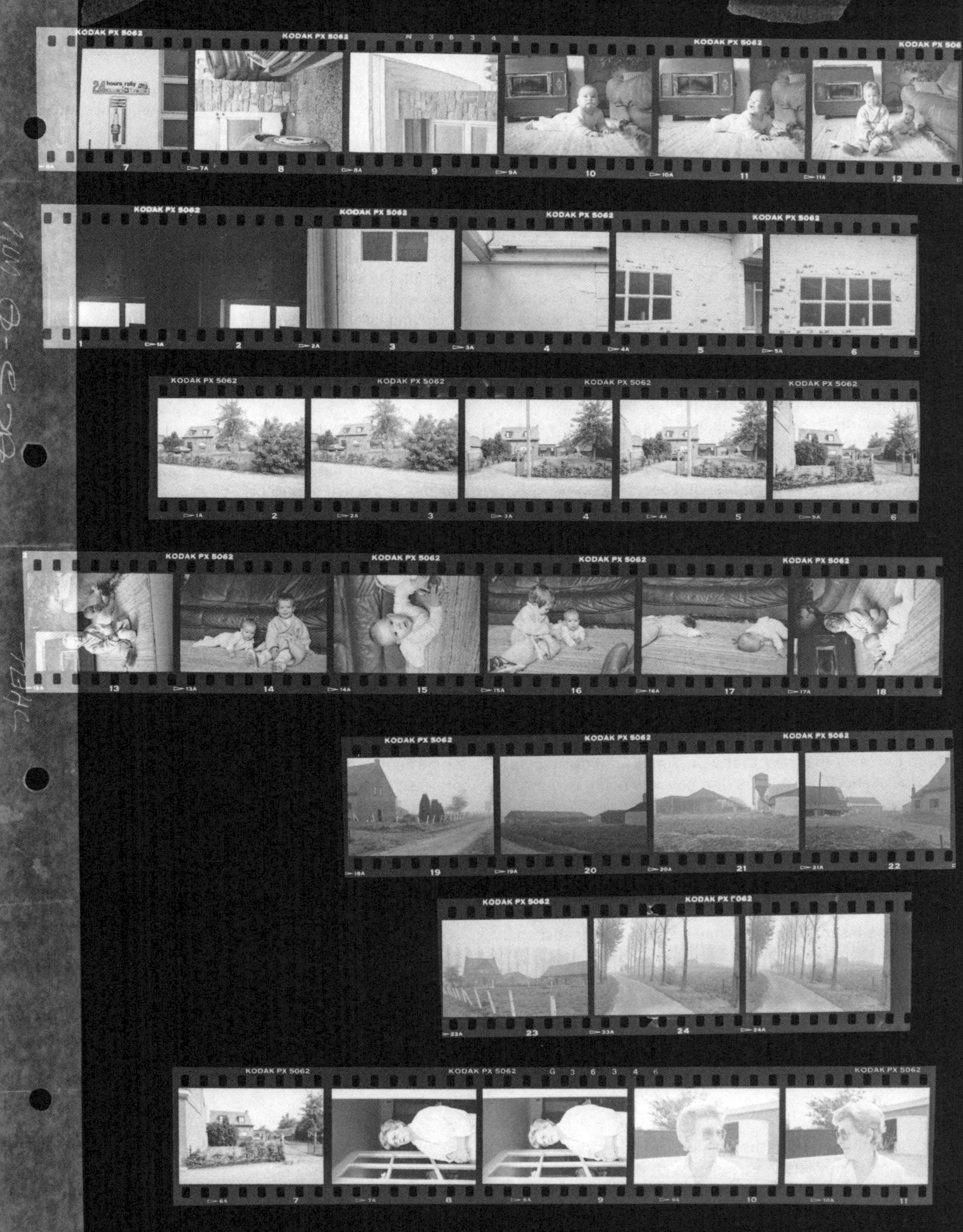

Episode 9 — The landscape

the archive shows	people trying to understand	the landscape they had shaped
people trying to understand	the landscape they had shaped	the archive shows
the landscape they had shaped	the archive shows	people trying to understand

Kodak introduced SAFETY FILM as an alternative to negatives based on the extremely flammable nitrocellulose (also known as cellulose nitrate, flash paper, flash cotton, guncotton, pyroxylin and flash string). The substance laid uncountable photographic archives to ashes. Once burning it is extremely difficult to extinguish.

ARCHIVE (8)
The archive contains seven images that can be labelled as panoramic pictures. However, this is only the case when the photographs are viewed in the archive, as strips of negatives. In order to see the panoramic construct, the viewer needs to be presented with two consecutive negatives. There are two kinds of panorama in the archive: the kind that originates due to the film jamming, and another that can only be attributed to a kind of laziness or a need for efficiency on behalf of the architect. Of the latter there are two examples in the archive. As the architect is documenting the situation as it is, it is compulsory to also document the context of the building or lot. In the case of these panoramas, he does this by simply pivoting from left to right, capturing the first and second photograph consecutively. On the filmstrip a panorama appears. On contact sheet 55, negatives 4 and 5 form such a panoramic picture. It has been snowing. An aubergine BMW is parked on the other side of the street and is cut in half by the separation between negatives 4 and 5. Apart from a slight kink in the landscape, the negative on the right is a perfect continuation of the one on the left. The fence around the orchard, the branches of the apple tree and the power lines connect implicitly in the void between the negatives.

The other kind of panoramic picture is caused by a technical error (the jamming of the film), followed by a moment of human determination (exerting force onto the lever to move it forward), in turn followed by a technical shortcoming (the film not advancing enough due to a tear between the sprocket holes). The result differs fundamentally from the other kind of panorama: there is no separation, no void between the negatives. Rather, there is a slight overlap: a thin, vertical strip of film that has been exposed twice, suggesting contiguity that might not be there. The two exposures might be from altogether different sites, but together they create a new landscape.

LANDSCAPE (6)
When things started getting out of hand – stagnated – the idea arose that the factories had something to do with it. Pollution. Small fragments of steel got kicked into the air and then deposited in the gardens, carried by the wind coming from behind our backs.

ARCHIVE (9)
There are three fires in the archive, or, rather, documents showing the devastation caused by three fires. Once on contact sheet 47, once on contact sheet 49 and once on contact sheet 53. The first appearance concerns a fire in a house. It's a *fermette*. The architect made a series of six photographs. One photograph documents the interior view of what appears to have been the kitchen. The beams carrying the first floor are charred, the oven is barely recognisable as such, there's a black cavity where the refrigerator used to be. The five other photographs show the outside of the house. The house has practically lost all of its roof tiles on one side. They are piled up on the paved driveway. Extending from every upper corner of each window, the fire has drawn black clouds on the facade. The roof ridge is sagging. The evidence of fire on sheet 49 is the remainder of a bonfire in a pasture. Two horses stand behind the fence, one of them looking at the architect. The third and last appearance of fire remnants is in a stable on a farm. The steel plates of the barn door are blackened and have bulged due to the heat. The roof of corrugated asbestos sheets is full of holes.

WEATHER (1)
In 'Reality would have to begin', Harun Farocki writes about civil engineer Albrecht Meydenbauer and his discovery of the use of photography for scale measurements. Meydenbauer argued that it was preferable and even more qualitative to measure buildings through photography than in situ. Farocki recognises a 'horror for the objectivity of the world' in Meydenbauer's aversion to the architect's measuring work at a construction site: 'At this mentally and physically strenuous occupation, the architect is exposed to the weather: sunshine or rainfall on his sketchbook, and when he looks up, dust in his eyes' (Meydenbauer, cited in Farocki, 2002, 159).

LANDSCAPE (7)
Smoke creeps between the church, the town hall, the retirement home, the day care and the social housing project. We are standing on the other side of the road when the gym hall burns down. An accident involving a contractor fixing the roof. The heat of the flames reaches our faces and we remember the orange glow, although one of us must have been too young to have any recollection of the catastrophe. Ash settles on the architect's Citroën BX.

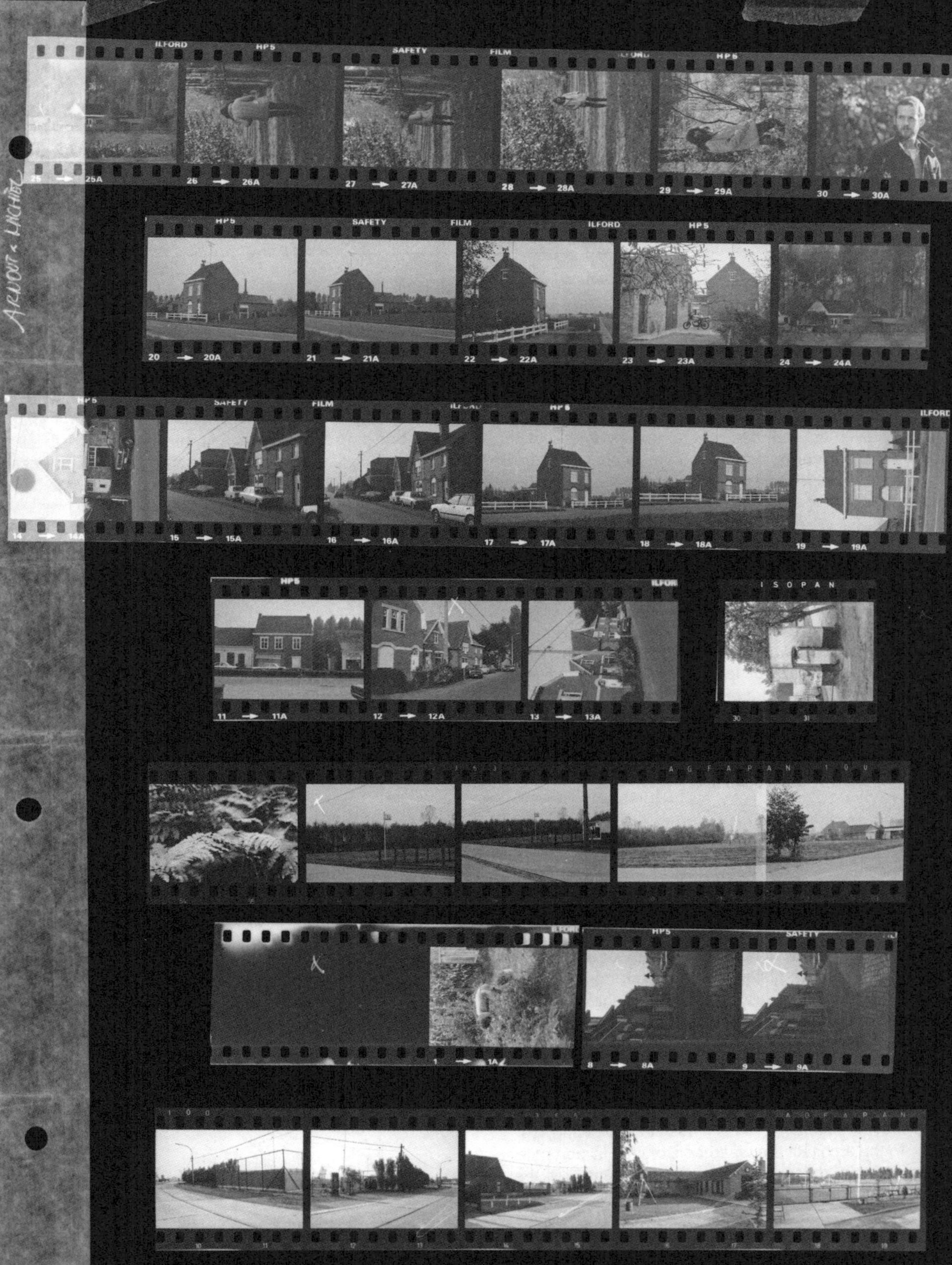

Episode 10 — Interior monologue #2

[a sigh]	he worries what the standstill will amount to	if it would ruin more than it preserves
he worries what the standstill will amount to	if it would ruin more than it preserves	[a sigh]
if it would ruin more than it preserves	[a sigh]	he worries what the standstill will amount to

As the impasse persisted, he (the architect) tried watching some television to ease his mind, but to no avail. 19h00: The Evening News. 19h30: Sports Magazine. 20h05: The Weather. 20h10: The Picture of Dorian Gray (A. Lewin, 1945). 22h: The Evening News (rebroadcast, on repeat). He must have fallen asleep. When he woke up, the streets in the city of G. had flooded, again and again. He turned off the TV and went to bed.

ARCHIVE (10)
The architect is sitting on a leather sofa. The black and white photograph (Kodak PX 5062) doesn't show it, but it's brown. He's holding one of us. The photographer is reflected in the convex glass of the television set. She – the architect's wife ('mom') – is wearing a dress. He was most often the one using the camera and therefore only appears eleven times in the archive: walking with one of us in a backpack during a holiday (contact sheet 19), looking straight at the lens, in the living room of our grandparents' house (20), looking into the distance like a film star, in a forest (27), sitting on a brown sofa holding one of us and looking worried (32), standing in the distance while mowing the lawn (38), holding a naked baby in a swimming pool (41), swimming in the same shallow swimming pool (41), sitting in the long grass on top of a cliff with his back against a wooden pole (44), wearing a beige Tenson jacket while drawing a construction detail (the photographer used the flash) (55), leaning against the edge of a table in the garden in front of a hornbeam hedge while holding our sister and looking at our dog (a Border collie called Supo) (61), walking along a small forest road covered in larch needles with our sister in the backpack that also appeared on contact sheet 19 (74).

MONTAGE (2)
Walter Benjamin criticises an approach of history that is characterised by an idea of progress or decline, and even of continuity: 'It may be that the continuity of tradition is mere semblance. But then precisely the persistence of this semblance of persistence provides it with continuity' (Benjamin, 2002, 486). One must be weary of the way 'continuity' functions, historically, and historiographically: 'That things are "status quo" *is* the catastrophe' (Benjamin, 473); 'Critical moment – the status quo threatens to be preserved' (Benjamin, 474).

WEATHER (2)
The weather conditions are subject to change, the negatives show. It's sunny, it rains, it has been snowing, it's windy. To the architect the weather is of little importance in the making of these photographic documents. Yet, the weather is documented.

CAMERA (4)
In 1994 the architect bought a Canon EOS 500 camera with a 35-80mm (4-5.6) zoom lens and a UV filter.

ARCHIVE (11)
He's wearing a digital watch. It looks like a Casio. It's impossible to read the time, no matter whether you are studying the high-resolution scan of the negative or the negative itself, with the aid of a loupe and lightbox.

The device had a stopwatch function. When we were around eight and ten, we used to compete in trying to start and stop the stopwatch in the shortest possible interval. The smaller the gap, the closer to zero. Sometimes the architect would also have a try. We once managed to get it down to 00:00:00:03. Neither of us dared to press 'reset' and try again.

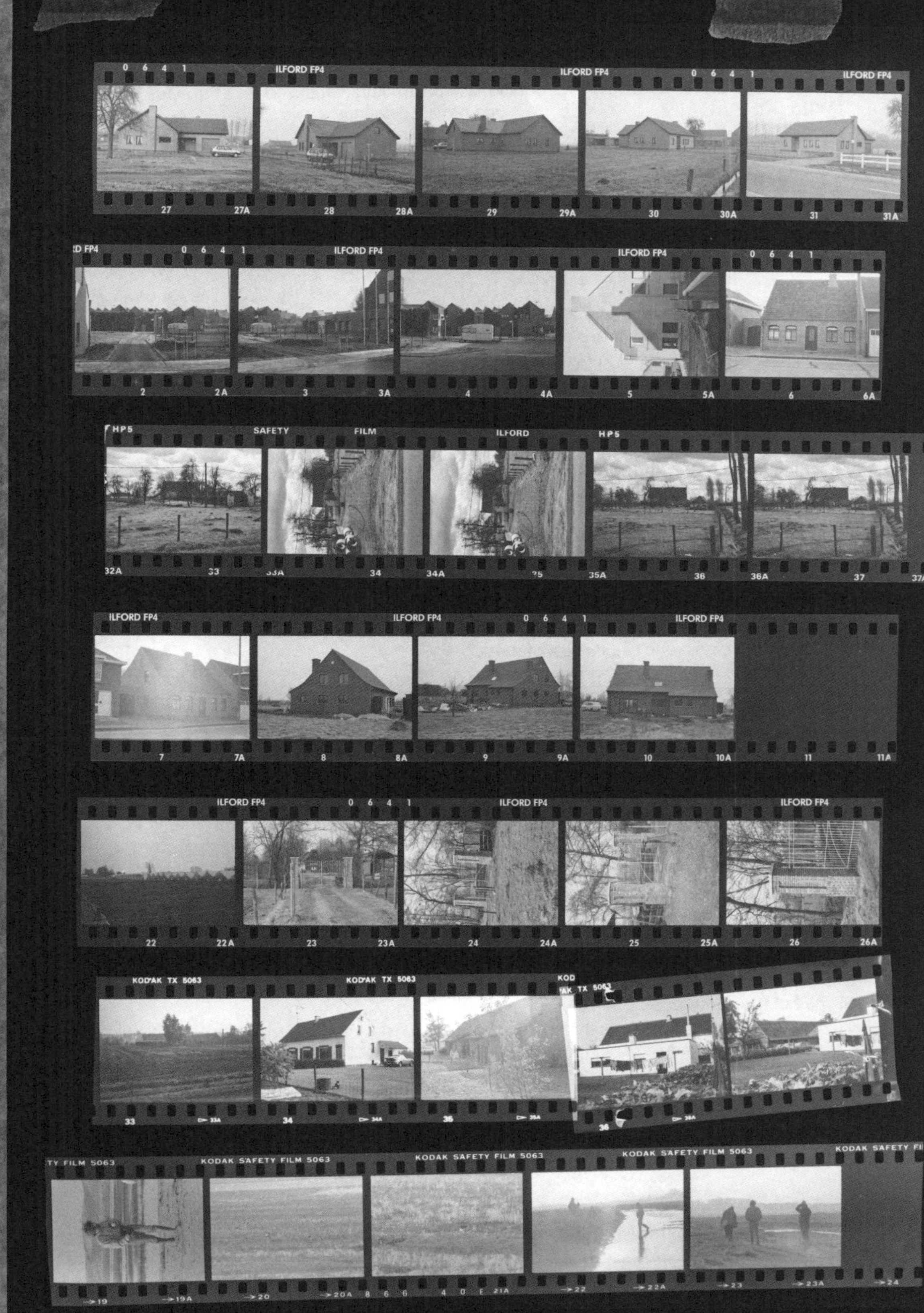
0 6 4 1
ILFORD FP4
27
27A
28
28A
29
29A
30
30A
31
31A
2
2A
3
3A
4
4A
5
5A
6
6A
HP5
SAFETY
FILM
ILFORD
HP5
32A
33
33A
34
34A
35A
36
36A
37
37A
7
7A
8
8A
9
9A
10
10A
11
11A
22
22A
23
23A
24
24A
25
25A
26
26A
KODAK TX 5063
33
34
35
36
KODAK SAFETY FILM 5063
19
19A
20
20A
21A
22
22A
23
23A
24

Episode 11 — The upheaval

a riot of masons, structural engineers and project developers	throwing unlaid bricks, chanting on the unpaved roads	WHAT'S UNCONSTRUCTED WILL RISE AGAIN
throwing unlaid bricks, chanting on the unpaved roads	WHAT'S UNCONSTRUCTED WILL RISE AGAIN	a riot of masons, structural engineers and project developers
WHAT'S UNCONSTRUCTED WILL RISE AGAIN	a riot of masons, structural engineers and project developers	throwing unlaid bricks, chanting on the unpaved roads

The riots would continue. They evolved into a weekly gathering. City squares became littered with building materials, like giant construction sites. The bricks, pipes and plywood piled up, turning into new, undesigned and seemingly uninhabitable architecture.

BOOK
Transferring the visual story made for the rotating billboard to the book forced the story into a new form. The following are some of the effects of the book on the story and those, in turn, of the billboard on the book:

- The billboard had a chronological order: a sequence based on episodes that followed one after another (each of which was based on three frames that were sequential on their own, but without a fixed starting point). In the book, the sequence had to be fixed on the level of the frames: whereas, for example, an episode on the billboard could be read in three ways (A-B-C, B-C-A or C-A-B), the book urged us to choose one of those three options. Mathematically speaking, the billboard's fifteen sequential episodes showed 3^{15} possible stories: 14,348,907 versions. This book presents one version – one sequence – of those.
- The format of the book is based on the format of the billboard: the dimensions of a frame define the dimensions of one spread (two pages). The scans of the contact sheets in the architect's archive have other dimensions and left spare space at the bottom of the pages.
- On the billboard, the text was centered on the bottom of each frame. The book's binding pushed these texts to the left or right page.
- Whereas the rotating billboard's properties – the three-sided prisms that constitute it – pushed the construction of the narrative into a logic built on the number three, the book took a more even approach, based on the number of pages in a section. The architect started using colour photography around 1992: half of the photographic negatives in the archive are in black and white. As the book's colour section had to be a multiple of eight – a consequence of the constraints of book printing with regard to the number of pages in a section – the last frame of the visual story could not be printed fully in colour as it was originally presented on the billboard (itself a colour negative, presented as a negative).

MONTAGE (3)
'It is the present that polarizes the event into fore- and after-history' (Benjamin, 2002, 471).

WEATHER (3)
In *The Snows of Venice*, Alexander Kluge wonders whether he can take the liberty to conjure up what the sky looked like on 31 December, 1799, as Schiller made his way to Goethe's house. He goes on by saying that, historically, there's a 'LACK OF SENSORY ATTENTION AT CRUCIAL MOMENTS'. There are exceptions, though, like the cameraman who was sent out to document the fireworks on New Year's Day, 2000. The camera was turned on prematurely. The batteries were used up by midnight, but 'certain gray tones, however, filtered through the cracks of its protective case, conveyed the motion of the walking cameraman, the transportation. The incompletely shut, low-information container was documented exactly. [...] To this day it provides inexact testimony as to the qualities of the leather of a twenty-first century carrying case and the precise sensitivity to light and dark demonstrated by a twenty-first century recording medium' (Kluge, 2018, 53).

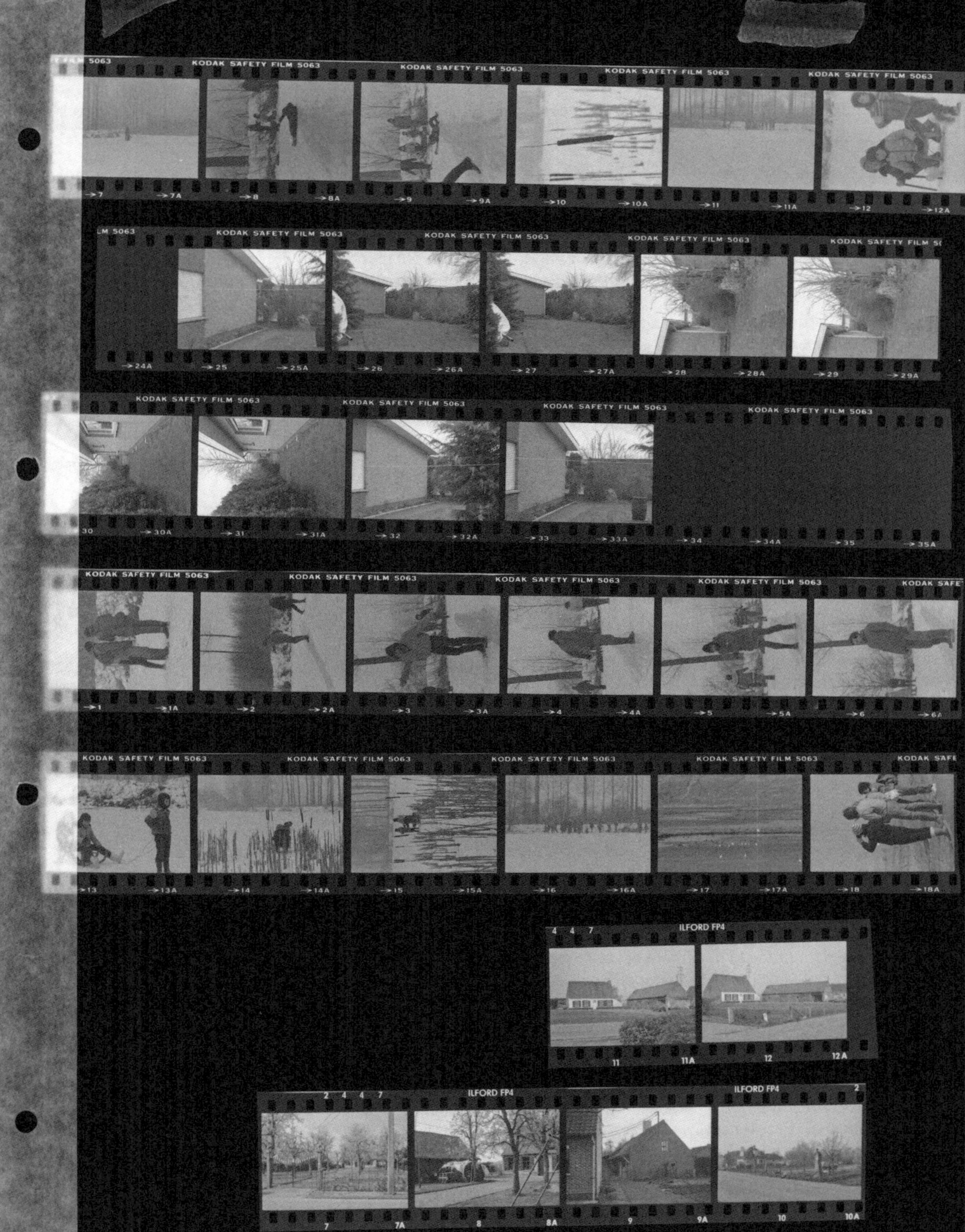

Episode 12 — Fissure

a fissure, it appears	in the plaster	like a cast
in the plaster	like a cast	a fissure, it appears
like a cast	a fissure, it appears	in the plaster

Seen up close, the crack in the wall seemed without scale and unfathomable. A hair, a pencil line, a gap, a crevasse.

HOLES IN THE ARCHIVE (1)
36 negatives in the archive document holes, cracks or cavities:

- 18 negatives show a crack in a wall.
- 8 negatives show a crack in a ceiling.
- 4 negatives show a substantial hole made in a brick wall.
- 2 negatives show a crack in a tiled bathroom wall (most likely a shower).
- 1 negative shows a crack running along a wall and continuing on a ceiling.
- 1 negative shows a long crack along the grain of an oak beam.
- 1 negative shows a bluestone windowsill with a missing part.
- 1 negative shows a vertical crack in a plastic garbage bin.

HERITAGE (1)
The Department for Conservation and Heritage's register grew exponentially. The usual categories (natural wonder, ruin, engineering marvel, settlement, garden, archaeological site, palace, etc.) no longer applied. Although the motives for preservation differed fundamentally, many experts stated that this ruling came close to some key articles in the Venice Charter for the Conservation and Restoration of Monuments and Sites of 1964, approved by the second International Congress of Architects and Technicians of Historic Monuments. Experts agreed, the value of the charter was undeniable. Still, there were two crucial flaws. First, there had been severe criticism surrounding the charter in the course of the last decades, especially concerning its opposition toward restoration and reconstruction – an approach that would, in time, become imperative. Second, the Venice Charter was based on a differentiation between what is heritage and what is not. Since the ruling, everything was an engineering marvel and therefore nothing was.

HOLES IN THE ARCHIVE (2)
Photographs were made to document appearances of non-matter as potential proof of an underlying structural deficiency, water leak or other problem. The photographs were also used to periodically check on their progression or standstill: the current state of the fissures was compared to the documented state at the time of the ruling.

HOLES IN THE ARCHIVE (3)
In the introduction to *Forensis, The Architecture of Public Truth*, Eyal Weizman talks about the significance of a structural crack. 'It's a good example,' he says, 'of an element that is both a sensor and an agent. Although such cracks may be seen as indicators of a structural problem external to themselves, they should not be understood simply as symptoms, but rather as material events that emerge as a result of evolving force contradictions around and within them. No crack can ever be reproduced; each is a unique combination between micro material inconsistencies and macro force fields. Cracks progress along paths of least resistance that tear through the places where the cohesive forces of aggregate matter are at their weakest' (Weizman, 2014, 16). Understanding structural cracks is a fundamental part in reading a building as information, as material in constant formation as opposed to the common approach of a building as a stable thing, an inert collection of material brought together through design. Structural cracks 'move through rock where a denser mineral concentration has settled. A column, beam, or floor might crack where the cement hardened around the odd cigarette butt thrown into the mix during the process of construction' (Weizman, 16).

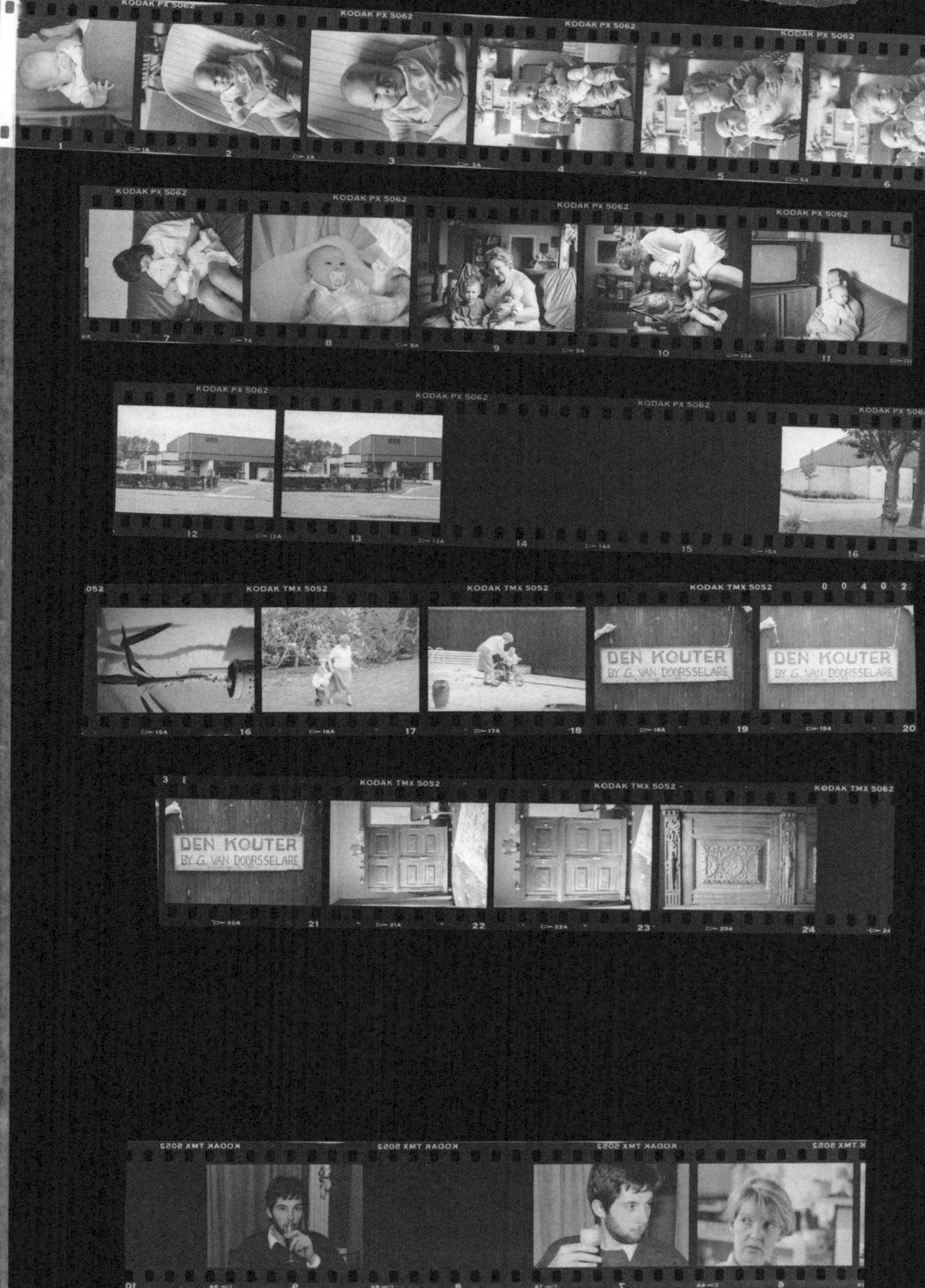

MICHIEL
DEN KOUTER
BY G. VAN DOORSSELARE

Episode 13 — Intensification

the situation deteriorates	as they start falling, the buildings, they panic	'THIS ISN'T HAPPENING'
as they start falling, the buildings, they panic	'THIS ISN'T HAPPENING'	the situation deteriorates
'THIS ISN'T HAPPENING'	the situation deteriorates	as they start falling, the buildings, they panic

When the rebar in reinforced concrete rusts, the expansive reaction ruptures the concrete, exposes the steel and accelerates deterioration. It is said that 'the concrete rots'. The rot is difficult to counteract, let alone preserve.

ARCHIVE (12)
Two buildings have collapsed, both of them barns. The one on contact sheet 41 appears to have been hit by a severe storm or a sudden gust of wind. The roof is lying in the dirt. Any underlying structure has disappeared, as if an immense vertical force rammed it straight into the ground. The collapse on contact sheet 88 is more partial. The middle purlin in the roof gave out, causing half the rafters and the roof tiles to plummet to the ground.

HERITAGE (2)
Excerpts from the Venice Charter for the Conservation and Restoration of Monuments and Sites of 1964:

Article 1. The concept of a historic monument embraces not only the single architectural work but also the urban or rural setting in which is found the evidence of a particular civilization, a significant development or a historic event. This applies not only to great works of art but also to more modest works of the past which have acquired cultural significance with the passing of time.
Article 2. The conservation and restoration of monuments must have recourse to all the sciences and techniques which can contribute to the study and safeguarding of the architectural heritage.
Article 3. The intention in conserving and restoring monuments is to safeguard them no less as works of art than as historical evidence.
Article 4. It is essential to the conservation of monuments that they be maintained on a permanent basis.
Article 5. The conservation of monuments is always facilitated by making use of them for some socially useful purpose. Such use is therefore desirable but it must not change the lay-out or decoration of the building. It is within these limits only that modifications demanded by a change of function should be envisaged and may be permitted.
Article 6. The conservation of a monument implies preserving a setting which is not out of scale. Wherever the traditional setting exists, it must be kept. No new construction, demolition or modification which would alter the relations of mass and color must be allowed.
Article 7. A monument is inseparable from the history to which it bears witness and from the setting in which it occurs. The moving of all or part of a monument cannot be allowed except where the safeguarding of that monument demands it or where it is justified by national or international interest of paramount importance.
Article 9. The process of restoration is a highly specialized operation. Its aim is to preserve and reveal the aesthetic and historic value of the monument and is based on respect for original material and authentic documents. It must stop at the point where conjecture begins, and in this case moreover any extra work which is indispensable must be distinct from the architectural composition and must bear a contemporary stamp. The restoration in any case must be preceded and followed by an archaeological and historical study of the monument.
Article 10. Where traditional techniques prove inadequate, the consolidation of a monument can be achieved by the use of any modern technique for conservation and construction, the efficacy of which has been shown by scientific data and proved by experience.
Article 11. The valid contributions of all periods to the building of a monument must be respected, since unity of style is not the aim of a restoration. When a building includes the superimposed work of different periods, the revealing of the underlying state can only be justified in exceptional circumstances and when what is removed is of little interest and the material which is brought to light is of great historical, archaeological or aesthetic value, and its state of preservation good enough to justify the action. Evaluation of the importance of the elements involved and the decision as to what may be destroyed cannot rest solely on the individual in charge of the work.

BILLBOARD (8)
The billboard was attached to the north side of a former welding factory. As a consequence of rain and pollution, the building showed signs of deterioration. As the billboard's display transitioned from one frame to another, and to another, the former factory must have slowly been changing, albeit imperceivably to the naked eye.

CAMERA (5)
The architect owned a tripod but hardly used it. The horizon is often a few degrees off level, mostly to the left.

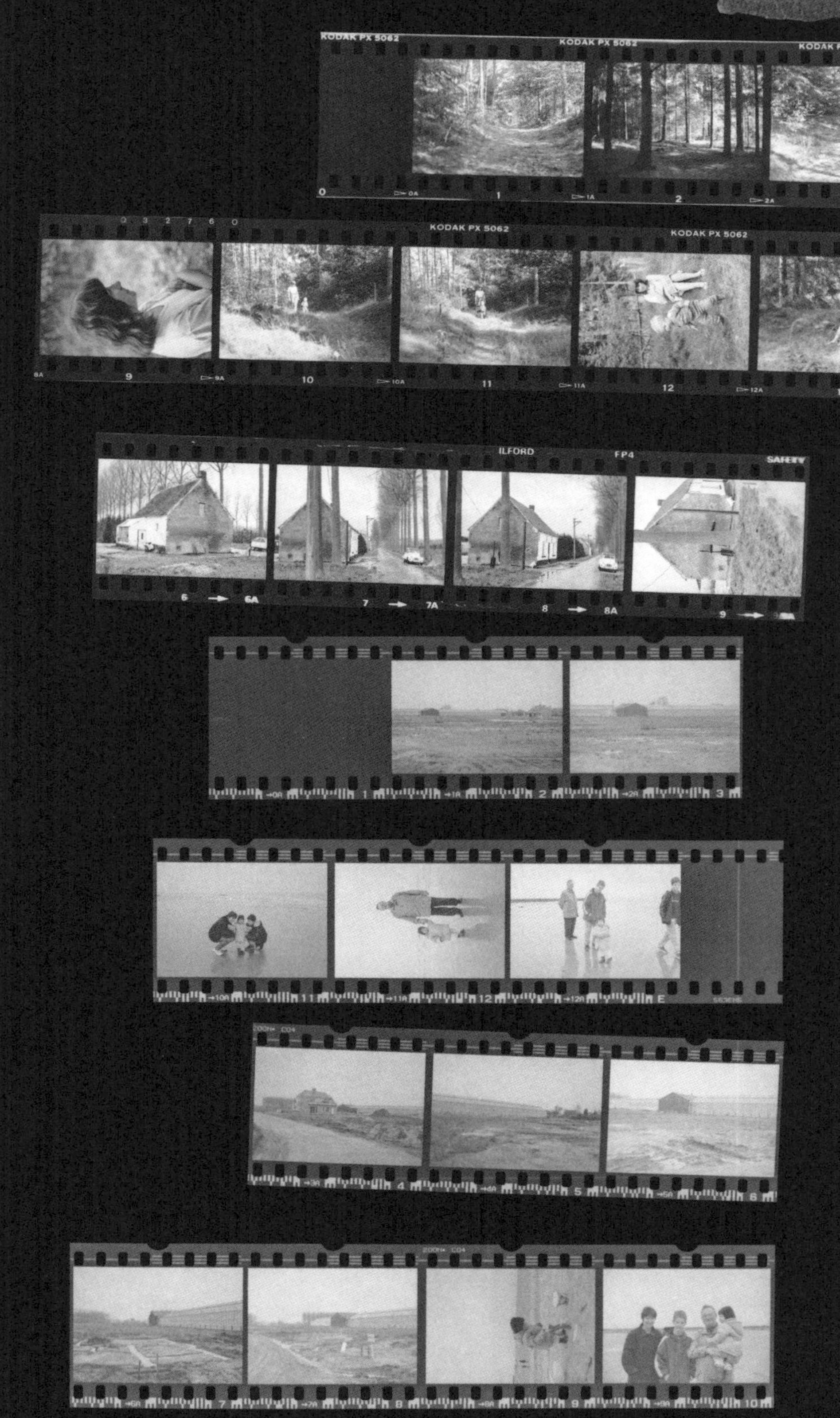

Episode 14 — Mise en abyme

look closer, closer still	no closer! don't you see?	it's right there, the first trace of the impasse
no closer! don't you see?	it's right there, the first trace of the impasse	look closer, closer still
it's right there, the first trace of the impasse	look closer, closer still	no closer! don't you see?

The scattered negatives on the lightbox show bricks, eaves and conifers, a farmhouse, poplars and family pictures. Two kids in bathrobes and pyjamas on the carpet. His shoes appear in the lower right corner of negative 16. The grain of the film and the rough fibre of the jute carpet become indistinguishable.

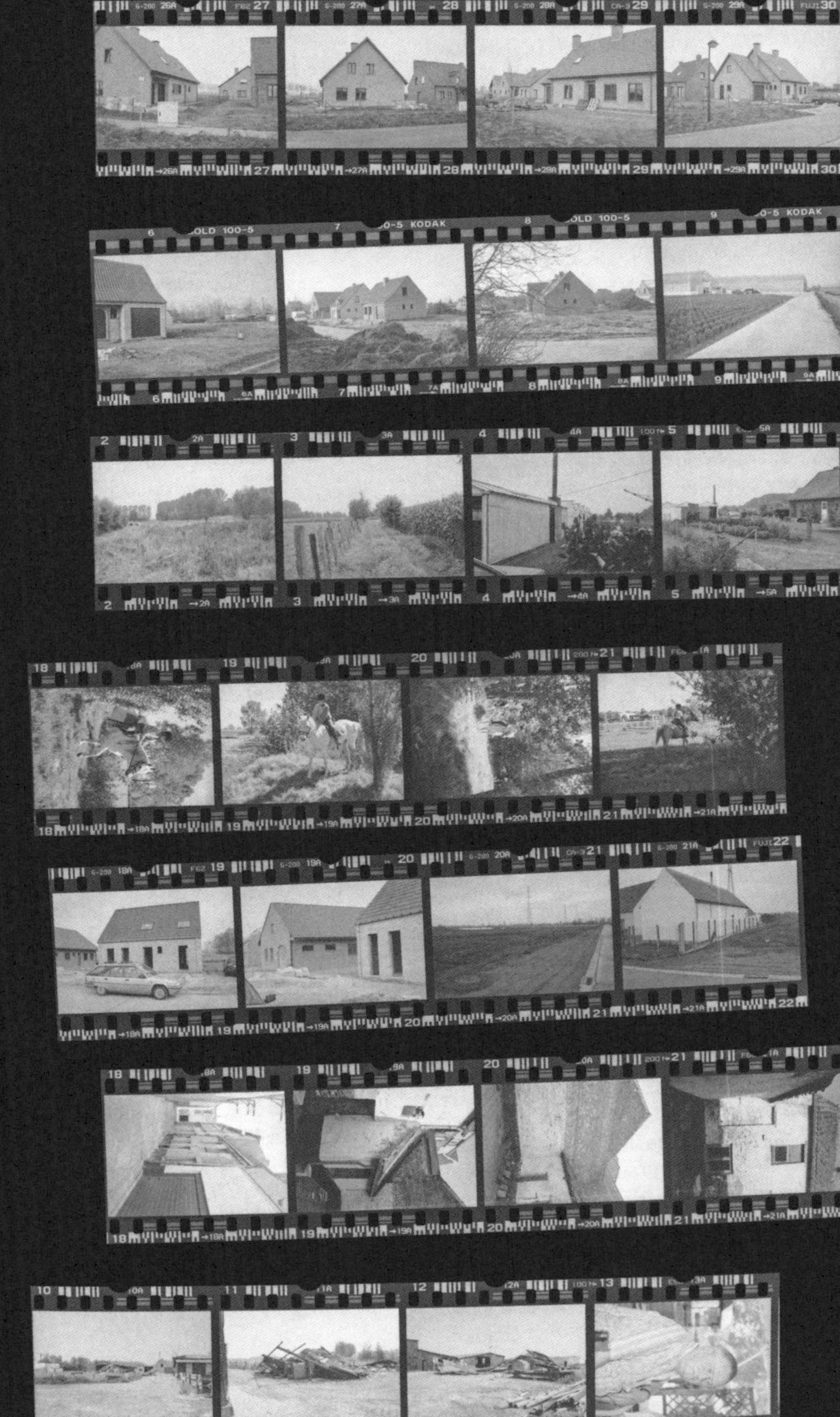

Episode 15 — The end

IS THE SITUATION	AS IT IS	THE SITUATION
AS IT IS	THE SITUATION	IS THE SITUATION
THE SITUATION	IS THE SITUATION	AS IT IS

The village sprawl grinds to a halt. In the middle of a purple lawn, two children are standing still. They appear to be looking at a pitchblack bench in the day care's garden. An impasse. At the horizon, beyond the poplars, greenhouses and fields, the grain silos, chimneys and pylones loom. The cooling tower's vapour goes straight up. It's a windless day.

MONTAGE (4)
'In order for a part of the past to be touched by the present instant <*Aktualität*> there must be no continuity between them' (Benjamin, 2002, 470).

DESCRIPTION
In 'Parable of the Palace', Jorge Luis Borges writes about the life-threatening peril of a perfect description. He tells the story of a poet who was shown around the emperor's palace. At the end of the tour, he recites a poem that describes the entire palace, 'whole and to the least detail, with every venerable porcelain it contained and every scene on every porcelain, all the lights and shadows of its twilights, and every forlorn or happy moment of the glorious dynasties of mortals, gods and dragons that had lived within it through all its endless past' (Borges, 1998, 318). Borges lists three outcomes: in the first, the emperor has the poet killed because he has stolen his palace. In the second, the palace disappears as the poet pronounces the last syllable. 'The world cannot contain two things that are identical' (Borges, 318). In the third outcome, the poet – a slave – died a slave and his poem fell into oblivion.

BIBLIOGRAPHY

Baetens, J. *Pour le roman-photo*. Brussels: Les Impressions Nouvelles, 2010

Barthes, R. *La préparation du roman I et II. Notes de cours et de séminaires au Collège de France 1978-1979 et 1979-1980* (N. Léger, ed.). Paris: Seuil/IMEC, 2003

Benjamin, W. *The Arcades Project* (K. McLaughlin & H. Eiland, trans.). Cambridge, Mass./London: The Belknap Press of Harvard University Press, 2002

Benjamin, W. 'The Work of Art in the Age of Its Technological Reproducibility. Third version', in: *Selected Writings. Volume 4: 1938-1940* (H. Eiland & M.W. Jennings, eds.). Cambridge, Mass./London: The Belknap Press of Harvard University Press, 2003, 251-283

Borges, J.L. *Collected Fictions* (A. Hurley, trans.). London: Penguin, 1998

Colomina, B. *Privacy and Publicity. Modern Architecture and Mass Media.* Cambrigde, Mass.: The MIT Press, 1996

Departement Omgeving. *Normen voor digitale aanvragen voor een Omgevingsvergunning. Stedenbouwkundige handelingen met architect* (version 3 November 2020). Online: https://www.omgevingsloketvlaanderen.be/sites/default/files/atoms/files/Normenboek%20digitale%20OMV%20aanvragen%20met%20architect_20201103.pdf, accessed on 3 January 2022

Edwards, E. *The Camera as Historian. Amateur Photographers and Historical Imagination, 1885-1918.* Durham/London: Duke University Press, 2012

Farocki, H. *Nachdruck/Imprint. Texte/Writings* (S. Gaensheimer & N. Schafhause, eds.). New York: Lukas & Sternberg / Berlin: Vorwerk 8, 2002

Haberman, C. 'Mt. Fuji: sacred, scenic and now crumbling', *The New York Times* (National Edition), 18 September 1984, A00001. Online: https://www.nytimes.com/1984/09/18/world/mt-fuji-sacred-scenic-and-now-crumbling.html, accessed on 9 April 2018

Forty, A. *Words and Buildings. A Vocabulary of Modern Architecture.* London: Thames & Hudson, 2004

Havik, K., Notteboom, B. & de Wit, S. (eds.). *Oase 98: Narrating Urban Landscapes*. Rotterdam: nai010, 2017

International Council on Monuments and Sites (ICOMOS). *International Charter for the Conservation and Restoration of Monuments and Sites (The Venice Charter 1964)*, 1964. Online: https://www.icomos.org/charters/venice_e.pdf, accessed on 12 December 2020

'Koninklijk besluit van 1 december 1975 houdende algemeen reglement op de politie van het wegverkeer en van het gebruik van de openbare weg . "Verkeersreglement"' [Belgian Highway Code], *Belgisch Staatsblad*, 9 December 1975

Lerner, B. & Kluge, A. *The Snows of Venice.* Leipzig: Spector Books, 2018

Lugon, O. *Le Style documentaire. D'August Sander à Walker Evans. 1920-1945.* Paris, Macula, 2011

Perloff, M. *Radical Artifice. Writing Poetry in the Age of Media.* Chicago: Chicago University Press, 1994

Roger, A. *Court traité du paysage.* Paris: Gallimard, 1997

Sekula, A. 'Photography between Labour and Capital', in: *Art Isn't Fair. Further Essays on The Traffic in Photographs and Related Media* (I. Steiner & S. Stein, eds.). London: Mack, 2020, 15-80

Tagg, J. 'Melancholy Realism: Walker Evans' Resistance to Meaning', in: *Narrative*, Vol. 11, No. 1, 2003, 3-77

Venturi, R., Scott Brown, D. & Izenour, S. *Learning from Las Vegas. The Forgotten Symbolism of Architectural Form* (Revised Edition). Cambridge, Mass./London: The MIT Press, 1977

Weissman, T. *The Realisms of Berenic Abbott. Documentary Photography and Political Action.* Berkeley: University of California Press, 2011

Weizman, E. 'Introduction: Forensis', in: Forensic Architecture (ed.). *Forensis. The Architecture of Public Truth.* London/Berlin: Sternberg Press, 2014, 9-32

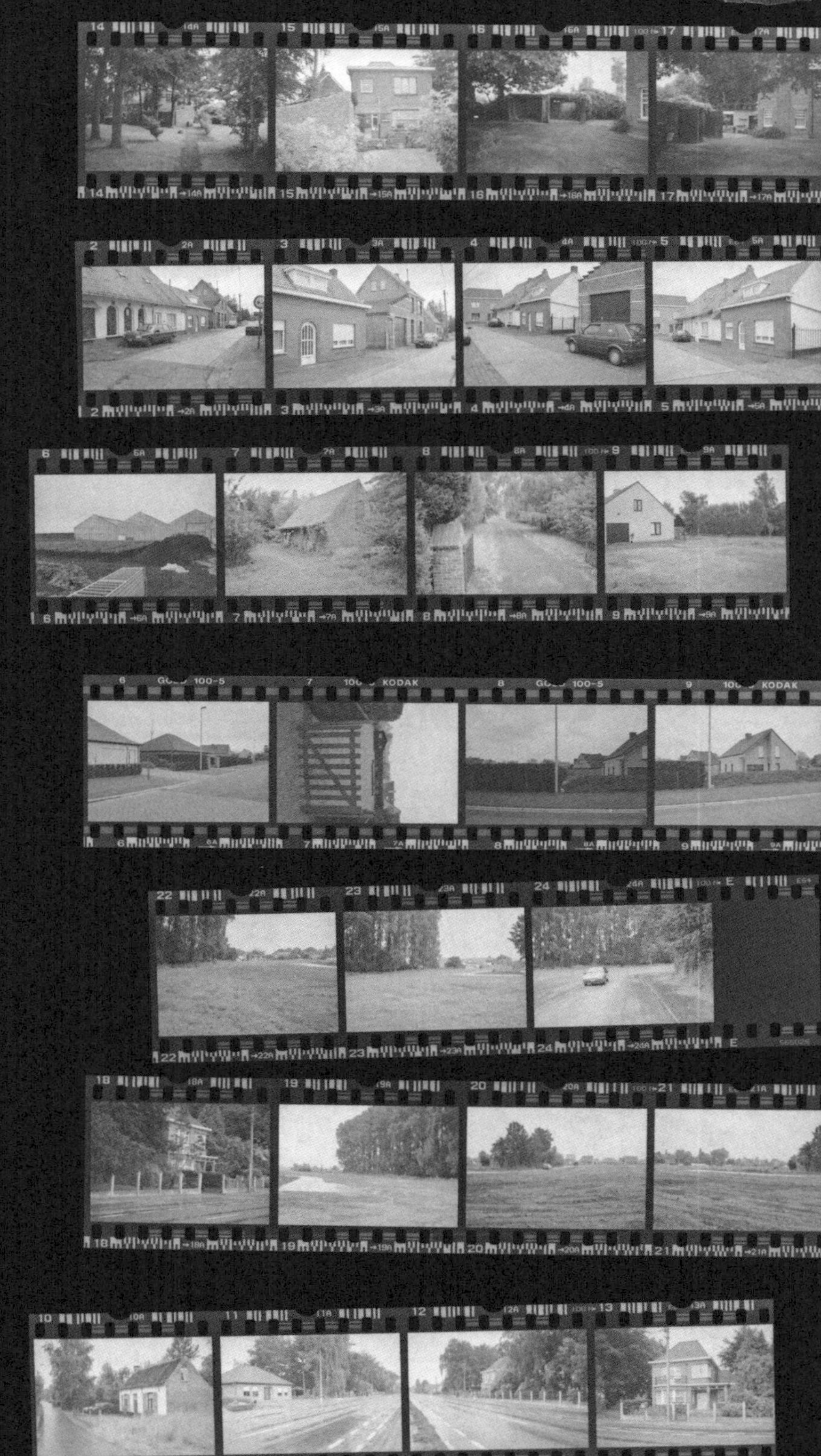

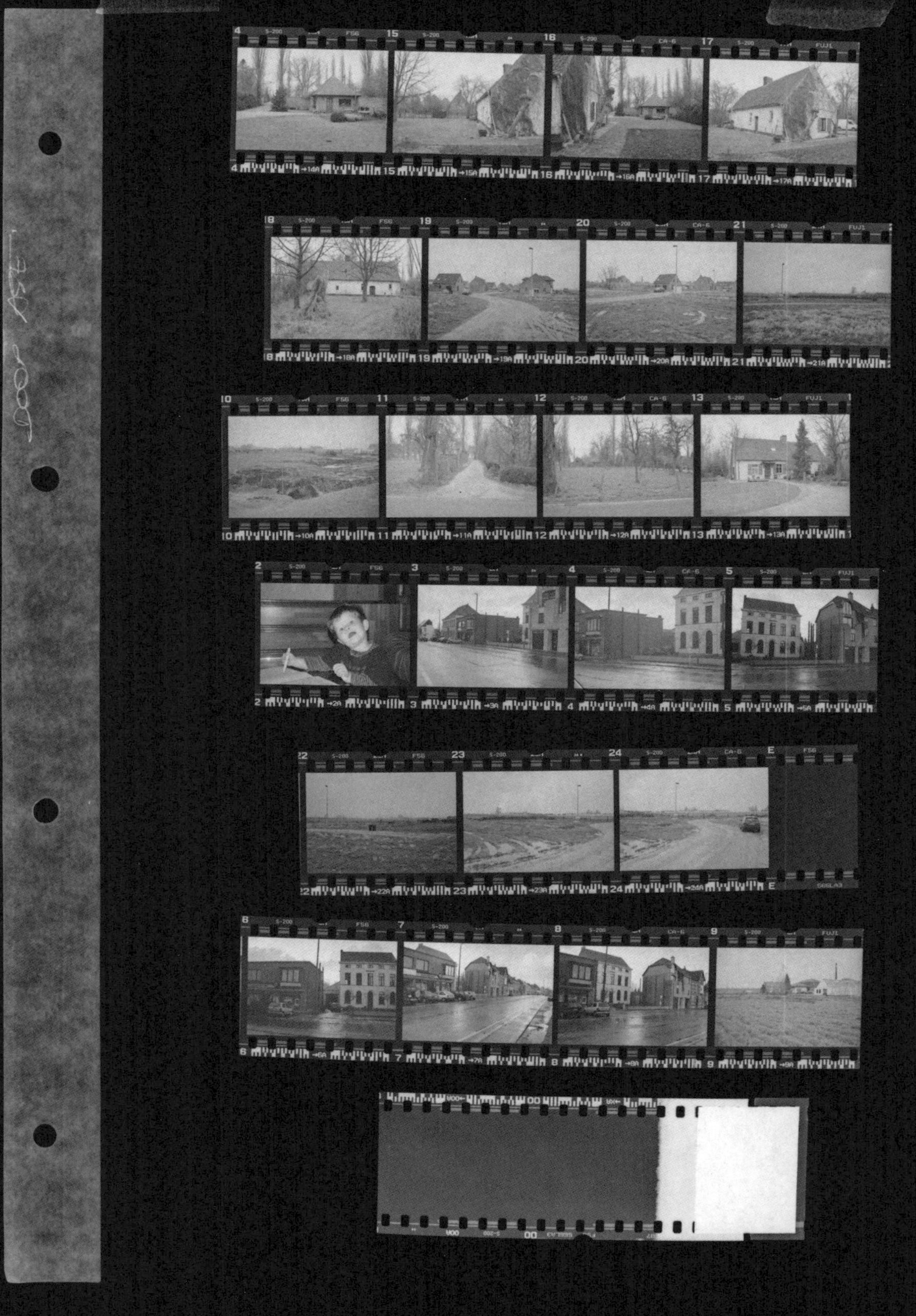

The Situation As It Is, 2022
Arnout De Cleene / Michiel De Cleene
APE#201
ISBN 9789493146983
Design: Haron Barashed, 019
Proofreading: Jonathan Beaton
Printer: Graphius, Ghent
Fonts: Times, Univers 55, Univers 65
Paper: Munken Lynx Rough 90g,
Maco Silk 90g
Edition: 999 (700 of which published together with 019's *Anything but certain* [APE#202])

The Situation As It Is was conceived as a visual story of fifteen episodes of three frames each. During the course of a year and a half (October 2020 until May 2022), those three-part episodes were presented on a rotating, three-sided billboard, mounted on the facade of art space 019 in Ghent, Belgium, along the R40, the inner city ringway.

Arnout De Cleene and Michiel De Cleene form research group De Cleene De Cleene. They focus on novel ways of approaching the everyday, by artistic means and from a cultural and critical perspective. A respective background in literature and photography is combined with a common interest in documentary practices.
www.decleenedecleene.be